RATIONAL-EMOTIVE THERAPY

RATIONAL-EMOTIVE THERAPY

A Skills-Based Approach

Russell Grieger, Ph.D.
and
John Boyd, Ph.D.

University of Virginia

With a Chapter by Albert Ellis, Ph.D.

VAN NOSTRAND REINHOLD COMPANY
NEW YORK   CINCINNATI   ATLANTA   DALLAS   SAN FRANCISCO
LONDON   TORONTO   MELBOURNE

Van Nostrand Reinhold Company Regional Offices:
New York Cincinnati Atlanta Dallas San Francisco

Van Nostrand Reinhold Company International Offices:
London Toronto Melbourne

Manufactured in the United States of America

Published by Van Nostrand Reinhold Company
135 West 50th Street, New York, N.Y. 10020

Published simultaneously in Canada by Van Nostrand Reinhold Ltd.

15 14 13 12 11 10 9 8 7 6 5 4 3 2 1

Library of Congress Cataloging in Publication Data

Grieger, Russell.
    Rational-emotive therapy.

    Bibliography: p. 265.
    Includes index.
    1. Rational-emotive psychotherapy.   I. Boyd,
John Donald, 1944-   joint author.   II. Ellis,
Albert, 1913-   joint author.   III. Title.
RC489.R3G74   616.8'914   79-9535
ISBN 0-442-22874-0

People are not disturbed by things,
*   but by the views which they take of them.*

*   Epictetus, 1st Century A.D.*

You cannot prevent the birds of
    sorrow from flying over your head,
but you can prevent them from building
    nests in your hair.

                        Chinese Proverb

Preface

Rational-emotive therapy (RET) has become one of the major approaches to psychotherapy during the last ten or fifteen years and is a foremost contributor to what Mahoney (1977) has called the emergence of a cognitive-behavioral model of intervention. The accord given to RET in its early phase of development (1955–1965) was largely due to the clinical efforts and writings of its founder, Albert Ellis, and his psychotherapeutic success as well as other RET practitioners. This face validity has now been supported with an impressive body of empirical evidence (Ellis, 1977b; DiGiuseppe, Miller, and Trexler, 1977) so that the scientific community has joined practicing psychotherapists in acknowledging RET as an innovative and viable approach to cognitive-behavioral intervention.

As RET has gained recognition, its theory and methods have been adopted and applied, in part or large measure, by thousands of mental health professionals including psychologists, psychiatrists, counselors, clergy, social workers, and psychiatric nurses. Parallel to this growing practice has been an increasing clamor for training in RET. Indeed, RET courses are now taught in many settings in addition to the Institute for Rational-Emotive Therapy in New York City, and attendance from professionals and students is exceptional for the multitude of lectures and workshops presented around the country by authorized RET instructors.

Two factors have, however, frustrated those seeking the requisite knowledge and skills for the competent practice of RET. One is the fact that RET has not been analyzed or explicated in terms of its composite techniques, and a model of RET training has not been developed that can be applied in a variety of training and supervision settings. Ellis (1971, 1973 a, b) correctly tells the RETer to be active, directive, educational, and the like, and he heeds his own advice (Becker & Rosenfeld, 1976). He likewise advocates the elegant solution of helping clients give up their disturbance-producing, irrational philosophies (Ellis, 1977f). Yet the fledgling RETer is left wondering just how to go about doing this. A second problem is the fact that most settings, hampered by time and manpower limits, are not equipped to do the intensive, emersion-type training that is done at the Institute for Rational-Emotive Therapy. These two factors make it difficult for the aspirant to gain RET expertise, thereby leading in many cases to amateurish therapeutic performances.

In this text we outline a skills-based model of rational-emotive therapy that fills the significant gap created by the two problems noted above. This RET model is based on the proposition that psychotherapy is a "craft" consisting of highly developed and refined skills which are employed to constructively influence the psychological state and behavior of clients. The proposition is in direct conflict with notions of psychotherapy as an ambiguous, interpersonal interaction, or an art. The skills-based rationale also reflects an applied scientific method; that is, psychotherapy is primarily the influence of one person's behavior upon another, and, as such, it can be studied in order to discover and identify those therapist behaviors (therapeutic techniques) which constitute the influence. To be studied are the crucial but subtle "performance characteristics" of each skill-behavior, including:

1. *Why* is it performed—the therapist's motive or the intended effect upon the client;
2. *When* is it performed—the timing of the skill within the session and within the entire therapeutic process;
3. *How* the skill is performed—the manner, style, or behavioral characteristics of the act (e.g., voice tone, facial expression, body posture, etc.).

We, likewise, view RET as a highly refined craft composed of an abundance of specific skills. Our skills-based approach, which we believe is reflective of the most accountable RET practice now being performed, conceptualizes these competencies as falling into four groups: (1) skills in rational-emotive psychodiagnosis and goal setting; (2) skills in facilitating client insight; (3) skills in the rational-emotive working through process; and (4) skills for helping clients engrain new, rational thoughts, feelings, and behaviors. Under ideal circumstances these four skill groups sequentially lead the client through the RET process. However, effective RET is not always characterized by the "ideal skill sequence," and we encourage therapists to remain flexible, moving between and among skill groups as client needs dictate. For this reason, it is imperative that therapists know why, when, and how each skill is to be performed. Armed with this, the therapist makes sense of the RET endeavor and therapeutically controls events rather than simply responding to circumstances.

After an initial chapter by Albert Ellis that overviews the basic RET theory of psychotherapy and personality change, we present four lengthy chapters which provide a detailed outline of the four skill groups. For each group, we present the purposes or goals of the skills (the "why"), a description of the skills-in-action (the "how"), precisely at what point to use them (the "when"), and various therapist and client roadblocks that can interfere with realizing the goals of the skill group. Then, in chapter six, we offer a transcribed therapy session in order to show exactly how these skills are pulled together to form the gestalt of the RET therapeutic process. Finally, we conclude the book with a chapter on issues in RET training and supervision (chapter seven), and a chapter on the understanding and application of RET to women and their special issues in RET (chapter eight), by Dr. Ingrid Zachary.

One last comment. While we sometimes explain basic RET concepts, we do not intend this book to be a primer of RET theory. We write this as a guide to doing RET and assume that the reader is familiar with the basic writing in RET's theory and practice. Excellent and extensive lists of recommended readings are provided by Ellis and Harper (1975) and by Ellis and Knaus (1977), and we refer the reader to these. We do believe that a thorough sampling of such lists and the following are extremely important, and we recommend them as prerequisite or concurrent reading to this text:

Ellis, A. *Reason and emotion in psychotherapy.* New York: Lyle Stuart, 1962.

Ellis, A. *Growth through reason.* Palo Alto, Calif.: Science and Behavior Books, 1971.

Ellis, A. *Humanistic psychotherapy: The rational-emotive approach.* New York: The Julian Press, 1973.

Ellis, A. *How to live with—and without—anger,* New York: Reader's Digest Press, 1977.

Ellis, A. Toward a theory of personality. In R.J. Corsini (ed.). *Readings in current personality theories.* Itasca, Ill.: Peacock Publishers, Inc., 1978.

Ellis, A., and Grieger, R. *Handbook of rational-emotive therapy.* New York: Springer Publishing Co., 1977.

Ellis, A., and Harper, R.A. *A new guide to rational living.* Englewood Cliffs, N.J.: Prentice-Hall, Inc., and Hollywood, Calif.: Wilkshire Book Co., 1975.

Goodman, D., and Maultsby, M.C., Jr. *Emotional well-being through rational behavior training.* Springfield, Ill.: Charles C. Thomas, 1974.

Maultsby, M.C., Jr. *More personal happiness through rational self-counseling.* Lexington, Ky.: Author, 1971.

Morris, K.T., and Kanitz, J.M. *Rational-emotive therapy.* Boston: Houghton Mifflin, 1975.

Rational-emotive therapy. *The Counseling Psychologist,* 7, 1977 (whole).

Russell Grieger, Ph.D.
John Boyd, Ph.D.

University of Virginia
Charlottesville, Virginia

Contents

RATIONAL-EMOTIVE THERAPY

1

An Overview of the Clinical Theory of Rational-Emotive Therapy

Albert Ellis, Ph.D.

In many respects rational-emotive therapy (RET) has a simple and easily exposited theory of human disturbance and of effective methods for helping people overcome their serious emotional problems. At the same time, this theory has many ramifications and complications. I shall try to briefly outline some of its main aspects in this chapter and shall assume that the reader has or will get more details in some of the main texts on the theory and practice of RET listed in the preface of this book. Later I shall outline its main hypotheses dealing with techniques of therapy and trust Drs. Grieger and Boyd to expand upon and illustrate them in more detail.

THE BASIC THEORY OF RET

The basic theory of RET has several important aspects, and includes a number of hypotheses, many of which have been at least partially confirmed by an impressive number of empirical, controlled studies (Ellis, 1977b). What follows are some of its more important assumptions.

Definition of Rationality

The term "rational" in RET has no absolutistic or invariant definition. It is assumed that virtually all humans have fundamental goals, purposes, and values; particularly to stay alive and, while surviving, attempt to be "happy" or "satisfied" in several main areas e.g., when they are by themselves, when they are communicating with other people, when they are in intimate relationships with a few others, when they are engaged in productive work of some sort, and when they are participating in recreational activities (e.g., art, science, music, sports, reading). If people choose to stay alive and to try to be happy, they act "rationally" or "self-helpfully" when they think, emote, or behave in any way that abets these goals; and they act "irrationally" or "self-defeatingly" when they sabotage their own goals. "Rational," "good," "responsible," or "moral" behavior mainly makes sense after humans have selected certain basic goals or purposes. *If* I want to survive happily or efficiently in a social group *then* it is "rational" or "good" for me to look out for myself *and* to try to get along fairly well with many or most of the other members of this group. But *if* I truly want to end my life or to live happily as a hermit, then "rationality" may well consist of my not looking out for myself or of my only looking out for myself and not trying to get along with others.

Definition of Appropriate or Undisturbed Emotions/Behavior

Appropriate or undisturbed emotions and behavior, like rational and self-helping thoughts, are again defined in terms of people's basic goals and purposes. Because virtually all humans, and especially those who are seen for psychotherapy, *do* seem to want to stay alive and to be happy by themselves, gregariously, in intimate relations, vocationally, and recreationally, and because there is a high degree of probability (though no certainty) that certain emotions will interfere with these goals, these emotions are usually designated, in RET, as "inappropriate" or "self-defeating." They could also be called "irrational," but it seems odd, in the English language, to call an emotion or state of feeling "rational" or "irrational." Consequently, the terms "appropriate" and "inappropriate" emotions are used. Some of the main positive "appropriate" emotions in RET are pleasure, joy, curiosity, love, and social interest, and some of the main negative "appropriate" ones are sorrow, regret, frustration, annoyance, and displeasure. The positive "appropriate" emotions help people get more of what they want (e.g., a better job or more recreational facilities) and the negative "appropriate" emotions help people avoid or eliminate what they do not want (e.g., a distasteful job or poor recreational facilities).

Some of the main positive "inappropriate" emotions in RET are grandiosity, rage, and mania; and some of the main negative "inappropriate" emotions are depression, anxiety, despair, self-pity, and feelings of worthlessness. The positive "inappropriate" emotions often have considerable immediate pleasure attached to them, but they frequently lead to later poor results (e.g., alienation of other people and foolishly waiting around for good things to happen by themselves). The negative "inappropriate" emotions usually are doubly destructive; they are unpleasurable feelings in themselves and they also tend to bring about poor results (again, alienation of other people and inertia). RET attempts to help people clearly distinguish or discriminate their "appropriate" from their "inappropriate" feelings, and often to intensify or abet the former while minimizing the latter. It definitely does *not* encourage states of apathy, overserenity, or nonfeeling.

The ABC's of Human Disturbance

RET holds that people practically never think, emote, or behave in a pure or monolithic way. Instead, when they "emote," they also think and act; when they "act," they also think and emote; and when they "think," they also emote and act. What we conventionally label "emotions" and "feelings of emotional disturbance" are largely— but not *exclusively*—the direct concomitants of people's thoughts, ideas, or constructs (Ellis, 1957, 1962; Ellis and Harper, 1961, 1975; Kelly, 1955; Phillips, 1956; Epictetus, 1899).

When people feel "emotionally disturbed" or act quite self-defeatingly fairly consistently after something unpleasant or frustrating has occurred in their lives, RET puts their disturbances in an ABC format. At point A, they have Activating Experiences of an obnoxious nature. They bring certain goals, purposes, or values to these A's (usually their basic goals of remaining alive and being happy in several ways) and they are balked or thwarted in achieving these goals. They then feel and act "disturbedly" at point C, their emotional and behavioral Consequences. For example at A, they fail at a task they consider important and get rejected by someone whose approval they distinctly desire; and at point C they feel hurt and depressed and withdraw from attempting the task again and trying to win this person's approval.

RET hypothesizes that, because of the manner in which most humans "naturally" think, as well as because of their prior learning experiences (with their parents, friends, teachers, books, etc.), they frequently if not usually conclude that A (Activating Experiences) directly "causes" or "creates" their C's (emotional and behavioral Consequences). But this is largely false. A definitely *contributes* to C, but only indirectly or partially "causes" it. Reactions at C, according to RET, are more importantly and more directly contributed to or "caused" by B—people's Belief System *about* what happens to them at A. They perceive A and draw *evaluative Beliefs* or *conclusions* about it (and about the basic goals or purposes they bring to A), and it is largely these evaluations or conceptions that "make" them feel and act in an "emotionally disturbed" manner at C.

First, most people, most of the time Believe (or tell or signal themselves) a set of rational Beliefs (rBs) at B: "I don't like failing and getting disapproved. I wish I hadn't. How annoying and obnoxious!" If they stayed only with these rational Beliefs (rBs) they would then only tend to have appropriate Consequences: feelings of annoyance, regret, sorrow, and frustration and ultimate determination to overcome these feelings by going back to their Activating Experiences of failure and rejection and changing them or avoiding them in the future.

When they have inappropriate Consequences (e.g., depression and withdrawal) at C, they also tell themselves and believe a set of irrational Beliefs (iBs): "I *must* succeed at A and get accepted by the people I like. How *awful* that I didn't. I *can't stand* failing and getting rejected! What a worthless person I am for having brought about these bad results!" Then they usually do little to help themselves go back to A and change the unfortunate Activating Experiences or they actually help make these A's even worse.

Musturbatory Thinking and Disturbance

Cognitive theories of emotional disturbance and psychotherapy— et. seg., those of Adler (1927, 1929), Beck (1976), Horney (1965), and

Kelly (1955)—tend to emphasize the irrational, illogical, and unrealistic elements in human thinking that lead to "emotional" disturbance. RET is somewhat more specific in this respect, as it hypothesizes that the most profound and pervasive forms of crooked thinking—or what Meehl (1962) has referred to as "cognitive slippage"—that lead to self-defeating Consequences are almost always forms of absolutistic evaluation of unqualified, shoulds, oughts, musts, commands, and demands. It is a natural, and probably biological, tendency of humans to desire their goals fulfilled at point A, the Activating Experiences that occur in their lives, and these desires, if they rigorously stick to them, rarely get them into serious emotional difficulties. But it is also a natural, and probably biological, tendency of theirs to insist that their goals *have to be, must be* fulfilled at point A, and if they foolishly go on to this kind of *musturbation,* they also invariably do get into serious emotional and behavioral problems.

Whereas other cognitive systems of psychotherapy emphasize different kinds of irrational thinking, such as overgeneralization, magnification, and attribution, RET categorizes the main irrational beliefs that people tend to hold, that very frequently "cause" or "create" dysfunction of emotional and behavioral consequences, under ten, eleven, or twelve major headings (Ellis, 1962; Ellis and Harper, 1961), and, more recently, it lists three major ones (Ellis, 1977a, 1979; Ellis and Grieger, 1977; Ellis and Harper, 1975; Ellis and Abraham, 1978), each with many derivatives.

1. I must do well and win approval for my performances, or else I rate as a rotten person.

- I must have sincere love and approval almost all the time from all the people I find significant.
- I must prove myself thoroughly competent, adequate, and achieving, or at least have real competence or talent at something important.
- My emotional misery comes almost completely from external pressures that I have little ability to change or control; unless these pressures change, I cannot help making myself feel anxious, depressed, self-downing, or hostile.
- If events occur that put me in real danger or that threaten my life, I have to make myself exceptionally preoccupied with and upset about them.

- My past life influenced me immensely and remains all-important because if something once strongly affected me, it has to keep determining my feelings and behavior today; my early childhood gullibility and condition-ability still remains, and I cannot surmount it and think for myself.
- I must have a high degree of order or certainty in the universe around me to enable me to feel comfortable and to perform adequately.
- I desperately need others to rely and depend upon; because I shall always remain so weak. I also need some supernatural power on which to rely, especially in times of severe crises.
- I must understand the nature or secret of the universe in order to live happily in it.
- I can and should give myself a global rating as a human and I can only rate myself as good or worthy if I perform well, do worthwhile things, and have people generally approve of me.
- If I make myself depressed, anxious, ashamed, or angry, or I weakly give in to the feelings of disturbance that people and events tend to make me feel, I perform most incompetently and shamefully. I must not do that, and I amount to a thoroughly weak, rotten person if I do.
- Beliefs held by respected authorities or by my society must prove correct and I have no right to question them in theory or action; if I do, people have a perfect right to condemn and punish me, and I cannot bear their disapproval.

2. Others *must* treat me considerately and kindly, in precisely the way I want them to treat me; if they don't, society and the universe *should* severely blame, damn, and punish them for their inconsiderateness.

- Others must treat everyone in a fair and just manner; and if they act unfairly or unethically they amount to rotten people, deserve damnation and severe punishment, and the universe will almost certainly see that they get this kind of retribution.
- If others behave incompetently or stupidly, they turn into complete idiots and ought to feel thoroughly ashamed of themselves.
- If people have the ability to do well but actually choose to shirk and avoid the responsibilities they should accept and

carry out, they amount to rotters and should feel utterly ashamed of themselves. People must achieve their full potential for happy and worthwhile living, else they have little or no value as humans.

3. Conditions under which I live must get arranged so that I get practically everything I want comfortably, quickly, and easily, and get virtually nothing that I don't want.

- Things must go the way I would like them to go, because I need what I want, and life proves awful, terrible, and horrible when I do not get what I prefer.
- When dangers or fearsome people or things exist in my world, I must continually preoccupy myself with and upset myself about them; in that way I will have the power to control or change them.
- I find it easier to avoid facing many of life's difficulties and self-responsibilities than to undertake more rewarding forms of self-discipline. I need immediate comfort and cannot go through present pain to achieve future gain.
- People should act better than they usually do, and if they don't act well and do create needless hassles for me, I view it as awful and horrible and I can't stand the hassles that they then create.
- Once handicaps exist in my life, either because of my hereditary tendencies or the influences of my past or present environment, I can practically do nothing to change them; I must continue to suffer endlessly because of these handicaps. Therefore life hardly seems worth continuing.
- If changing some obnoxious or handicapping element in myself or my life proves hard, that difficulty ought not exist. I find it too hard to do anything about it; I might as well make no effort, or very little effort, to change it.
- Things like justice, fairness, equality, and democracy clearly have to prevail; when they don't, I can't stand it and life seems too unbearable to continue.
- I must find correct and practically perfect solutions to my problems and others' problems; if I don't, catastrophe and horror will result.
- People and external events cause practically all my unhappiness and I have to remain a helpless victim of anxiety, depression,

feelings of inadequacy, and hostility unless these conditions and people change and allow me to stop feeling disturbed.

- Since I managed to get born and now remain alive, my life has to continue forever, or just about as long as I want it to continue. I find it completely unfair and horrible to think about the possibility of my dying and no longer having any existence.
- As long as I remain alive, my life has to have some unusual or special meaning or purpose; if I cannot create this meaning or purpose for myself, the universe or some supernatural force in the universe must give it to me.
- I can't stand the discomfort of feeling anxious, depressed, guilty, ashamed, or otherwise emotionally upset; if I really went crazy and wound up in a mental institution, I never could stand that horror and might well have to kill myself.
- When things have really gone bad for me for a reasonably long period of time and no guarantee exists that they will change or that anyone will take over my life and make things better for me, I simply can't bear the thought of living any longer and have to seriously consider killing myself.

RET also stresses three main forms of thinking that are "logical" derivatives of the basic irrational *musts,* and that are very frequently "causat've" or "creative" of dysfunctional emotional and behavioral Consequeqces: (1) *Awfulizing* ("It is *awful,* or *terrible,* or *horrible* that I am not doing as well as I *must!*"); (2) *I-can't-stand-it-itis* ("I *can't stand, can't bear* the things that are happening to me that must not happen!"); (3) *Worthlessness or shithood* ("I am a worthless person if I don't do as well as and win as much approval as I must!"). Grieger and Boyd will show in the next chapter how all this combines in various ways to produce the inappropriate negative feelings of anxiety, depression and despair, shame and worthlessness, and rage and hostility that contribute to most emotional and behavioral disturbances.

Self-Responsibility for Feelings

RET holds that both environmental conditions and hereditary or biological tendencies contribute significantly to healthy and unhealthy emotional reactions, and that for these reasons, humans frequently or usually *tend to* act and react in certain disturbed ways; but that they are also born and reared with some element of "free" choice or decision making. They can, albeit with difficulty, observe their own thoughts, feelings, and behaviors; can decide to behave somewhat differently; and can actualize this decision if they also decide to follow it up with concrete, ongoing, steady action to change themselves. Although they rarely are *totally* responsible for their own feelings, they also are rarely simply "conditioned" or "made to" think, feel, and act in specific ways. Although they do not *fully* make themselves (physically or emotionally) disturbed, to some degree they *choose* to do so, and can therefore choose to overcome their disturbances. They can do this by working on their irrational thinking, their inappropriate emoting, and their dysfunctional behavior. Most elegantly, pervasively, and permanently, however, they can probably do so by working hard and consistently at changing their basic philosophic premises: their absolutistic musts and their other forms of irrational beliefs. In any event, they are usually more self-conditioned and then conditioned from without; and they therefore can choose to do a great deal of effective self-reconditioning.

Biological Basis of Human Disturbance

RET tends to emphasize, more than most other systems of psychotherapy do, the strong biological basis of human "nature" and human disturbance (Ellis, 1976a,b). This view is not necessary for the effective use of RET in the treatment of psychological problems, since a therapist can choose to believe that clients are disturbed mostly because of their past experiences or environmental conditioning and can still be a strong RET practitioner. I personally believe, however, on the basis of many years of clinical experience as well as pursuing much research data, that most humans are born with a strong predisposition to think crookedly, to emote inappropriately, and to behave dysfunctionally—just as they are also born, as Maslow (1974), Rogers (1961), and a number of other humanistic psychologists have pointed out, with strong predispositions to love, to reason, to have peak experiences, and to actualize themselves. This does not mean that they are fated or doomed to behave neurotically but that they easily and "naturally" do so in many ways on numerous occasions, and that they have great difficulty in preventing themselves from doing so.

Some advantages of acknowledging the powerful biological (as well as sociological) tendencies of people to defeat their own ends and to behave in a disturbed fashion are these: (1) it explains why virtually all humans in all parts of the world often behave neurotically; (2) it explains why some exceptionally bright individuals still foolishly defeat themselves; (3) it explains why it is so difficult for most people, including those who devote considerable time, energy, and money to psychotherapy, to make fundamental changes in themselves; (4) it explains why so many people who make psychotherapeutic progress later fall back to their old dysfunctional ways; (5) it explains why insight into how one is defeating oneself is not enough and why constant work and practice at interfering with ineffectual patterns of behaving is required for maintained change; and (6) it leads therapists and clients to have more realistic expectations about psychotherapy.

The Ubiquity of Emotional Disturbance

Along with hypothesizing that humans have strong biological predispositions toward emotional disturbance, RET also tends to hold (though not dogmatically) that what we normally call "emotional disturbance" and "human irrationality" are exceptionally widespread, and that virtually no one fails to have a considerable degree on innumerable occasions. Although severe neurotics, borderline personalities, and psychotics may well be exceptionally and rigidly disturbed, the rest of the "normal" population often holds many irrational beliefs and acts dysfunctionally in several important respects.

RET's hypothesis about the ubiquity of emotional disturbance is one reason why it strongly advocates educational rather than merely therapeutic methods of tackling such disturbance. It holds that most members of the populace tend to have some kinds of dysfunctional addictions (e.g., smoking, drinking), and procrastination, anxieties, compulsions, obsessions, depressions, inhibitions, defenses, hostilities, and feelings of worthlessness; and that therefore a public education policy of disseminating some of the main elements of RET to the general populace would effect a great deal of prophylaxis and treatment of emotional ills.

Payoffs and Defenses

RET largely agrees with various psychodynamic thinkers that humans frequently get rewards or payoffs for their disturbed behaviors, and that therefore they may resist giving them up (Berne, 1964). It also agrees with the psychoanalysts that people often set up defenses against disturbed feelings, and instead of letting themselves feel anxious, guilty, or angry, they use rationalization, avoidance, projection, false attribution of "causes," and other games or defenses to hide their failings or the feelings that would accrue if they admitted such failings (Berne, 1964; A. Freud, 1975; S. Freud, 1965).

Unlike Eric Berne, however, who hypothesized that people frequently get very dramatic or delicious payoffs when they stay with their neurotic symptoms—for example, delight in their self-righteous feelings of hatred against their parents or mates—RET hypothesizes that their main and incredibly frequent payoff is simple ease. They frequently realize that ridding themselves of their disturbed symptoms, such as rage or overeating, would help them considerably, but they also realize, fully or partially, that it is much easier for them, especially in the short run, to bear with these symptoms than to fully face and concertedly try to extirpate them. Their resistance to change, therefore, may stem from pleasurable payoffs, or, as the Freudians would allege, it may stem from their hating their mother or their therapist and refusing to change for that daughter-of or son-of-a-bitch. But it is much more likely to stem from their low frustration tolerance: their stubborn refusal to go through immediate pain to get future gain. Their main payoff is instant comfort, which undramatically and insidiously prevents them from working at therapy and surrendering their disturbances.

As for defensiveness, RET agrees that it frequently exists but hypothesizes that it originates in self-damning attitudes toward failure and not from childhood experiences. If people did not savagely berate themselves, and consider themselves pretty worthless individuals when they lied, stole, acted incompetently, failed sexually, achieved poorly at school or at work, and committed other "stupid" or "shameful" acts, they would hardly bother to rationalize and go through other defensive or repressive maneuvers to deny these acts and to pretend that they behaved well.   Whereas psychoanalysis assumes that gradually showing people that they are defensive, in the course of the analysis building trusting, long-term relationship with them, will significantly help them to become less defensive, RET assumes that the better road to helping them in this respect is to get them to see the irrational beliefs (iBs) that underlie their fears of failure and their subsequent self-downing. Thus, if I am defensive about a poor public presentation that I make at one of my speaking trips throughout the country, and I claim that it was really a good presentation, or that I didn't have too much time in which to prepare it and was forced to speak to a highly prejudiced audience, I am most probably ignoring the reality of my negative feelings about them because: (1) I would consider myself something of a worm if I admitted that, without any good extenuating reason, I gave a poor talk; and (2) I think that I can't bear the "horrible" discomfort I would feel if I made myself anxious about giving such a poor talk.

In RET, I would be shown not only that I held these two important irrational beliefs, but I would also be shown how to keep vigorously Disputing them, until I gave them up. I would presumably then wind up with the philosophy: "Yes, I gave a poor public presentation this time, and may even do so again in the future. Too bad! I'm still fallible and imperfect! Now how can I take more pains to make a better presentation in the future, and to accept myself as a fallible human, even if I do badly again next time?"   Then I would no longer be defensive.

THE RET THEORY OF PERSONALITY CHANGE

As I have noted in an essay, *Toward a Theory of Personality* (Ellis, 1978a), arriving at a theory of personality is by no means the same thing as arriving at a theory of personality change. As the previous section of this chapter shows, RET has several basic assumptions regarding how humans operate and particularly how they become disturbed or, better, how they manage to disturb themselves. But it also has major hypotheses about what therapists had better do to help clients change themselves, and thereby minimize or eliminate their "emotional" disturbances. Let me consider some of these hypotheses in the following presentation, and let Grieger and Boyd elaborate on them and show exactly how to go about doing them later in the book.

Therapeutic Goals of RET

RET has two somewhat different, though overlapping goals: inelegant and elegant change. Inelegant change largely consists of some kind of symptom removal. Clients come to therapy with feelings of anxiety or depression, with dysfunctional behaviors like compulsive overeating or apathetic withdrawal, and with disordered thinking such as lack of concentration or obsessive–compulsive rumination. One goal of RET is to help them minimize or eradicate these symptoms, and thereby to live, presumably, longer and happier lives. It therefore targets certain "abnormal" or "unhealthy" emotions and behaviors, and tries to show clients how to work at changing these.

Elegant change in RET goes much beyond this kind of symptom removal, and aims at a significant lessening (rather than a complete removal) of clients' *disturbability*. It is assumed that, for whatever reason, these clients come to therapy with a strong basic tendency to keep disturbing themselves, not only in the target areas first presented to the therapist, but quite probably in several other important areas as well. The assumption is that if they can be helped to make a profound change in their philosophy of life, if they largely give up their demanding and their *musturbating,* and if they are determined to keep working indefinitely at maintaining rational thoughts, appropriate feelings, and efficient behaviors, they will ultimately (possibly in a year or more) begin to reach the point where they automatically react differently, and presumably healthfully, to the obnoxious Activating Experiences that occur in their everyday affairs. Thus, if they fail at some important task and get rejected by someone whose approval they distinctly desire, they will tend to feel distinctly sorry and sad, and quite frustrated and annoyed, but will only rarely or slightly feel worthless, hostile, and self-pitying. Moreover, because they are regretful and irritated, rather than depressed and horrified, they will quickly start plotting and scheming to do something constructive so that they can succeed next time and have a better chance of winning the approval they want, and they will literally work at doing constructive things.

Elegant change toward lesser disturbability, then, includes people becoming significantly less gullible and absolutistic, facing grim reality in a more optimistic (but not pollyannaish) fashion, and being more inclined toward *working* out solutions to whatever problems life brings. It is more of a basic attitudinal or philosphic change than any-thing else, but it goes hand in hand with a determination and a follow-up action to either modify existing conditions for the better or else gracefully lump them with a minimum of wailing. It is an anti-awfulizing, anti–demanding, anti–indulgent, and anti–whining *outlook*. And when it really exists, it leads first, to the fairly consistent maintenance of symptom removal; second, to the stubborn refusal to create more symptoms; and third, to a vital absorbing interest in enjoying, as much as one can, the rest of one's existence. This is the fundamental goal of RET for most clients, and when it is only partially reached, as is alas often true, this at least is the goal that the therapist hopes the clients will keep striving for.

If the goals of RET that I have just stated seem a little too vague or general, here are some more specific aims. Assuming that most humans, including RET clients, distinctly want to stay alive and be happy, and assuming that they can best do so by emoting appro-priately, thinking rationally, and behaving self-helpingly, RET hypothesizes that these goals are much more likely (though not necessarily) to be achieved by people's striving for the following kinds of subgoals:

Self-interest. Emotionally healthy people are largely interested in and true to themselves and secondarily to others, in general and to a few selected others in particular. But, because they have their "being-in-the-world," they had better not be *too* self-absorbed or "selfish." Instead they had better act kindly, considerately and have what Adler called 'social interest' in others, because they want to enjoy freedom from unnecessary pain themselves and because they would like to create the kind of a world in which the rights of others, as well as their own, are not needlessly curtailed.

Self-direction. Healthy individuals assume responsibility for their own lives, are able to work out most of their own problems with a good degree of independence, and while often wanting or preferring the cooperation and support of others, do not *need* or absolutistically *demand* dependency.

Tolerance. Well-functioning, rational humans give others *the right to be wrong.* While disliking or abhorring some others' *behavior* they do not condemn or damn *them,* as persons, for this displeasing behavior.

Acceptance of Uncertainty. Emotionally mature men and women accept the fact that we live in a world of probability and chance, where there are not, nor probably ever will be, any absolute certainties, and they realize that it is not horrible—indeed, in many ways it is fascinating and exciting—to live in such a probabilistic, uncertain milieu.

Flexibility. Healthy people tend to remain intellectually flexible, are open to change, and unbigotedly view the infinitely varied people, ideas, and things in the world as permissible and acceptable.

Scientific Thinking. Nondisturbed individuals are sufficiently objective, rational, and scientific, and they are able to apply the laws of logic, of empiricism, and of the scientific method not only to external people and events, but to themselves and the results they get from their own interpersonal and intrapersonal relationships.

Commitment. Healthy and rational people are usually vitally absorbed in something outside themselves, whether it be in people, things, or ideas. They preferably have at least one major creative interest, as well as some human involvements, which are highly important (but not sacred!) and around which they structure a good part of their lives.

Risk-taking. Emotionally sound persons are able to take risks, to ask themselves what they would really like to do, and then to try to do this, even though they may fail. They are adventurous (though not necessarily foolhardy); are willing to try almost anything once, to see how they like it; and look forward to some breaks in their usual life routines.

Self-acceptance. Healthy rational–emotive people are glad to be alive and to accept themselves just *because* they are alive, *because* they exist, and *because,* as live individuals, they almost invariably have some capacity to enjoy themselves and to ward off unnecessary pain. They do not equate their worth or value to themselves on the basis of their extrinsic achievements or on what others think of them, and they preferably do not rate their selves, their totality, or their being at all, but *accept* their existences and endeavor to enjoy life.

Non-utopianism. No one, in all probability, is likely to reach the point where she/he is never frustrated, and consequently never feels sorrowful, regretful, or annoyed; it would seem unhealthy if anyone ever did. But humans are neither likely to achieve perfect joy or happiness, on the one hand, nor total lack of anxiety, depression, despair, self-downing, and hostility, on the other. Even when we know that these negative emotions are foolish and needlessly self-defeating, it is unlikely that we shall ever be able to eliminate them entirely. The best we can do is to minimize their frequency, intensity, and duration. Perfect mental health seems like a chimera—at least, as long as humans remain much the way they are!

RET and Self-Acceptance

As briefly noted, RET takes a much different view of self-acceptance than many other forms of therapy which try to promote people's feelings of "self-esteem" or "self-confidence." In the original edition of *A Guide to Rational Living* (Ellis and Harper, 1961), I firmly took the view that people could accept themselves or consider themselves valuable or worthwhile simply because they were alive, and not because they did anything to "prove" their worth, such as performing adequately or being loved by others. This is a good pragmatic definition of human worth, because those who employ it will virtually never feel worthless—unlness they do so after their death!

Philosophically, however, accepting oneself as worthwhile because one is alive does not work too well, since one can just as easily say that one is worthless because one is alive. Both definitions are tautological and are not empirically verifiable, except that the first one works pretty well and the second, pretty badly in terms of how disturbed one feels when one employs it. A better solution, which I hinted at in *Reason and Emotion in Psychotherapy* (Ellis, 1962) but finally adopted a little later (Ellis, 1971, 1973a) is that of helping people to refuse to rate themselves, their totality, their essence, or their being at all, but only to rate their specific traits, deeds, and performances. The latter are rated in terms of the good or bad results they bring in regard to people's basic goals or values.

Thus, if my basic goal is to stay alive and to be happy when I am by myself, with others, and engaging in intimate relationships with a few others, then I can rate some of my traits (e.g., intelligence, discipline, and healthfulness) as "good" or "worthwhile" and I can rate some of my other traits (e.g., depression and hostility) as "bad" or "less valuable." For the former traits will tend to help me achieve my basic goal and the latter will tend to sabotage my achieving it. If I have good intelligence, however, I am not necessarily an intelligent or good *person*—since I don't always act intelligently or well. And if I have considerable hostility, I am not necessarily a hostile or bad *person*—since I don't always act hostilely or badly.

Some of the main reasons why rating my "self" or "person" is illegitimate and undesirable include: (1) If I rate my acts and traits, I can see whether they are beneficial or harmful to my purposes, and help change some of them. If I rate my "self" or my "being" I become self-centered rather than problem-centered and distract myself from improving my disadvantageous traits. (2) Because I am fallible and have many failings, and I rate myself in terms of some of my important traits, I will tend to give myself a poor rating and have low self-esteem. (3) I will often tend to become obsessed with my self-ratings and try to prove myself rather than be and enjoy myself. (4) I *am* not, nor do I *equal,* any of my individual acts or characteristics. I am I—a very complex, ongoing, ever-changing *process.* How can I legitimately give a single, global rating to this process?

(5) Self-rating leads both to deifying myself at times and to devili-fying myself at other times; to idolatry and to damnation. But I am a human, not a god or a devil. (6) Some of the most severe emotional disturbances, such as anxiety, depression, and feelings of inadequacy, are almost inevitable concomitants of self-rating.

For reasons such as these, RET helps people to see that *they* are not good nor bad, worthy nor unworthy. They had better honestly and accurately rate their performances, but in no way try to evaluate their "selves." If they do so, it is hypothesized, they will tend to feel minimally disturbed and maximally enjoy their existences.

RET and Longrange Hedonism

RET accepts the philosophy of hedonism—that pleasure is a principle good and can be taken as the main goal of action. But, it does not advocate a stance of immediate gratification or shortrange hedonism at the expense of pain tomorrow; rather it encourages longrange hedonism or the seeking of pleasure today *and* the non-sabotaging of tomorrow's satisfactions. Just as it emphasizes low frustration tolerance and discomfort anxiety in the creation of emotional disturbance, it does stress minimizing these tendencies by vigorous and persistent cognitive, emotive, and behavioral ap-proaches. Thus, if clients procrastinate about activities that they would like to accomplish (such as writing onerous reports or finish-ing papers or theses), the RET therapist shows them that they are not only rationally telling themselves that "It's hard to do these tasks!" but that they are usually also irrationally insisting, "It's *too* hard *and* it *shouldn't be* that hard!" They are shown how to Dis-pute these irrational beliefs (iBs) and to give them up. Simultaneously, they are shown how to use emotive methods (such as rational-emotive imagery) and behavioral methods such as penalizing them-selves by burning a twenty or a hundred dollar bill every time they do not spend, say, a minimum of an hour a day working on the report or the paper to help them stop procrastinating and to change their shortrange hedonistic philosophy (Ellis and Knaus, 1977).

Secondary symptoms of discomfort anxiety are also tackled in RET. Thus, if clients procrastinate because they are anxious about writing an imperfect report or paper, and they then awfulize about the uncomfortable feeling of anxiety that they bring on when they attempt to write it, they are shown that they are telling themselves irrational beliefs (iBs) along these lines: "If I attempt to do this report, I know that I will become anxious and that I'll suffer enormously while laboriously working on it. I *can't stand* this kind of anxiety! I *must* not be so uncomfortable! Therefore, I'll find some excuse not to write the report." Again, such clients are shown how to Dispute their secondary symptoms—their discomfort anxiety—by challenging and questioning their irrational beliefs (iBs): "Where is the evidence that I *can't stand* anxiety? Will the ensuing discomfort kill me? Will it destroy *all* possibility of my being happy? Won't it be better if I face this uncomfortable anxiety now, for an hour or so, rather than living with it forever—and never getting the report done? Why *must* I never be uncomfortably anxious? It's hard to face and uproot my anxious feelings, but what makes it *too* hard?"

At the same time, clients with secondary symptoms of discomfort anxiety are shown, by RET emotive methods, how to accept themselves with their unpleasant, self-created feelings, and how to use behavioral methods (such as in vivo desensitization, in the course of which they implosively make themselves anxious until they *see* that this feeling does not destroy them) to overcome their horror about their uptightness. As usual, RET tries to help clients make a profound attack on their shortrange hedonism that brings about both primary symptoms (e.g. procrastination) and secondary symptoms (e.g., discomfort anxiety about procrastinating).

Comprehensive Aspects of RET

RET has always emphasized the enormous importance of thinking in contributing to people's emotional reactions and their behavior, but it has also emphasized that emotion significantly influences thinking and behaving and that action influences emoting and thinking (Ellis and Harper, 1961). Although RET has sometimes been accused of getting on the behavior therapy bandwagon, this is false. In the classic presentation of RET, *Reason and Emotion in Psychotherapy* (Ellis), published in 1962 and compiled from talks and papers originally given from 1956 to 1960, many references are given to RET's use of learning theory, to homework assignments, to in vivo desensitization, and to skill training (see, for example, pages 196, 201, 258–259, 311, 327 and 333–335). And in *The Intelligent Woman's Guide to Manhunting* (Ellis, 1963), I took the pioneering stand that women could be just as assertive in seeking a mate as could men, and that they could train themselves to be highly assertive without being aggressive.

All psychotherapies are actually cognitive, emotive, and behavioral in their techniques, in that they implicitly if not explicitly use all these three major modalities (Ellis, 1968). Since I first started employing RET in 1955, after I had largely abandoned psychoanalysis and psychoanalytically-oriented therapy for a few years prior to that, RET has always used several emotive and several behavioral methods with virtually all its clients. More importantly, it has used them on theoretical rather than on practical grounds, and has used them to try to effect an elemental or basic philosophic change in clients' behavior.

If, for example, an RET client has a severe phobia in regard to riding in elevators, this person would be given a variety of cognitive, emotive, and behavioral methods, including anti-awfulizing about the hassles and hazards of elevator rides, readings in RET antimustur-bational literature, rational-emotive imagery, shame-attacking exercises, and in vivo desensitization preferably in a flooding rather than a gradual manner. The emotive and behavioral methods would be used, in this case, not merely because they work to help remove elevator phobias but because they tend to help the client radically and basically change his or her philosophy about the "horror" of facing "dangerous" conditions and the "terrible pain" or being confined and frustrated. In vivo desensitization in particular, as Emmelkamp, Kuipers, and Eggeraat (1978) have indicated, may show phobics that nothing terrible does happen when they face "frightful" events, and may actually lead to a greater cognitive change than may more overtly cognitive methods.

RET, then, has always been comprehensive, multimodal, and cognitive-emotive-behavioral, and as the years go by it becomes more so, since it adopts or adapts many different kinds of therapeutic procedures, ranging from encounter group methods to special modes of operant conditioning, as these become available. It holds many theoretical assumptions, as I hope this chapter shows, but under its theoretical umbrella, it is able to encompass many highly "eclectic" therapy techniques.

Active-Directive Methods of RET

RET hypothesizes that active-directive methods of therapy—such as confrontation, probing, challenging or disputing irrational beliefs, teaching procedures, giving emotive exercises, and assigning homework tasks—help more clients more effectively than more passive and unintrusive approaches (Ellis, 1962, 1977b). Here again, it is assumed that because people naturally make themselves disturbed, because they actively keep repropagandizing themselves with irrational Beliefs and dysfunctional behaviors (or nonbehaviors), forceful intervention on the part of therapist is more likely to help them change themselves than is a more nondirective methodology. Consequently, RET therapists, particularly those trained at the Institute for Rational-Emotive Therapy in New York and Los Angeles, are encouraged to adopt a vigorous active-directive approach.

RET and Self-Management Methods

While RET employs many behavioral methods and teaches these to its clients, it assumes that these methods are often best employed when clients control their own behavior than when they allow themselves to be controlled by a therapist, teacher, other individual (Ellis, 1969b, 1973a,b; Goldfried and Merbaum, 1973; Kanfer and Goldstein, 1975). RET therapists, therefore, try to help clients to select their own target behaviors to change, and to pick their own reinforcements and penalties when they want to modify some of their disturbed ideas, emotions, and practices (Ellis, 1977a; Ellis and Abraham, 1978; Ellis and Grieger, 1977; Ellis and Knaus, 1977; Ellis and Harper, 1975).

Choice of Behavioral Change

RET adopts what is sometimes called a "soft determinism" approach: assumes that all human behavior, including emotional disturbance, is largely determined by hereditarian and environmental conditions or influences and that therefore pure free will does not seem to exist. It also assumes, however, that humans still have a distinct degree of choice or will and can, with considerable amounts of determination and work, partly change how they think, feel and act (Ellis, 1962, 1973a,b; Greenwald, 1976; Horowitz, 1971; Rychlak, 1976). Because of this ability, they can choose to work (or not to work) in therapy at helping themselves, and they can thereby choose to change some of their most "natural" and long-practiced disturbances and to actualize their potential for greater enjoyment and personality growth.

RET therapists try, therefore, to show clients that they do have some degree of choice in overcoming their disturbances and that if they choose to see what they are doing to upset themselves and to work, cognitively, emotively, and behaviorally, to refuse to upset themselves in the future, they can significantly help themselves improve. "Will-power", in RET, is defined not merely as the determination to change but the determination to *work* at changing oneself and the *actual work* that one does to follow up this determination.

Disputing of Irrational Beliefs

While RET hardly invented the disputation of irrational beliefs— since philosophers from Socrates onward have specialized in this kind of disputation—it has, among all major psychotherapies, specialized most in this respect.

Disputing makes use of the scientific method of challenging and questioning shaky or untenable hypotheses that clients hold about themselves, about others, and about the world. Thus, clients may fail at an important task and get rejected by others at point A (Activating Experiences); may tell themselves several irrational beliefs (iBs) at point B (e.g., "I *must* succeed at A and get accepted by the people I like. How *awful* that I didn't! I *can't stand* failing and getting rejected! What a worthless person I am for having brought about these bad results!"). They, then tend to bring about inappropriate Consequences (e.g., depression and withdrawal) at point C.

If these clients are of normal intelligence and not in any unusual category (e.g., very young or quite old), an RET therapist would proceed with Disputing: "*Where* is the evidence that you *must* succeed and get accepted by the people you like? *Prove* that it is awful if you don't. In *what* way can't you *stand* failing and getting rejected? *How* does your having brought about these bad results make you a worthless person?"

When this kind of active, persistent disputing is carried on until the clients give themselves the "correct," empirically validated answers, and when they really and strongly believe these answers, they wind up with E, a set of new cognitive, emotive, and behavioral Effects. Cognitively, E consists of these kinds of radically changed or new conclusions or premises on the part of clients: "There is no evidence that I must succeed and get accepted by the people I like—though there is evidence that it would be highly *preferable* or *desirable*. It is not awful if I fail and get rejected—only distinctly inconvenient and frustrating. I definitely can *stand*, though I'll never *like* failing and being rejected. I am never a worthless person for failing—but only a person who has failed in this instance, and who may well fail in the future; and I am still, as such a person, undamnable and quite "deserving" of getting whatever advantages may accrue to me now and tomorrow."

When clients arrive at these cognitive or philosophic Effects, at point E, they almost always tend to feel sorry, regretful, and annoyed at what has happened to them, at point A (their Activating Experiences)—and this is their new emotive Effect or eE. They also tend to act on this new appropriate emotion and to do something, if they can, to change the situation at A so that they improve their lot and feel happier about life—and this is their new behavioral Effect (bE). The cognitive technique of Disputing, in RET, and of teaching clients how to dispute their own irrational beliefs (iBs) whenever they subsequently experience obnoxious events at A and feel emotionally upset at C, is the most typical and perhaps the most often used method of RET. Again it is hypothesized that when this method is successfully used with emotionally disturbed clients, they will get the most lasting, most elegant, and most profound kinds of cognitive, emotive, and behavioral change. It is not assumed that all or even most disturbed people can or will consistently use disputing to help themselves with their problems, but it is assumed that those who do, will be more benefited in certain ways than will those who effectively employ rational self-statements, distraction procedures, autosuggestion, or other cognitive methods.

Homework Techniques

RET almost invariably emphasizes consistent and radical homework assignments, and tries to help clients do these assignments in their head, through imaging, and (especially) in vivo. It starts with the assumption that humans naturally and easily disturb themselves and have difficulty overcoming these biological tendencies; it further assumes that they therefore had better practice, practice, and practice still more various anti-disturbing methods—cognitive, emotive, and behavioral. It tries to help clients continually, virtually every day to do homework in the form of actively seeing and Disputing their irrational Beliefs (DiBs). It helps them forcefully and vigorously, in roleplaying or in real-life situations, acknowledge and express their feelings, and train themselves to feel differently and more appropriately. It gives them in vivo desensitizing behavioral assignments, in the course of which they deliberately face "fearsome" situations, refrain from doing compulsive acts, and make themselves stay in obnoxious circumstances in which they exhibit low frustration tolerance.

RET, moreover, encourages clients to do their homework assignments repetitively and floodingly. Individuals afraid of riding on buses or subway trains, for example, would be urged to take rides many times—and to start doing so immediately, preferably twenty or thirty times a day, and preferably under the "worst" conditions (e.g., when the trains or buses were crowded, if that is what they feared most). The RET hypothesis is that the more often and the more "painfully" these "dangerous" tasks are attempted, the more the clients are likely to see that nothing much happens to them and that the "danger" is largely imagined.

Self-Disclosure and Shame Attacking Techniques

RET hypothesizes that ego anxiety is highly correlated with feelings of shame, guilt, embarrassment, humiliation, and self-downing, and the more people squarely face and change the irrational Beliefs behind these feelings, the less emotionally disturbed they will tend to be. It therefore emphasizes, especially in its group therapy, many kinds of self-disclosing, risk-taking, and shame-attacking exercises. In the course of the last-named exercises, for which RET is fairly famous, individuals are encouraged to do something in public (in the therapy group itself or, preferably, outside the group) that they consider exceptionally "shameful," "embarrassing," "foolish," or "humiliating." In the course of doing these "shameful" things, they prove to themselves that they really are not shameful and that they can be done with relative comfort and self-acceptance. Thus, they may yell out the stops in subway trains, buses, or elevators; ask for sex-related items in a loud voice in drug stores or other shops; or walk a banana on a red ribbon on a sunny day when the streets are fairly crowded (Ellis, 1977a; Ellis and Grieger, 1977).

Educational and Information Giving Methods

RET has always been an educational and information-giving procedure. It stresses the fact that people do not necessarily require individual or group therapy to overcome some of their serious emotional disturbances, but that they can also be appreciably helped by various psychoeducational procedures, including lectures, discussions, classes (for children and adults), workshops, bibliotherapy, audiovisual techniques, and other techniques (Bokor, 1971; Sydel, 1972; Taylor, 1975; Zingle, 1965). RET is frequently frankly didactic during regular therapy sessions, and it hypothesizes that rational-emotive procedures can be taught and learned in many educational ways.

Humorous RET Techniques

RET assumes that people largely disturb themselves not when they make something important and have strong desires to achieve in that area (for that, actually, is a healthy or "good" trait in most instances) but when they *exaggerate* the significance or importance of something and take it *too* seriously rather than just seriously. One of its main techniques, therefore, consists of using humorous attacks on people's irrational beliefs (iBs). To this end, RET therapists frequently use the humorous techniques of taking clients' nutty ideas to ridiculous extremes, reducing them to absurdity, employing paradoxical intention, and using various kinds of puns, witticisms, irony, whimsy, evocative language, slang, and deliberate use of sprightly obscenity to help these clients see the ridicule of their philosophies—but not, of course, *themselves.* (Ellis, 1977d). In this respect, RET goes along with a number of other therapists who have stressed the use of humourous sallies on clients' irrationalities (Berne, 1964; Farrelly and Brandsma, 1974; Frankl, 1966; Greenwald, 1975, 1976; Haley, 1963; Klein, 1974, Whitaker, 1975).

Humanistic-Existential Approach to Therapy

RET accepts humanistic-existential framework, but it combines the "humanism" of the Association for Humanistic Psychology with that of the "humanism" of the American Humanist Association. With the latter group, it assumes that all humans are human—not superhuman nor subhuman; that at present they all seem to live and die; and that they had better assume that this is their life, make the most of it while it lasts, and not count on any kind of physical immortality. With the former group, it takes the humanist-existentialist position that people largely create their own world and give meaning to their lives; that they had better define their own freedom, cultivate individuality *and* social interest, live in dialogue with others, accept their experiencing as highly important, be fully present in the immediacy of the moment, and learn to accept limits in life and their ultimate demise (Braaten, 1961; May, 1961; Hartman, 1967).

Because, however, of its realistic and active-directive outlook on how humans had better accept themselves and live successfully with others, it tends to endorse the active methods employed by existentialists like Viktor Frankl (1966, 1968) rather than the more passive existenial encounters between clients and therapists used by therapists like Carl Rogers (1961) and Rollo May (1969). Existenialists such as Buber (1962) and Heidigger (1962) tend to be, in their own way, fine propagandists who very active-directively *teach* the principles in which they believe. RET, too, tends to *show* and *demonstrate* to people how they can fulfill themselves more humanistically (Ellis, 1972).

Problem Solving

Since RET is a highly cognitive-oriented form of therapy, it has always stressed the therapeutic technique of problem-solving. Clients are induced to see that their "emotional" and "behavioral" disturbances partly or largely arise from the ineffectual problem solving they have done and to acquire better methods of thinking things through. While they are being helped to dispute and change their basic irrational beliefs, at point B, they are also helped to go back to the events that are going badly in their lives, at point A, and to figure out better solutions to some of these occurrences. RET therapists do not hesitate to help their clients with this kind of practical problem solving, as long as it is accompanied by solid challenging and disputing of irrational beliefs (Ellis, 1962, 1971, 1973, 1977a; Ellis and Harper, 1975; D'Zurilla and Goldfried, 1971; Goldfried and Davidson, 1976; Goldfried and Goldfried, 1975).

Skill Training

As is the case of problem solving methods, RET also has always espoused the training of clients in some of the skills in which they are deficient—as long as this training is accompanied by uprooting their basic irrational Beliefs. The trouble with the skill training movement, recently so popular in therapy, is that in many instances it *only* provides people with better skills—such as assertion training and communication skills—with the apparent hope that this training will help them think better about themselves and get along better in life. It frequently does—but not very elegantly. For many individuals, who acquire personal or social skills in therapy, wrongly conclude, "I now am a better person *because* I am more skilled and *because* people will now accept me with these skills." Their self-acceptance, in these instances, is still highly dependent on their competence and their approval by others, and is in great danger of collapse should they subsequently prove to be less skilled and less approved.

In RET, people are shown how to accept themselves *whether or not* they perform well in certain areas and *whether or not* others like them. As they start gaining this kind of *un*conditional self-acceptance, they are frequently also taught social, personal, assertive, academic, and other skills. In the case of a man I saw for therapy in the 1950's who had a profound fear of dating women and who was given the homework assignment of dating several of them, I reported as follows: "While Caleb was seeing these women, the therapist went over with him in detail his behavior with, and his reactions, to them. He was given specific information and instruction as to how to make dates; what to expect from the women; how to understand them and their problems; how to avoid being discouraged when he was rebuffed; what kinds of sexual overtures to make and when to make them, etc. His mistakes and blunders were gone over in an objective, constructive manner, and he was shown how, instead of blaming himself for these mistakes, he could put them to good self-teaching uses" (Ellis, 1962, p. 259).

RET agrees with therapists like Haley (1976) and Spivack, Platt and Shure (1976) that problem solving is very useful in psychotherapy, and agrees with therapists like Liberman and his associates (1975, 1978) that skill training can also help many clients; but it puts both problem solving and skill training solidly within a philosophic framework, and uses them in conjunction with helping clients to change their fundamental irrational Beliefs. It hypothesizes that this combined cognitive-behavioral approach will be more effective with most clients than problem solving or skill training approaches used by themselves.

LIMITATIONS OF RET

RET attempts to gracefully accept the limitations of all psychotherapy—including RET (Ellis, 1962). Because it assumes that people have strong biological predispositions to be disturbed in the first place, and that these require lifelong self-help effort to minimize or overcome, it also assumes that psychotherapy will often be relatively or utterly ineffective. It takes the unutopian view that individuals with severe disturbances are virtually never completely cured—they are merely significantly improved. They almost always have the innate tendency to lose some of their gains and to create quite new symptoms and even when they are "elegantly" improved by RET techniques, they only acquire the tendency to disturb themselves much less in the future. But never, not at all!

Because of the inherent limitations of humans, RET hardly works with certain disturbances, such as extreme mental deficiency, childhood autism, acute schizophrenia, dyslexia, epilepsy, and acute mania. It frequently can help individuals with these disorders to accept themselves *with* their handicaps, and thereby to prevent them from increasing their extreme disabilities. It can often beautifully deal with their secondary symptoms: their disturbances *about* their original disturbances. But it only partially helps with their basic disorders, and sometimes very partially.

Elegant forms of RET—such as teaching clients how to use the scientific method and how to Dispute their irrational Beliefs (iBs)— are ideal, and often work remarkably well in relatively brief periods of time with severely neurotic individuals. But because of the limitations of many clients, as well as the limitations of RET itself and RET practioners themselves, these elegant methods are often inapplicable to certain clients, or help effectuate only limited gains. Too bad! RET therapists had better, at least for the nonce, accept this reality and do their best to live with, and do as effective therapy as they can do under these limiting conditions.

SUMMARY

RET has a distinct set of hypotheses about human personality and the main "causes" or influences on the creation of emotional disturbance and it also has a set of hypotheses about which psychotherapeutic techniques are likely to be most effective in helping people overcome or minimize their severe problems. I created it in the mid 1950's against opposition from virtually all other popular schools of therapy then extant. Today, however, it has become an important and integral part of one of the mainstreams of psychotherapy: the new movement that stresses (1) active-directive techniques, (2) encountering-type confrontation, and (3) cognitive-behavior therapy. In its general or inelegant form, it significantly overlaps with and in some ways is practically synonymous with cognitive restructuring, cognitive-emotive-behavior-therapy, multimodal therapy, semantic therapy, philosophical therapy, and humanistic-existential therapy. In spite of its distinct theoretical framework, it is quite eclectic in its treatment techniques and employs a large number of thinking, affective, and behavioral methods.

In its more elegant form, RET emphasizes a clearcut understanding by clients of their basic irrational beliefs (iBs), particularly their absolutistic *shoulds* and *musts*; and, in addition to using a wide range of cognitive, emotive, and behavioral methods, it especially employs logical Disputing, philosophic restructuring, semantic analysis, and teaching clients to use the scientific method to uproot their irrational Beliefs and dysfunctional behaviors.

RET makes a valiant attempt to state its hypotheses in distinctly operational and testable terms, and it has, therefore, already inspired a large number (close to a hundred) outcome studies using control groups to test its clinical efficacy. Almost all these studies have shown that groups of individuals treated with RET make significantly greater changes in personality adjustment and symptom removal than do control groups treated with no therapy or with other forms of therapy (DiGiuseppe, Miller, and Trexler, 1977; Smith and Glass, 1977; Murphy and Ellis, 1979; Zingle and Mallett, 1976).

Literally hundreds of controlled experiments have also been done that test some of the main clinical and personality hypotheses of RET and more than 90 percent of these experiments tend to substantiate these hypotheses (Ellis, 1977b). Impressive evidence therefore exists to support both the clinical validity of RET and allied cognitive-behavior therapies as well as the general hypotheses of rational-emotive therapy.

Research in RET and cognitive-behavior therapy is, however, still in its formative stages. Many RET hypotheses—such as its assumptions that philosophic Disputing of irrational Beliefs and that helping people to rate only their traits and deeds and not their "selves" or "persons" will lead to better therapeutic results—are yet to be substantially tested; and considerably more investigation in these areas is desired. One of the basic tenets of RET is that the effectiveness of therapeutic techniques had better be checked and validated (or invalidated) by scientific experimentation, and not merely devoutly subscribed to on the basis of brilliant clinical intuition or of popular practice.   For all its tested "validity" so far, RET had therefore better not rest on its laurels, but instead encourage continual evaluation of its own and other therapy theories by the most rigorous scientific procedures.

2
Rational-Emotive Psychodiagnosis

All psychotherapists begin with an attempt to understand the dynamics of their clients' problems. Efforts are made to determine what motives, drives, values, defenses, complexes, fixations, regressions, attitudes, and so on propel people to act and feel as they do. A differential diagnosis is formulated hopefully suggesting goals, that when reached, indicate that the client is cured, or at least has changed for the better.

Many psychotherapists insist on collecting a great deal of diagnostic data about their clients. Some subject their clients to a lengthy and formal assessment procedure that, in its most complete version, goes something like this: the social worker obtains a definition of the presenting problem, characterizes the client's current social and physical environment, and gathers a rather lengthy social history; the psychologist conducts a battery of tests that typically include various measures of intelligence and personality; and the psychiatrist conducts a rather lengthy mental status examination. When all this is completed, everyone writes a report of their findings and assembles to "staff" the client.

A good many other psychotherapists eschew this formal psychodiagnostic method. Rather than relying on such a structured procedure, they use such procedures as roleplaying, hypnotic regression, and leisurely free associations to allow the diagnostic data to gradually emerge. They, too, spend a great deal of time trying to reach a differential diagnosis.

In light of the growing body of research that shows the many serious difficulties with traditional methods of psychodiagnosis, it is truly unfortunate that clinicians continue to engage in these behaviors. This is not the place for a lengthy review of literature that outlines the questionable validity of clinical diagnostic methods, nor do we have the time for a thorough discussion of the problems with the medical conceptualization of psychopathology.   The interested reader may turn to many sources, such as Bersoff (1971, 1973), Mischel (1973), and Peterson (1968), for a discussion of these matters.   Suffice it to say that traditional psychodiagnostic procedures are generally invalid, usually unnecessary, and often conducted for the wrong reasons. To wit:

". . . The real reason many clinicians conduct psychological examinations is that someone expects it of them. All too frequently, they administer and interpret Rorschachs, code MMPI's, and prepare reports for no clear reason beyond the scheduled expectation of a staff conference, the knowledge that they are going to be asked what 'the psychologicals look like,' and prescience of an embarrassed silence if they have nothing to say. . . Many clinical psychologists have been caught in an irrational system which requires useless answers to meaningless questions. . ." (Peterson, 1968, p. 32).

In almost complete contrast to traditional clinical practice, the rational-emotive therapist is relatively unconcerned with differential diagnosis, except perhaps in distinguishing psychotic from non-psychotic individuals. Rather, s/he primarily focuses on uncovering clients' irrational beliefs or philosophies, understanding how these ideations uniquely contribute to the clients' problems, and determining what to do to help clients resolve their problems. Only information directly relevant to treatment is gathered and the DSM II is left in the bathroom for more casual reading.

Furthermore, the rational-emotive therapist rarely turns to the various objective and subjective tests on the market. Instead, the RETer finds only three diagnostic "tools" indispensable. One is a thorough knowledge and appreciation of the crucial role that cognitions play in impacting both behavior and affect. A second is an in-depth understanding and sensitivity to the basic irrational ideas that individually and in combination constitute the core of emotionally disturbed states. A third is confidence in the validity of the various RET premises and a commitment to understanding clients from this perspective.

This chapter describes what rational-emotive psychodiagnosis is all about. In it, we will present an overview of the dynamics of the more common emotional concerns that clients present. We will help the reader to conceptualize the rational-emotive psychodiagnostic process and suggest ways to begin the client in RET. Finally, we will present some therapist problems and client resistances that may undercut the smooth initiation of rational-emotive therapy.

UNDERSTANDING PSYCHOPATHOLOGY

It is beyond the scope of this book to review the cognitive perspective on psychopathology in general. Neither is it possible to paint a thorough etiological picture of the cognitive slant on particular areas of psychopathology. There are already many resources that in part do this job and a text entirely devoted to the cognitive interpretation of psychopathology, titled *Cognition and Emotional Disturbance,* is now being prepared by myself (R.G.) and one of my colleagues, Dr. Ingrid Zachary.

Nevertheless, we feel it important to spend some time sketching the dynamics of some of the major forms of emotional disturbance. While it is often easy for the seasoned RETer to understand the client in relatively short order, the data that clients present is often voluminous, frequently confusing, and sometimes downright misleading. And, the basic clinical theory of RET, which appears simple at first blush, contains complexities and subtleties that can make the psychodiagnostic process very difficult, particularly for the novice.

To us, an understanding of psychopathology encompasses three areas. These include: (1) the type or category of problems the client presents; (2) the irrational ideas that cause and maintain the client's disturbed behaviors and feelings; and (3) secondary symptoms that clients may develop about their emotional and/or behavioral problems. We will discuss each of these in turn.

Problem Categories

Determining what does and does not constitute psychopathology is a debatable point, but it is one that is essential in deciding how best to help people. Some problems clearly call for psychotherapy while others could better be handled with guidance, advice, case management, or some form of environmental manipulation.

In making this determination, we find it useful to group client concerns into three categories. Category one has to do with *career concerns.* What do I want to do with my life? Do my interests and talents match? What is the job market for someone with my aptitudes? These are weighty questions that certainly deserve attention. Yet by themselves, they hardly constitute psychopathology; and, unless accompanied by emotional or behavior problems, like severe anxiety or prolonged procrastination, they certainly are not the province of psychotherapy.

A second category involves *environmental concerns* or *problems in living.* These are concerns about outside events and can be anything from a leaky faucet to an obnoxious spouse. It is typical for clients to initially present these types of problems to the therapist. They want the therapist to either help them change the circumstance or to change it for them. While troublesome, these do not define a person as disturbed, and unless also accompanied by emotional problems, hardly call for psychotherapy as we normally view it.

The third category of concerns are *emotional and behavioral* ones. It is the emotional disturbances—the depressions, angers, guilts, anxieties, and poor frustration tolerances—and it is the dysfunctional behaviors—the procrastinations and the like—to which psychotherapy generally attends and which is the distinct province of RET.

In making these distinctions, we must emphasize that our theoretically discrete treatment of these categories is not how they always exist in real life. Quite frequently clients have manifestations of two or even three categories, and the therapist must distinguish between them. Furthermore, clients may have emotional problems *about* vocational or environmental concerns. In these cases the therapist's psychodiagnostic task is indeed challenging because multiple problems and their relationship to each other must be determined.

Rational-emotive therapy is primarily designed to resolve emotional disturbance, and therefore it is not the treatment of choice for vocational and environmental problems. When clients bring these latter two problem types to the RETer, s/he will either refer the client to a counselor specializing in such areas, or administer appropriate counseling and guidance methods.

If the client presents a complex problem consisting of multiple and interacting problem categories, the RET therapist conceptualizes the entire problem area, ferrets out the emotional-behavioral aspects, and enters rational-emotive intervention. This therapy target is chosen first, even if the RETer is skilled in resolving environmental and vocational problems, because of a theoretical proposition which is central to RET. The proposition is that most people can constructively resolve or successfully cope with environmental and vocational concerns if unincumbered by emotional problems. For the minority who can't, emotional problems should still be treated first so clients are better able to make use of counseling and guidance methods for their other concerns. And, RET also holds that relieving practical problems before emotional problems tends to rob clients of their motivation to solve their emotional problems, leaving them more comfortable yet still disturbed.

Thus, in first understanding psychopathology, the RETer tries to determine whether the client has a career, environmental, or emotional-behavioral problem and, if a career or environmental problem exists, whether or not an emotional or behavioral problem about the career or environmental problem exists as well. If a career or environmental problem exists alone, then an appropriate referral is made or simple counseling or advice is given; but, if an emotional-behavioral problem is uncovered, or if an emotional problem is found to be superimposed on top of one of the other type problems, practical advice or problem-oriented counseling is temporarily withheld, and attention is first given to the emotional-behavioral concerns that are problematic in and of themselves and that may inhibit solving or even exacerbate the career or environmental problems. Once the therapist has determined that the client's concern falls within the province of rational-emotive therapy, the next step is to detect what irrational ideas the client holds that causes him or her to be disturbed.

Irrational Ideas and Psychopathology

If you are an RETer, you assume on theoretical and empirical grounds that human emotional disturbance stems from seeing the world distortedly because of, and according to, invalid ideas, beliefs or philosophies. The experienced RETer will listen to clients' complaints and begin making assumptions about what irrational ideas are part and parcel of their disturbance.

As has already been stated in chapter one and elsewhere (Ellis, 1962, 1971, 1973b, 1977a, 1977b), there is an infinite variety of thoughts people can think to disturb themselves. But, when these emotionally disturbing ideations are analyzed, as has been done by Albert Ellis throughout his clinical career, there emerges a fairly limited number of fundamental irrational ideas that cause almost all forms of emotional disturbance. These ideas include the three major types of musturbation or demandingness, awfulizing, I-can't-stand-it-itis, and self-rating.

These, then, are the basic irrational ideas behind psychopathology in general. But, what about the various psychopathologies? How do these basic irrational ideas manifest themselves, for instance, in anxiety problems or anger problems? While we do not have the time to spell this out in great detail, as that would constitute a text all its own, we will briefly overview the dynamics behind several common client problems, and refer the reader to Ellis (1962, 1971, 1973a,b, 1977a) and to Grieger and Zachary (in press) to study in more depth psychopathology from a cognitive perspective.

Anxiety. Anxiety problems are probably the most frequent ones that propel people to psychotherapy. In addition to more obvious manifestations, such as general nervousness and unreasonable fears of taking tests and public speaking, anxiety is central to all the traditional neurotic disorders, to most forms of sexual dysfunction, to the various psychophysiological disorders, and to many instances of procrastination. Understanding what is behind anxiety, and the myriad ways people use to defend against it, is clearly essential to clinical work.

In the most general sense, anxiety can be viewed as an internal warning signal that one is in imminent danger of not getting or of losing something thought to be needed (Ellis, 1977a). This position contains several important elements. First, people feel anxious when they anticipate something aversive or obnoxious happening in the near future. Distant events are usually not so troublesome, nor are those that can be put off or avoided. Second, and perhaps most crucial, this proposition implies that anxiety occurs when the potential danger or loss involves a highly prized, essential entity whose loss is viewed as serious, *catastrophic*, and highly destructive. We do not become anxious over the prospect of losing something we care little about. Finally, anxiety is characterized by the person feeling him/herself helpless to deal or cope with the situation or concern in question. When one believes oneself capable of mastering and controlling the situation, anxiety is minimized.

Now, beyond this general definition, how do RETers conceptualize the dynamics of anxiety problems? While recognizing that people can and do make themselves anxious in a myriad of ways, anxiety involves three "fantasies." A first fantasy contains a belief in a *"have to,"* that is, a belief that something *must* occur, as in "I must be approved." A second fantasy is that the "have to" will not take place or happen. And, a third fantasy is that it will be *awful if* the "have to" fails to happen. These three fantasies are usually centered around approval anxiety (AA), ego anxiety (EA), and discomfort anxiety (DA).

Approval Anxiety. Approval anxiety has to do with the importance people place on being accepted by others and the necessity for performing well in order to gain that acceptance. We all find it advisable to do well and to periodically obtain the approval of selected others; finding it desirable, we sometimes concern ourselves about possibly doing poorly and receiving disapproval. The person with approval anxiety, to the contrary, determines that approval is more than merely desirable; he or she deems it essential to do well and win approval virtually all the time, and he or she views it as a calamity if approval is not generated or if disapproval actually results.

To put it into RET terms, approval anxiety stems from people avidly believing that: "I must do well and win the approval of others, or else I can't stand it." They possibly also hold one of the main corollaries of this irrational belief (Ellis, 1977a, p. 40–41), including the ideas that:

(1) "I must have sincere love and approval almost all the time from virtually all the people whom I find significant or important in my life."

(2) "I must prove myself a thoroughly competent and adequate achiever or at least have a real skill or talent in something important to me."

(3) "I must continue to rely and depend on other people. Because I remain weak in this respect, I shall also continue to need and rely on certain sets of superstitious and religious ideas in order to survive times of great stress."

(4) "I can and should give myself a global rating as a human, and I can rate myself as good and worthy *only* if I perform well, do worthwhile things, and have people generally approve of me."

(5) "I must never question the beliefs, attitudes, or opinions held by respected authorities or by my society, family, or peer group because they certainly contain a real validity. If I do question them, people should rightly condemn and punish me."

Once people buy into these irrational ideas, their "gooses are cooked." For, *"needing"* love and approval, or more accurately, *believing they need* love and approval, they will view any possibility or hint that disapproval may be forthcoming as a catastrophe that cannot be borne. They will then worry incessantly about upcoming situations lest they perform poorly and incur disfavor; they will drive themselves mercilessly to do well and gain favor; they will experience anxiety in the situation for fear of doing something stupid; they will develop all sorts of self-defeating strategies to avoid threatening situations; they will rationalize their failures by blaming others and fate for their poor performances; they will literally cause themselves a variety of psychosomatic pains; and, ironically, they will probably perform more poorly because of their anxiety.

Ego Anxiety. Ego anxiety is a kissing cousin to approval anxiety. It stems from self-rating, or when people feel that their self or personal worth is threatened. They believe that they *must* or *should* perform well and/or be approved by others in order to accept themselves (the critical criteria), and that it is *awful* or *catastrophic* when they don't perform well and/or are not approved by others as they *must* be. Ego anxiety is usually accompanied by feelings of anxiety, depression, shame, guilt and worthlessness.

An example we like to present to our clients, that captures the dynamics of ego anxiety, has to do with two waitresses who serve a rude customer. The waitress who only carries food on her serving tray feels very little discomfort and virtually no anxiety when approaching the obnoxious customer's table. But, the waitress who carries both food *and* her self-worth on the tray experiences a great deal of anxiety (ego anxiety), for she has more than a few moments of unpleasantness at stake in dealing with this person, she also has her "self" at stake.

Discomfort Anxiety. Most of us want the easy life. We want to enjoy ourselves, avoid pain and difficulty, get what we want without too much effort, hassle or delay, and experience unhappiness infrequently and then only in mild degrees. Then, when frustrated, we react with displeasure, moan and groan for a while, and quickly get on with the business of life.

It is becoming apparent to many cognitive therapists (Ellis, 1977a, 1977b, 1978c; Ellis and Knaus, 1977) that a good proportion of the population goes beyond just wanting things to go well; a good many people *demand* that things go well and view it as *utterly tragic* when things do not. Discomfort anxiety consists of hypertension that results when people see that their comfort is threatened and believe (1) that they *should* or *must* get what they want (and *should not* or *must not* get what they don't want) and (2) that it is *awful* or *catastrophic* when they don't get what they must. Rather than merely disliking hurt or pain, and wanting comfort, these people neurotically fear or dread pain and experience self-pity, impatience, and low frustration tolerance as well.

Both approval anxiety (AA) and ego anxiety (EA) are usually dramatic, powerful feelings that often seem overwhelming, while discomfort anxiety (DA) is often less dramatic but perhaps more common. It tends to be specific to certain "uncomfortable" or "dangerous" situations—and consequently shows up in such phobias as fear of heights, of open spaces, of elevators, and trains. But it can also easily generalize to uncomfortable *feelings* themselves—such as the feelings of anxiety, depression, and shame. Thus, DA may be a primary symptom e.g., anxiety about elevators—or a secondary symptom e.g. anxiety about feeling anxious about elevators.

A personal example can perhaps make this clear. I (R.G.) used to play college basketball and used to frequently fly around the country to various games without giving flying a second thought. I enjoyed the adventure of traveling to new and exciting places, the peacefulness and solitude of being in the air, not to mention the opportunity to meet attractive stewardesses (as they were then called) roughly my age. I had a ball. Then, after graduating, I did not fly for almost a year and when I did, I had the unfortunate experience of taking a flight that was particularly rough, one in which I became extremely frightened.

I had no problem until I discovered at my next opportunity to fly that I was extremely afraid, and I acted on my fear—I literally stopped flying. I did not go on vacations that were beyond driving distance, I avoided professional conferences and conventions, and I let friendships slip because of mileage. Nothing seemed to make it better, not even doing RET on myself. I told myself, to no avail, that it was not awful to die, that no one can live forever, that life should be lived to the fullest, and a score of other things designed to get me up in the air.

Fortunately, one day I realized what my fear was all about. I was not actually afraid of flying, rather I was afraid of experiencing those anxious feelings when I flew. When I really started listening to what I was telling myself, I found it was something like: "My God, I'll feel miserable in the air. I hate that. Its awful. I can't stand to feel so terrible." And, worse: "If the plane goes down, the agony of that dreadful minute or so of panic will practically kill me before the crash does." There it was. I was not afraid of crashing or even dying, but of emotional discomfort. And I viewed the discomfort as worse than the potential physical suffering. And, it was only when I began to realize that I could easily tolerate the anxiety that I could relax and enjoy flying once again.

As a secondary symptom, discomfort anxiety may generalize to almost *any* kind of anxiety. Thus, people may first feel anxious about going in elevators and then feel anxious about feeling anxious about elevators. But they may later worry about whether they are *also* going to feel anxious about trains or escalators; and they may therefore actually make themselves exceptionally uncomfortable (anxious) about *many* forms of anxiety (discomfort), and become pandemically anxious (as in agoraphobia). Or they may at first feel anxious about a specific event e.g., about entering an elevator—and later, realizing that they may well become anxious about that event, they may also make themselves anxious about any symbol of that event e.g., a picture of an elevator—or about any thought of that event e.g., the thought, "Suppose I have to take an elevator when I visit my friend. Wouldn't that possibility be *awful!*"

Because it is less dramatic than approval anxiety and ego anxiety and because it may be a secondary rather than a primary symptom, discomfort anxiety is often unrecognized and may be wrongly labeled as ego anxiety ("I would be a rotten person if I experienced anxiety when I entered an elevator!) or as a general or "free-floating" anxiety ("Since I am not a rotten person when I am afraid of elevators and since I know that I won't get hurt or die in an elevator, I don't really know what I am afraid of, and therefore I must have 'free-floating' anxiety").

Guilt and Self-Downing. Although anxiety and depression problems comprise the heart of most clinical practices, feelings of guilt and low self-worth are probably more noteworthy in terms of the damage they do. This is so because feelings of worthlessness or low self-esteem, besides being debilitating in and of themselves, create a multitude of other problems as well. In this regard Ellis (1972) writes:

"Almost all modern authorities in psychotherapy belive that the individual's estimation of his own value, or worth, is exceptionally important and that if he seriously denigrates himself or has a poor self-image, he will impair his normal functioning and make himself miserable in many significant ways. Consequently, one of the main functions of psychotherapy, it is usually held, is to enhance the individual's self-respect (or "ego-strength," "self-confidence," "self-esteem," "feelings of personal worth," or "sense of identity") so that he may thereby solve the problem of self-evaluation."

When an individual does not value himself very highly, innumerable problems result. He frequently will focus so intensely on what a rotten person he is that he will distract himself from problem-solving and will become increasingly inefficient. He may falsely conclude that a rotter such as he can do virtually nothing right, and he may stop trying to succeed at the things he wants to accomplish. He may look at his proven advantages with a juandiced eye and tend to conclude that he is a "phony" and that people just haven't as yet seen through him. Or he may become so intent on "proving" his value that he will be inclined to grovel for others' favors and approval and will conformingly give up his own desires for what he thinks (rightly or wrongly) they want him to do (Ellis, 1967; Hoffer, 1955; Lecky, 1945; Nietzsche, 1965). He may tend to annihilate himself, either literally or figuratively, as he desperately tries to achieve or to please (Becker, 1964; Hess, 1966; Watzlawick, 1967). He may favor noncommitment and avoidance, and become essentially "nonalive" (May, 1967). He may sabotage many or most of his potentialities for creative living (Gardner, 1964). He may become obsessed with comparing himself to others and their achievements and tend to be status-seeking rather than joy-exploring (Farson, 1966; Harris, 1963). He may frequently be anxious, panicked, terrified (Branden, 1964; Ellis, 1962; Coopersmith, 1968; Rosenberg, 1962). He may tend to be a short-range hedonist and to lack self-discipline (Hoffer, 1955). Often he may become defensive and thus act in a "superior," grandiose way (Adler, 1964; Anderson, 1962, 1964; Low, 1967). He may compensatingly assume an unusually rough or "masculine" manner (Adler, 1931; Maslow, 1966). He may become quite hostile toward others (Anderson, 1964; Low, 1967). He may become exceptionally depressed (Anderson, 1964). He may withdraw from reality and retreat into fantasy (Coopersmith, 1968; Rosenberg, 1962). He may become exceptionally guilty (Ellis, 1967; Geis, 1965). He may present a great false front to the world (Rosenberg, 1962). He may sabotage a number of special talents which he posseses (Coopersmith, 1968). He may easily become conscious of his lack of self-approval, may berate himself for having little or no confidence in himself, and may thereby reduce his self-image even more than he has done previously (Ellis, 1962; Ellis and Harper, 1967). He may become afflicted with numerous psychosomatic reactions, which then encourage him to defame himself still more (Coopersmith, 1968; Rosenberg, 1962).

This list is hardly exhaustive since almost the entire psychotherapeutic literature of the last fifty years is more or less concerned with the harm an individual may do himself and how badly he may maim or destroy his relations with others when he condemns himself, makes himself feel guilty or ashamed about his acts or inactions, and otherwise lowers his self-image. This same literature illustrates the corollary proposition almost endlessly; namely, that when a human being somehow manages to accept, respect, and approve of himself, in most instances his behavior changes remarkably for the better: his efficiency considerably improves, his anxiety, guilt, depression, and rage lessen, and he becomes much less emotionally disturbed."

Helping people consistently appraise themselves so that they almost invariably accept or respect themselves is relatively easy once the dynamics of guilt, feelings of worthlessness, and self-downing are understood. Feelings of guilt and worthlessness result from people downing or denigrating their value as human beings, or, to say it somewhat differently, from evaluating themselves as totally bad. Guilt and feelings of worthlessness directly result from a two-pronged attack on oneself. The first attack occurs when people note that they have done something wrong or inept, concluded that it was undesirable to have done that, and judge the *act* as bad. This leads to feelings of regret, sorrow and disappointment, and to efforts to rectify or change the act. The second attack, however, leads directly to the guilt and feelings of worthlessness.   These occur when individuals judge themselves as bad for engaging in the act. They note the wrongdoing, believe that it was a *horrible* thing that *should* not, *must* not have been done, and *condemn* themselves totally. Guilty persons thus negatively evaluate, and hence down their total beings as a result of some real or imagined poor performance, trait, or quality. In the process, they call themselves not only bad, but *always* bad and deserving of damnation for being bad.

Depression. Most therapies treat all other symptoms of depression as secondary to the affective disturbance. RET, on the other hand, views the distorted ideas of the depressed person as central to the development and maintenance of depression with its affective, motivational, and physical symptoms. The reader will certainly want to turn to Beck (1961, 1963, 1964, 1972) Beck and Shaw, (1977), Ellis (1962) and Seligman (1975) for discussions of cognitive inter-pretations of depression. We will present the ideas of Paul Hauck (1973) who offers perhaps the purest RET model of depression. He cites three types: (1) self-blaming depression;   (2) self-pitying depression; and (3) other pitying depression.

Self-Blaming Depression. We have just talked about the relationship between self-downing and guilt. A blood brother to guilt and a major consequence of self-downing is depression. For, to quote Hauck (1973),

"...if you are constantly cutting yourself down, hating yourself, thinking that you are the worst human being alive and that you should be horse-whipped every Tuesday and Thursday afternoon, you will get depressed just as sure as there are mental hospitals in the United States. It makes practically no difference what you blame yourself for, just as long as you give yourself a good tongue-lashing over it. . . Just blame yourself and you have a depression coming on.   And if you blame yourself mightily, you will become quite disturbed, probably feel like crying, become silent and moody, and you may even want to jump off the Brooklyn Bridge." (p. 22)

Self-pitying Depression.   Enough said about self-blame.   A second major way clients get depressed is to feel sorry for or pitying of themselves.   Self-pitying depression results when a person is confronted with frustration and responds with the following two irrational ideas: (1) I *must* have what I want and *must not* have what I don't want; (2) its *awful* that I don't get my way.   Holding these ideas, and being thwarted, this person whines about how cruel the world is, how difficult it is for such a poor wretch as s/he to have to deal with reality such as it is, and how tragic it is not to get what is wanted. Thus, suffering is guaranteed.

I (R.G.) was recently presented with a quite unusual case of a person suffering from self-pitying depression.   Harriet consulted me for being, in her words, "out of control about eating."   It seemed that, after having led a rather spartan culinary life and being regularly engaged in a heavy jogging regimen for years, she had begun to gorge herself to the point of gaining some twenty pounds.   Her concern about her overeating had recently turned to alarm when she started sticking her finger down her throat to throw up at the end of a meal, in order to continue eating.

A brief look at her recent history will give some insight into the dynamics of all this.   She had for years lived a rather comfortable life—a spacious house, membership in a country club, a maid once a week, leisurely luncheons with friends, children at private school— until her husband left her and the children.   At this point her whole life changed.   She had to give up her home and move to a two bedroom apartment; she had to take a job, she no longer could afford her maid; she lost the company of a man she loved and who kept her from loneliness, and so on.   All in all, she lost pretty much all the comforts she had been used to.   In her eyes, life became rather deprived and unsatisfying.

All of this certainly proved disconcerting, to say the least, and presented difficult frustrations to her.   However, she added emotional problems to these hardships by adopting the following line of thought:

"These hardships and hassles are *horrible;* I am used to all sorts of satisfactions and I *shouldn't* have to experience this; it's unfair for me to have to put up with this and I *shouldn't* have to; life is so *awful* for poor little me." Without going into how she downed herself for her eating problem, it is easy to see how she made herself depressed about her circumstances. In short, she developed self-pitying depression.

Other Pitying Depressions. Another way people depress themselves is to awfulize about the misfortune of others, by being both concerned *and* overconcerned about the suffering of others. Other-concern involves wanting things to go well and seeing it as unfortunate when they do not. Other-overconcern, or other-pity, derives from two irrational ideas. The first one, that we have to be upset about the problems others confront (or else we are awful); the second, that the misfortune or suffering of others is too horrible to bear.

A brief example will illustrate this. I (R.G.) am currently working with a somewhat depressed mother, referred by a school psychologist, to provide her help in disciplining her rebellious seven year old. A major part of both her depression and her lax disciplining style is her overconcern for her child's reaction when punished. It seems that when spanked or denied something he typically goes to his room and wails that no one loves him and how unhappy he is. And, like a trained puppy, Mom falls for this blackmail. She quickly depresses herself by concluding how horrible life is for her little baby and almost immediately gives in to him. The net result is for the cycle to repeat itself and for her to make herself depressed quite frequently.

Anger and Aggression. RET sees anger as the mirror opposite of guilt. As the reader will recall, guilt stems from irrational ideas people hold about themselves. Anger ideation is also the opposite of anxiety. Anxiety results from *self*-oriented irrational ideas, particularly with regard to future events, whereas anger generally (though not always) results from *other* directed irrational ideas with regard to things other people have already done.

Angry people almost inevitably take at least three major irrational stances. The first is an appraisal that the action of another is an assault against some rule, value or standard (Beck, 1976) that *should* not, *must* not happen. The picture one gets is of an arrogant rule-maker riding roughshod over the universe clinging to the irrational belief (or one of its main derivatives) that others *must* treat me fairly, kindly, and considerately or they rate as rotten.

The second stance angry people take is to perceive the action of the other as *serious,* to label it negatively and to conclude that it is so *awful* as to be beyond understanding. While a husband's glance at an attractive woman's figure seems trivial to most, the wife who concludes that it is a terrible thing that he has no right to do would almost certainly make herself angry.

The third stance common to anger is to *evaluate the person* who engaged in the offensive act *as rotten,* as per: "Because you did this *terrible* thing that you *should not* have done, I *condemn* you as a shit and will cause you as much suffering as I can muster."

The assumption throughout all this is that angry people Jehovistically impose absolute, arbitrary demands on others. They honestly, yet erroneously believe themselves to be the center of the universe so that others must cater to their wants and desires lest they be worms. Yet, while this is true for most, if not all angry people, we often find that two other irrational themes already discovered are central to a number of other emotional disturbances. These stimulate the ideas enumerated above and fuel the anger reaction. One has to do with self-worth and the other with frustration tolerance.

Self-Worth Anger. Often lurking behind anger reactions is a threat to one's feelings of worthiness. People prone to self-worth anger typically hold the irrational idea that their self-worth depends on how well they do in winning love, approval and acceptance. Individuals who hold this idea quite often interpret the negative actions of others as somehow threatening their self-worth. With self-worth, the basic pawn at stake, these people reflexively, immediately and absolutely *demand* that the acts *should not* happen. They conclude deep down: "His actions communicate that he finds me insignificant; if that is true, it makes me insignificant; he therefore *shouldn't* do that to me, *the SOB!*"

A double level problem thus operates in what we call self-worth anger. On the more conscious, accessible level the typical "shoulding" and "condemning" takes place. At a less conscious and accessible second level looms the predisposed tendency to generalize from the negative actions of others to self-worth. Instead of immediately accepting the validity of the insult and turning inward to condemn the self, as guilty and depressed persons would do, these people turn on and condemn the other person in the picture. The turning on of the other person or event is a self-protective action that serves to prevent people from facing feelings of worthlessness.

Let us illustrate with a clinical example that we think is self explanatory. Carol was a member of an RET group who wanted to overcome her anger problems. Not being a wilting lilly, she quickly took advantage of the group situation. She readily acknowledged the fact that she "shoulded" other people and condemned them as rotten for behaving in the particular ways she did not like. She also acknowledged the irrationality of these stances and with our help correctly thought them through. But, she did not improve.

Then, in one group session Carol discussed how angry she had become at a woman who rented a room in her house. It seemed that this woman used Carol's iron and left her kitchen untidy, despite the fact that she repeatedly told her to not do either. After she and the group again went over the same ground as before, the following interchange took place between Carol and the therapist.

Therapist: We don't seem to be getting anywhere here. Let me ask you a question, Carol. Do you find this woman's behavior positive, negative, or neutral?

Carol: Well, negative, of course.

Therapist: Then, finish this sentence for me: "I don't like her using my iron, *particularly* since I've told her not to, because . . ."

Carol: (pause) Because it discounts me.

Therapist: What do you mean when you say it discounts you?

Carol: She invalidates me.

Therapist: That sounds a little mystical to me. Do you mean that she somehow devalues your worth by ignoring your wishes?

Carol: Yes. That's exactly right.

Therapist: Well, aren't you confusing her negative value of you, assuming that that is true, with *your own* value of yourself

	as a person? Aren't you putting your self-worth on the line depending on whether she obeys you or not?
Carol:	In a way, I guess I am.
Therapist:	With that being at stake, I can see why you are so angry at her and why you would demand that she toe the line. It's a logical reaction from an illogical premise. But, isn't the real problem the fact that you don't really accept yourself?
Carol:	Yes. I guess that is the problem.

Thus, a core component of many angry reactions is individuals equating their intrinsic value with the extrinsic value others hold of them. Negative treatment or regard by others is often magically taken by these people as a threat to their self-worth. Then, out of fear of worthlessness to which they are rarely aware, they vehemently demand different treatment and hastily condemn the culprit for treating them that way.

Low Frustration Tolerance Anger. Often hiding behind and fueling anger is low frustration tolerance. Low frustration tolerance (LFT) results from the following irrational idea:

The world (and the people in it) must arrange conditions under which I live so that I get everything that I want when I want it. And further, conditions must exist so that I don't get what I don't want. Moreover, I usually must get what I want quickly and easily.

Things are fine for people who hold this irrational idea when life is smooth and easy. But, when confronted with hassles and hardships, these people are prone to become either self-pitying and depressed, as in "what's the use," or outraged. So, again, a double level problem often exists when people get angry. On the more conscious level, the angry person engages in the typical shoulding toward, awfulizing about, and condemning of the frustrating person or set of circumstances. On the deeper, less conscious level, the person believes that things should always be easy, smooth and hassle free, and he or she thinks in the following manner: "This hassle is *too much to be bearable;* it is such a hassle that it *shouldn't* exist, particularly for me;

and you and the world are *rotten* for subjecting me to such a hassle." All in all, LFT anger is a scream of outrage against any semblance of unfairness, injustice, or hassle.

To sum, anger generally stems from a person holding irrational ideas about others. When confronted by angry clients look for what rule or *should* they are imposing on others, what form of *awfulizing* they attach to the others or to their acts, and how they *damn* the other. Equally as important, be sensitive to cues that your angry clients hold elements of self-downing or LFT anger, for they often are behind the angry themes and actually provide the impetus and energy for the anger. If you find them, it will be best to work directly with them, for they represent the key to the anger and probably a more core problem.

Problems About Problems

Problems about problems are the dynamics behind some of the common problems clients present to the therapist. As mentioned earlier, it is the rare client who presents only a single problem. Rather, clients usually develop secondary symptoms of disturbance that overlay their primary symptoms; or, to say it differently, they develop emotional problems about emotional problems. When people feel and behave in a disturbed manner at C (their emotional or behavioral Consequence), they very frequently make this C into another or secondary A (event), and then they create a secondary disturbance (or further disordered Consequence) about it. Thus, once they fail at an original A and feel depressed, worthless, and withdrawn at the original C, they tend to observe their C-state and think and feel as follows: A (Activating Experience)—"I am depressed and withdrawn." rB (rational Belief)—"I don't like these results. How annoying!" aC (appropriate Consequence)—Sorrow and annoyance about being depressed; determination to do something to overcome this inappropriate feeling. iBs (irrational Beliefs)—"I *must* not be depressed and withdrawn! How *awful*! I *can't stand* it! I am pretty worthless for having brought them about!" iC (inappropriate Consequence)—Depression about feeling depressed. It might be humorously said that they bargain basement shop and buy two problems for the price of one.

Secondary symptoms of emotional disturbance usually exacerbate primary symptoms, and they largely interfere with people clearly perceiving how they tend to create these primary symptoms and what they can do to uncreate them. Tertiary symptoms may also arise. Some individuals see that they are depressing themselves about their original feelings of depression, condemn themselves severely for doing this, and feel depressed about being depressed about being depressed!

Seven year old Markie recently demonstrated a classic example of how one develops a problem about a problem. His mother stupidly allowed him to see the movie Jaws II, which contained a number of scary and vivid scenes of people being eaten by a shark. As she might have suspected, he found this very frightening and could not go to sleep that particular night. Putting this into RET language, he frightened himself by thinking fearful, awfulizing thoughts about this movie. This represented the first or original problem. As kids are wont to do, he came out of his bedroom several times telling how scared he was, until on the fourth occasion, he started crying. Interestingly enough, on this occasion, he told a completely new story about how stupid he was for not using enough common sense to avoid going to that particular movie and for not "using his head" like his Dad regularly admonished him to do. In essence, he downed himself (1) for going to the movie, and (2) for getting so frightened. In doing this, he caused himself a guilt problem about his fright problem.

Brenda V. represents a clinical example of a person who developed tertiary emotional problems about an original emotional problem. She entered therapy with such severe anxieties that she had almost completely withdrawn socially and was on the verge of dropping out of college. It became obvious that her anxieties resulted from ego anxiety in that she believed that she must do well in all her performances and be approved by almost all the people she encountered or she would be a thoroughly worthless person. In the jargon, we labeled her problem as "a severe case of chapter 10," referring to chapter 10 of A New Guide to Rational Living (Ellis and Harper, 1975), "Tackling dire needs for approval."

We would have had a simple time of therapy had this been Brenda's only problem, but this was not the case for she developed a three-level problem. At level 1, as stated previously, she made herself anxious about rejection, failure, and self-worth, and she responded by either withdrawing from social contacts or by passively going along with what anybody wanted her to do. Then, she developed a secondary problem about her original problem; she noted her anxiety reaction, making it a new A, and further upset herself by awfulizing about her anxiety, thus creating an additional emotional effect, or a new C. In essence, she made herself anxious about being anxious. Finally, at level 3, the tertiary problem, she further noted her anxieties, creating yet another A and further upset herself by awfulizing about them and condemning herself for having them, thus creating another emotional consequence of depression. The net effect for her was to snowball a single problem into three separate, yet intimately related problems.

In RET, we look for evidences of both primary, secondary, and tertiary problems. If we find both two or even three, as is very frequently the case, we are able to understand the client's disturbed feelings more fully and clearly, to be more effective at helping him or her to see the irrational Beliefs behind problems and to surrender them.

SKILLS IN RATIONAL-EMOTIVE PSYCHODIAGNOSIS

Before outlining the skills of rational-emotive psychodiagnosis, it is prudent to set forth a few prefacing remarks that will put the diagnostic process into proper perspective. One such remark concerns the questions of "when" does the therapist conduct a diagnosis and "how much time" does it require. In RET, the diagnostic process begins with the first session of therapy, and, depending upon the therapist's expertise and the complexity of the client's problems, it can take from ten minutes to several sessions. Expert RETers, Albert Ellis being the prime model, can usually establish a fairly complete diagnosis and begin intervention early in the first session; less experienced and able clinicians may naturally use more time than this for their psychodiagnosis. It is a mistake to think that diagnosis requires a long time to establish and that it must be perfectly established before intervention can begin. To the contrary, a diagnosis can be set early and altered as information relevant to diagnosis dribbles into the therapist's head throughout the RET process.   After one or two interviews the RETer usually has enough information to correctly conceptualize the client's problems. This diagnostic picture is then sharpened as therapy progresses and as the client discloses more information.

Another prefacing remark: the overall therapy situation may dictate how and when to use diagnostic skills. The skills sequence described in this chapter pertains to a "standard" therapy situation where a client has sought the therapist's help and is motivated to some degree to work toward problem resolution. Many therapists do not enjoy the benefits of a motivated client and a clearly defined therapy situation, psychodiagnosis as well as treatment may be delivered in something other than textbook fashion. Such is reality; the skills of rational-emotive psychodiagnosis may have to be adopted and delivered in innovative ways per difficult circumstances. But we strongly believe that most of the skills described in this chapter are essential to rational-emotive psychodiagnosis and should no be compromised.

Last, it is helpful for readers to remember that there are two main goals in rational-emotive psychodiagnosis. One is to *categorize* the client's problem; that is, to clarify whether it is a career concern, or an environmental problem, or an emotional-behavioral concern.

The second goal, pursued only if the client has an emotional-behavioral problem, is to accurately conceptualize the client's dynamics into the ABC's which constitute the problem.

In the remainder of this section we will outline and explain the key skills which are employed during the psychodiagnostic process. Topics will include the therapist-client relationship, skills in categorizing client problems, techniques for pursuing the ABC's, the skill of formulating and presenting a diagnosis proper, and the steps in setting RET goals.

The Client-Therapist Relationship

A multifaceted skill which stands at the forefront of an initial RET session and the beginning of psychodiagnosis is the establishment of a client-therapist relationship which is conducive to effective psychotherapy.   Rational-emotive therapy does not propose a "standard relationship" to go along with its theory and methods, for therapists are usually more effective when using their own unique personality attributes than when imitating the personal style of an "expert" clinician. Yet, there are conditions seeming to characterize the users of RET, which we will express in the next chapters, and there are some conditions and qualities which are widely accepted as being clinically advantageous. These latter characteristics are deserving of the therapist's attention, and will be addressed here, for contrary to RET critics, RET practitioners *are* sensitive to the client-therapist relationship.

Credibility. A client attitude and relationship condition which helps .determine the choice of a therapist is credibility or expertness. Such things as the recommendations of former clients, public presentations, the authorship of books and articles, endorsement from other mental health professionals, and of course professional licensing, all contribute to the client's pretherapy attitude of credibility and the predilection to choose a therapist.

Once the client sits down, the therapist's behavior will confirm or contradict the client's pretherapy attribution of expertness; and this is where RET shines, for an RET therapist is active and vigorous in his/her interventions in the first session. By getting right to work, the client is sensitively yet firmly led into a productive diagnostic exploration of the problem(s). Consequently, the client is inclined to think that the therapist is truly interested in him/her, and, of even greater impact, the client is led to perceive that the therapist is competent. There is no fumbling around, prolonged and unnecessary chit-chat, or sparring back-and-forth in terms of the relationship. A message is implied via the therapist's demeanor and actions "I am here to help you resolve your concerns; I know how to do that, so let's get started." Such a message spawns credibility.

Facilitative Conditions. More controversial than credible, which most therapy approaches agree to, is the place of facilitative conditions within the client-therapist relationship. These conditions of *empathy, unconditional respect, warmth,* and *genuineness* are thought by those of client-centered persuasion to be indispensable to the client-therapist relationship. The conditions are widely endorsed by eclectics and therapists of numerous theoretical orientations as being a highly desirable variable in psychotherapy, and research has supported their instrumental effect in psychological help giving (Carkhuff, 1969).

In RET, the conditions do have a role, but it is a role which differs from that played elsewhere. Empathy, for example, is considered important in RET, and during the initial session and diagnostic phase we recommend conveying understanding to the client through specific techniques (to be discussed later). But RET moves quickly to uncover the self-talk and philosophic meanings behind a client's emotions, data which is most crucial to clients' sense of well-being. Thus, the RET therapist does not spend a prolonged period of time conveying lower levels of understanding (e.g., reflection of feelings), though this is done to some extent as the therapist helps clients identify the activating events and emotional upsets in their problems. Rather, the RETer quickly goes to a profound level of understanding, or empathy, by attending to the heart and soul of the client's psychological being (e.g., the personalized meanings or philosophies behind the feelings). In doing this, the therapist displays a level of empathy, almost from the start, that is most facilitative of a sound relationship.

Unconditional respect, like empathy, takes on a distinct role in RET. The RET therapist respects the rights of clients, and does have a sincere and humanistic interest in helping them alleviate their emotional suffering. These attitudes of respect and caring are expressed in subtle and sundry ways. But also conveyed to clients is a total acceptance of them, while perhaps not accepting their symptoms. The attitude conveyed is: "I accept you no matter what stupid thing you've done or ways you're acting; what I don't accept is the fact that you cannot change that way of acting, and I'll do my best to help you in that regard." There is a tacit and explicit message from the therapist that clients are seen as fallible mistake-makers, but that they are not judged as bad because of it. Hence, they receive acceptance and respect that is most genuine and respectful.

The client-therapist relationship is clearly very important to RET, but for reasons which differ from those espoused by more relationship-oriented therapies. Clients can expect the RET therapist to express genuine interest and accurate empathy, but they will learn that s/he does not consider them "special" and deserving of tender loving care. Rather, they are accepted as people, regardless of their problems, and attention is quickly turned to a mutual problem solving effort.

Categorizing Client Problems

After perhaps some initial get acquainted talk, the RET therapist directly asks what problems prompted the client to seek help. It is at this point (if not before) that psychodiagnosis begins, and the first order of business is to categorize the client's complaints into career, environmental, or emotional-behavioral concerns. As already discussed, RET is especially designed for emotional-behavioral problems. If, therefore, the client has a purely environmental or career concern, RET will not be the treatment of choice; some form of counseling and guidance activity would be more appropriate, and the therapist can either administer this treatment (if s/he is qualified) or refer to a counselor who specializes in practical and career concerns.

A typical categorizing situation that we frequently encounter is the client who has multiple problems and/or problems about problems. Clients having multiple problems might present two or three different types of problems to the therapist, such as:

1. I'm having a difficult time finding a job, I need some help. I don't like my present job, but what else can I do? *(Career Concern)*
2. How can we manage to live happily in such a small house, where do we put all the kids so there's some privacy? *(Environmental Concern)*
3. Also, my mother-in-law is driving me nuts. Last weekend I lost control of my emotions and caused a big scene. I just can't go on like this. *(Emotional Concern)*

Problems about problems is a categorizing situation similar to having multiple problems, except that the problems are not discreet and they are psychologically related to each other. There are three common ways that clients can have problems about problems:

4. A practical problem about an emotional problem.

   Example: "My boss tells me that my work is slipping and my job is in jeopardy. But I'm so nervous that I can't sleep at night, and when I get to work I'm dead tired. And I spend all day worrying about my personal problems instead of producing."

5. An emotional problem about a practical problem.

   Example: "I've become so upset living in this tiny house, I'm just a nervous wreck!"

6. An emotional problem about another emotional-behavioral problem.

   Example: "I get so nervous when I speak in public. I'm just a jerk who can't do anything right."

In the foregoing six situations, the RET therapist would categorize the client's complaints into one of the categories and then direct his or her attention to the emotional-behavioral concerns, if they exist. The reason for such categorizing is simple: if therapists try to simultaneously deal with multiple problems, they will add to clients' confusion and their own frustration. Rational-emotive therapy helps clients clearly articulate and think through their emotional-behavioral problems, and it is unethical to entertain their tangled network of problems. Categorizing is a crucial step in reducing the complexity of client difficulties, and it opens the door to further diagnosis of emotional-behavioral problems.

How to Categorize. The skills of categorizing client problems are mostly conceptual, accomplished by simply offering pointed leads, listening to the client's responses, making judgments, and communicating the judgments to the client. This therapy excerpt illustrates how a therapist might categorize a client's problems during an initial session.

Client 1: There's been a lot of things bothering me—ever since my divorce things have been bad.

Therapist 1: What kind of things are bad for you? Tell me about them.

Client 2:   Well, I guess my social life or lack of it is really the worst, and my job, the one I just started, it's a big mistake.

Therapist 2:   So, you are dissatisfied with your social life, and unhappy with your new job. Let's look at the social life first. What's bothering you there?

Client 3:   It's not having a permanent relationship, and being lonely. But when I get a date I feel clumsy, I haven't dated for fifteen years . . . . during my marriage. I get uptight, and things don't go well.

Therapist 3:   This is certainly an appropriate thing to bring into therapy, and we can get started on it right away. But what about your job problem, let's just overview it and see if we should deal with it too. What exactly concerns you about your job?

Client 4:   It's not what I expected, I took the job thinking it would be like my other one, and now that I know it's not, its difficult, I'm still stuck with it!!

Therapist 4:   How long have you been working on it?

Client 5:   A week and a half.

Therapist 5:   Un huh. I think I'm beginning to see your concerns. There seems to be three. Your social life is one, a job that might not be right for you is another, and . . .

Client 6:   Yea, I . . . . I guess . . . . that's right.

Therapist 6:   OK. We can certainly attend to these things. But, I also hear you are having emotional problems about what I would call these practical problems or problems in living. You seem to be very upset about being alone and dating again, and you are also disturbed about things not working out well in your job.

Client 7:   I agree . . . But, what can I do about the job? What if it doesn't fit me?

Therapist 7:   Then we can face that and find another one for you. Maybe you can even consult with a vocational counselor. But, right now I'd like to explore a bit further

> with you your emotional problems about these
> practical problems.

This excerpt is a discussion of the client's problem categories, and it took place very early in the initial session. Note that the client begins by overtly presenting environmental concerns (Client 2) and career concerns (Client 3). The therapist asks questions to draw out the client (Therapist 1, 2, 3, 4), all the while listening both to the content and to the affective elements intertwined with the content of the client's messages. He articulates them to the client in terms of their career/environmental categories (Therapist 5) and emotional category (Therapist 6). He then goes on, after identifying the emotional problem for himself and for the client, to direct the discussion to an investigation of the irrational ideas behind the emotional problems (Therapist 7). We want to emphasize that it is *also* commonplace for the therapist to include an explanation of the client's problem categories in the diagnosis proper.

Pursuing the ABC's

The search for the ABC's of client problems begins the moment the person enters therapy. In this pursuit, the therapist acts both as an opportunistic listener and as an equally active interrogater. From the moment the client begins talking, the RETer begins placing the presented data into its respective A, B, or C niches. In doing all this, an arsenal of skills (in addition to the RET theory of emotional disturbance) may be expended, a few of which are crucial and will be reviewed.

Listening Skills. All therapists listen, but they do not listen for the same things. Client-centered therapists listen predominantly to feelings and self-dynamics; psychoanalytic therapists listen for symbolic representation of unconscious psychosexual striving; gestalt therapists are usually in search of blocked emotions; and rational-emotive therapists listen for the A's, B's, and C's of client problems.

Listening for Activating Events. One of the components in client problems which RETers listen for is activating events (A)—those antecedents and situational conditions which precede and seem to contribute to (although not directly cause) clients' emotional and behavioral symptoms. The main skill in listening for A's is to sort out and unscramble them. Events are frequently expressed in multiples, along with information about other problem components and other information which is irrelevant to the problem. This excerpt from a woman complaining of depression is illustrative.

"Well, things haven't been going well in general. First the car broke down, and I had told him to have it repaired, but as usual he didn't listen; and when he said I'd have to find my own ride, I told him off!!! Oh was I angry. . . .but then he didn't come home that night, and, and, my mother told me to leave him, and I've just been depressed all week."

There is a great deal of information in this brief excerpt. The client communicated feelings of frustration, anger, and depression. She articulated four events—the car breaking down, her husband telling her to find her own ride, her husband staying away from home overnight, and the mother telling her to leave her husband. Some of these events were more directly related to anger and frustration and some to depression. The first skill would be to hear the four discreet events. Then, to ascertain the part they played in each of the feelings, the therapist would inquire further with pointed leads.

Listening for Emotions and Behavior. As the RET therapist listens for and investigates activating events, s/he simultaneously listens for the symptomatic emotions and behavior which form the core of the client's distress or difficulties. Clients vary widely in the extent to which they can accurately express their feelings and describe the behaviors which make up their symptoms. Some articulate clients, particularly those having had previous therapy, are surprisingly helpful, while others express only that they are upset, overwhelmed, falling apart, and so on. Thus the task of listening for emotions and behavior may be easy or challenging.

One guideline to follow when listening for C's is to use events as a cue. Whenever you hear an activating event, quickly listen for how the client felt and acted toward that event. While listening, also *observe*. Nonverbal behavior is a tip off to clients' emotions.

Another guideline is to remember that there are only a limited number of major emotions—anxiety, anger, guilt, depression, and frustration. Therefore the therapist is not looking for an uncommon, esoteric emotional state; the search is for those basic upsetting emotions which all of us experience.

Congruence between emotion and behavior is also a helpful listening guideline. Because emotion and behavior are contingently linked together, knowing one will often illuminate the other. When a client says she "told off" her husband, we can infer that she was angry. If she says she felt fearful, we would expect avoidant and non-assertive behavior, or under certain conditions, defensive aggression. If the client denied having anger toward the husband, yet made disparaging remarks to him, we could be fairly sure that she was nevertheless angry. In these instances, behavior is a clue to emotion, and vice versa.

Listening for emotions and behavior requires skill and confidence, for often clients will not admit to the emotions and behaviors which the therapist sees and hears. It is advisable to keep in mind that denial is a frequent dynamic in client problems, and the therapist need not force the client to agree with his/her diagnosis, nor is the client's confirmation necessary to form a diagnosis from which to launch intervention. To the contrary, RET therapists should not be surprised if they are alone in their diagnosis.

Returning to the therapy excerpt from the depressed client, here are some tentative hypotheses about C's which can be garnered from listening to the client's limited dialogue. These hypotheses could be substantiated by soliciting more dialoque from which the therapist would carefully listen for emotions and behavior.

Activating Event (A)	Emotion and Behavior of Client (C)
Car breaks down	Irritated toward husband because she had told him to have it repaired. May have expressed this irritation via "I told you so" statements, and perhaps "How am I supposed to get to work?" (These statements would probably stimulate anger in the husband)

Husband says: "Find your own ride to work!"	Irritation quickly turns to livid anger, which is expressed in a verbal tirade.
Husband intentionally stays away from home over night.	Guilt and/or depression and/or anger. (These need to be clarified)
Mother told daughter to leave the husband. (Time of occurrence needs to be clarified)	Depression, perhaps also some anxiety when client thinks about leaving.

Listening for Irrational Ideas.   Having discussed how the therapist listens for events, emotions and behaviors, we arrive now at the most crucial issue in psychodiagnosis—listening for irrational ideas. In the beginning of this chapter, we presented many of the irrational ideas which spawn emotional and behavioral disturbance, and in this section we want to talk about how to hear and identify these ideas.

Before therapists can hear irrational ideas they must truly understand the dynamics of psychopathology and be familiar with how people express the ideas behind their pathology. I (J.B.) remember my first introduction to RET, and my subsequent search for literal and verbal expressions of irrational beliefs. Nowhere could they be found, and I became skeptical of RET. Later this skepticism was dispelled when I learned that irrational ideas are often expressed in disguised or implied forms.

How does the RET therapist hear irrational ideas? The skills-based answer to this question is (1) to infer and hypothesize the B's after A and C are known, and (2) to listen for disguised and implicit expressions of B.

Inferring B's requires a thorough knowledge of and sensitivity to the basic irrational ideas and how they interact to produce emotional disturbances. This skill, then, is basically conceptual. What the RET therapist does is fall back on his or her theory and experience, uses this base to make inferences about what irrational ideas are likely given the A and C presented, and takes a (hopefully educated) guess as to what is going on in the client's head.

A continued illustration with the depressed client excerpt will show the skill of inference. Previous illustrations have shown that through leads, the therapist has solicited information from the client, and listening skills have turned up some A's and C's. Now we are ready to infer the irrational B's. An A and C sequence which seemed to be worthy of therapeutic attention was the client's high degree of anger and consequent verbal attack when the husband told the client to find her own ride to work. The diagnostic question in the therapist's mind would be: What could the client say to herself about A that would create C? By examining the four themes of irrational ideation, we can hypothesize some very tenable irrational B's.

Demandingness: He *should* have fixed the car, and since he didn't, then he *should* at least find me a ride to work. I *shouldn't* have to put up with this.

Awfulizing: He *never* does anything I ask, he *doesn't care* about me at all, he *doesn't do a thing* to help our marriage last; and that is terrible of him.

Can't Stand It: This is more than I can (and should have to) bear; it's just got to stop or else!!

Condemnation: How dare that insensitive and incompetent *bum* talk to me like that. He *deserves to be hurt* and I'm the one to do it!!!

To verify our hypotheses we could inquire and listen for supporting evidence, and the irrational B's would either be changed or developed further. As the therapist listens for this, s/he will also hear implicit and disguised expressions of irrational ideation. *Rhetorical questions,* for example, are filled with emotion, and implicit within them is an irrational idea. Here are several such common rhetorical questions with the implicit meaning in parentheses.

How can that be!

(It *shouldn't* be; it's *awful* to think it might be)

How could he do that?!

(He *shouldn't* have done that terrible thing, and *he's terrible* for having done it.)

What kind of person would do that?!

(He's a real *louse* for doing that!)

What's the use in trying?!

(Thing are so *awful* and *hopeless* that there's no sense in trying;
I am such *a hopeless incompetent* there's no reason for me to
attempt difficult tasks)

Do you mean I have to put up with this?!

(I *can't tolerate* this; it must stop; it's unfair that its happening
and that you expect me to withstand it.)

Incomplete sentences are another form of disguised irrational
ideation which the therapist can listen for in pursuit of B's. In this
form of expression, the client emotionally makes a statement which
leads up to, but stops short of the expression of an irrational idea. If
the therapist is listening closely for B's, the unspoken idea can be
"heard"—i.e. the meaning can be inferred. These incomplete sentences
are illustrative.

He didn't fix the car. . .

(. . . as he *should* have done)

I forgot to do that. . .

(. . . and I'm a terrible person for doing that)

It's scary, if he decides to leave me. . .

(and my life would end, I wouldn't know what to do because I
need him to lean on, I couldn't make it alone)

An *incongruity between B and C* is also a clue to denied and
disguised irrational beliefs. This arises when the client presents an
emotion, such as anxiety, anger, depression, guilt, or frustration,
and presents the idea that could not possibly lead to that particular
feeling. This discrepancy alerts the therapist to question the accuracy
of the client's reported feelings and/or ideas. In such an instance, the
therapist would probe for the "real" feelings and/or would continue
an investigation for the "correct" irrational B. Often the irrational

B is near the surface, and the client's phony B may actually represent a rationalization of it.   If the therapist can merely identify the irrational component, implicit and disguised within the phony rationalization, a diagnostic coup will be accomplished.

Pointed Leads.   Another significant skill in pursuing ABC's is the pointed lead, a direct and concise question or statement.   It directs the client's dialogue to the ABC's of the problem situation and elicits specific informational content.   Pointed leads tend to facilitate an increase in concreteness as the session progresses.   Examples of pointed leads are:

"Under what circumstances do you have these upset feelings?"

"Describe the events that led up to these feelings."

"Tell me how you felt in those situations; put words to your feelings."

"Feeling that way, how did you act, what did you do?"

"What was going through your mind.   What were you thinking when you began to feel that way?"

It is most frequent that clients give discernable information to these questions that allows the therapist to get to their ABC's If clients responded in a completely desirable fashion to pointed leads, such as the above, all the time, the diagnostic task would be quite easy.   But this is sometimes not the case, for clients are often extremely upset and prone to escalate their emotions as they try to describe their problems.   Thus, it is imperative that the RET therapist sensitively interrupt clients' amorphous emotional monologues with pointed and directive leads in order to keep them focused and to correct their distorted perceptions of what the therapist has asked. If this is not done, the client will often ramble for long periods while the therapist passively listens to a plethora of irrelevant information.   The following therapy excerpts demonstrate the use of directive, pointed leads when the client begins to go astray.

EXCERPT ONE

Therapist: Under what circumstances do you have these upset feelings?

Client: All the time!! That dame never stops! She's the worst excuse for a wife you could imagine. Do you know what kind of a nut she is, she. . .

Therapist: Wait a minute, now. Are you saying that you *always* have this upset, that it *never* ceases.

Client: Well, of course not.

Therapist: O.K. then, let's be specific, think hard now, in the last day or two, in what situations have you become really upset?

EXCERPT TWO

Therapist: Tell me how you felt in those situations, put words to your feelings.

Client: It was terribly upsetting, just awful!

Therapist: *How* did you feel? Angry? Fearful? Guilty?

Client: Oh, I don't know, it was just stressful.

Therapist: Stressful. . . . .what kind of feelings make up your stress?

EXCERPT THREE

Therapist: What was going through your mind. What were you telling yourself during that incident?

Client: I just thought why did this happen to me?

Therapist: That was *after* the incident, but *during* it, what did you think the first time you saw him?

As illustrated by the above excerpts, the RET therapist must often be quite pointed in structuring the therapy session and keeping the client focused. As intriguing and compelling the clients' emotional outpourings may be, the RET therapist must be vigilant against becoming seduced into passive listening. Only by sensitively yet rigorously keeping the client focused can the RET therapist uncover the client's ABC's, which is the heart of RET.

Reflective and Clarifying Responses.   While the primary purpose of the diagnostic process is to understand the client's problems and provide targets for intervention, a secondary and very important aspect is the therapeutic gain it provides for the client.   This is why we earlier referred to RET psychodiagnosis as a therapeutically investigative enterprise: it is investigative since data collection is a prime purpose; it is therapeutic because clients often find the questions and responses of the therapist helpful in clarifying what their problems are and in beginning them on the way to recovery. To all the above, we also recommend adding therapeutic value through reflective and clarifying responses.

By prudently offering reflective and clarifying responses during diagnosis, the RET therapist can promote empathy and rapport with the client.   A clearer understanding of problems is gained as the client hears the ABC's and other core issues mirrored back. Further, discourse is encouraged, which in turn provides more diagnostic data.   Clarifying techniques also offer the advantage of double-checking the therapist's perceptions with those of the client.

A word of caution accompanies our comments about reflective and clarifying techniques, however, because too many of these techniques can lead the therapy session astray, particularly if the focus is on the A's and C's.   Reflection and clarification of A's and C's, without equal or more attention to the B's, encourages clients to conclude that A causes C.   Such a conclusion produces and/or reinforces emotional irresponsibility and an external locus of control. These therapy segments show that reflective and clarifying responses can be integrated into psychodiagnosis for a therapeutic influence on the client.

EXCERPT ONE

Client: He just ignores all the things that need fixing, and I pester him to fix them, but it's like he ignores them just to spite me. . . . .he really doesn't care. . . .

Therapist: So one of the problem situations that is repeatedly played out is that you "pester" him to fix something and he doesn't do it, then you conclude that "he's trying to spite me and he doesn't care about me."

Client: Well, wouldn't he at least try if he did care?

Therapist: Not necessarily. I can think of many circumstances under which he would not fix those things you want him to, yet would maintain caring for you. The key idea here, and the most important issue, is that you are telling yourself that "he must do what I ask or else he doesn't love me."

Client: All I know is that I'm miserable.

Therapist: What are your feelings?

Client: (Silence). . . .(mumbling) I don't know (head down, slumped in chair, no body movement)

Therapist: Maybe you're feeling right now like. . . .there's no way out of this mess. . . and, I must be a lousy person. . . . because my husband doesn't even care, and there must be something wrong with me to get myself into this.

Explanation: The first and fourth therapist responses are reflective and clarifying. The first one tries to summarize the central issue in what the client has disclosed—she draws a certain conclusion, a questionable one, from her husband's actions. Response four is more reflective and empathic. Seeing that the client has become depressed, perhaps due partly to the previous confrontive statement, the therapist mirrors the client's inner feelings and meanings. . . . those B's which are producing the depression. It is advisable for the therapist, later, to begin intervention on the client's ideational themes of hoplessness and self condemnation, for this early excerpt indicates that the client puts herself down whenever the therapist places on her the responsibility for her thoughts, emotions and behavior.

EXERPT TWO

Client: . . . and when she tells me for the umpteenth time that I shouldn't have married him I just about go through the roof.

Therapist: You feel very angry.

Client: Oh do I!

Therapist: Do you express it. . . do you tell her how you feel or what you think?

Client: No, of course not.

Therapist: So mother takes a shot at your husband, and you for marrying him; you don't like her remarks, but you never say so.   What's stopping you—why do you think you shouldn't say something?

Client: Well you just don't talk to your mother that way!

Therapist: You think that you don't have the right to disagree with your mother, or ask her to stop putting down your husband and marriage.

Client: (Silence). . . . maybe that's it.

Therapist: Besides this conflict with your mother, what are some of the other situations in your life that are giving you trouble?

Explanation: The first therapist response is a reflection of feeling, the third is a clarifying summary, and the fourth is a reflection of the client's irrational B. These responses facilitate client insight, but the therapist does not go further into intervention because the diagnosis is not completed.   Response four is a lead which solicits more information about other ABC's.

Review of the Psychodiagnostic Process

The RET skills covered thus far in the chapter form a smooth flowing process and interaction when practiced by a competent therapist. A client comes to the first therapy session in an upset and bewildered emotional state, and the therapist puts the individual at ease with structuring statements, and an accepting interested, and professionally credible demeanor. Beginning questions solicit the client's explanation of his/her problems, and the therapist gathers further information through pointed leads. Problems are gradually untangled and assigned to three diagnostic categories (career, environment, or emotional-behavior problems). This categorization may be shared with the client as a method of preliminary goal setting and so further dialogue is directed at emotional-behavioral concerns. Regardless of whether the categorization is or is not shared, the therapist turns the diagnostic investigation toward the ABC's of the client's emotional-behavioral problems. Pointed leads, discriminative listening, and reflective-clarifying responses are employed to gather information about the ABC sequences and situations which comprise the client's problems. When the therapist believes that the core ABC's of the client's main problems have been identified, this information is summarized into a conceptual picture which we are calling a *diagnosis proper.*

Psychodiagnosis Proper and Goal Setting

The end product of the skills and processes delineated above is a diagnosis proper or the development of a "total" conceptual schema, created by the therapist, which categorizes the client's problems and explains them in terms of their composite ABC's. It is the outcome product of the diagnostic information gathering process.

Included in a diagnosis proper is the conceptualization of clients' main problems and their categories, and of the events (A), (B) ideas, and (C) emotions and behaviors, which comprise the problems. Problems may be overlapping, there may be many ABC sequences within each problem, and the sequences themselves may be interwoven. This may sound complex, and indeed the entire network of client problems can reach difficult proportions, but the one element which reduces the monster to a manageable beast is the B! People disturb themselves with only a relatively small number of irrational themes and ideas; their problems seem complex because of the disguised and ingenious ways in which they apply these irrational beliefs in a multitude of different situations.

To illustrate a diagnosis proper, the case of the depressed woman previously presented will again be offered. Readers can consult earlier pages where diagnostic information was gathered via the therapist skills of listening for activating events, listening for emotions and behavior, and listening for irrational ideas.

Client's Problem Statement. "Well, things haven't been going well in general, first the car broke down, and I had told him (husband) to have it repaired but as usual he didn't listen, and when he said I'd have to find my own ride I told him off!!!! Oh was I angry. . . but then he didn't come home that night, and, and, my mother told me to leave him, and I've just been depressed all week."

Psychodiagnosis Proper. The client is a middle aged housewife who presented the major complaint of being depressed (C) following a week of arguing and domestic dispute with her husband (A). A further investigation revealed a long-standing discord between the client and her husband, characterized by the wife's anger and de-mandingness regarding the husband's lack of interest in home main-tenance and the practical chores she wants him to perform. Her anger is expressed in a continual flow of judgments, and she creates a great deal of anger by condemning the husband for not meeting her expectations. Thinly veiled behind the anger are strong feelings of being unloved and unwanted, and a real sense of being discounted and hence put-down by her husband's perceived lack of commit-ment to the home and marriage. She clearly experiences ego anger, characterized by such irrational ideas as: "He acts as if he doesn't care for me; I need this and he should be caring; It's awful that he doesn't and it's awful of him, the bastard." Though the client does express genuine affection for the husband and a desire to save the marriage, her intentions are masked by the aggression she displays toward the husband when in his presence. She is skeptical of his caring for her, and tells herself that his refusal to do home chores is an indication that he doesn't love her.

A secondary emotional problem, or emotional problem about her interpersonal and emotional problems, is the client's guilt and depression for having contributed to the dispute. She notes her anger and the effect it has on her marital relationship (original C), and creates a new problem about it by putting herself down. Also complicating the client's problem is her mother's strong criticism of the husband and the marriage, a significant force, since the client desperately wants her mother's approval and is quite fearful of hurting her mother. Thus she is caught in a conflict; if she attains happiness in her marriage, the mother will disapprove, and when she attacks the husband, she loses his love but gains mother's. A feeling of hopelessness and desperation prevails.

Rational-emotive therapy will be directed at the irrational themes or ideations which cause the client's emotional-behavioral problems. Anger and aggression toward the husband, arising from demandingness and condemnation, and fueled by a threat to her needs for his love and her own tendency to equate her value with her husband's value of her, is one problem the client wishes to assault; another is the issue of guilt and self condemnation about contributing to the marital discord. The competent administration of RET to this client, given cooperation and hard work by the client, will result in a dissipation of her anger and aggression toward the husband, and an increase in constructive assertive behavior. By resolving anger and aggression, the client will be freer to cope with her marital problems, and therapy could help her learn to communicate more effectively with her husband. Change can also be expected regarding the client's anxiety about approval needs and self-rating, particularly with regard to fears about losing the husband's and mother's love. If the client can overcome her irrational approval demands, she will arrive at an emotional autonomy which allows her more energy to enhance her relationship with her husband.

Goal Setting. Immediately after the therapist formulates a diagnosis proper, s/he tells the client what options are available *and* which one(s) are recommended. The options available to RET clients are:

1. To work on emotional-behavioral concerns, and when resolved, turn therapy toward any environmental and career problems remaining.
2. To work on emotional-behavioral problems about other emotional-behavioral problems.
3. To work on environmental and career concerns and avoid therapy.

The third option is not recommended because a central proposition in RET is that people can more easily and capably handle practical dilemmas when not burdened with emotional distress. Time and again we have seen clients' practical concerns disappear as they resolved emotional problems. So, the RET therapist recommends that clients rid themselves of emotional problems and thereby free their energy and natural coping talents for practical tasks.

In goal setting, we find it helpful to simply set out the problems for the client in terms of their category and their levels. We show them that they have career and/or environmental problems and irrational problems about these, and we recommend that they deal in RET first with their emotional problems.

Here are two examples of setting therapy goals. The first one occurred at the end of the initial session with our depressed woman client; the second example is a goal setting segment initiated midway through an initial session with a depressed male client. This latter segment illustrates how quickly an RET therapist can diagnose the core issues (ABC's) of a problem and turn therapy toward these targets.

EXAMPLE ONE—DIAGNOSIS AND GOAL SETTING

Therapist: In this first session we've identified and explored your main concerns, and I'd like to summarize these as we close.

Client: O.K., I think we did get to most of the things that have been bothering me.

Therapist: One concern, probably foremost in your mind, is the continuing rift with your husband. For you personally it consists of being very angry at him, and feeling as though he doesn't love you.

Client: Yes.

Therapist: Actually, I hear you having two concerns here. One, your husband doesn't do the sort of things you'd like him to do—take care of the house, and so on. But, two, you have an emotional problem about that practical problem: you get yourself quite angry at him for all this, which first makes you terrifically upset and probably adds to your husband's "bad" behavior.

Client: And I feel awful for the anger.

Therapist: Right. And that's another problem, on top of the
             practical one and the emotional one. You get yourself
             guilty about the anger, and in effect create other emo-
             tional problems about the first two problems. So,
             you've got three problems here. Do you see what I'm
             saying?

Client: Yes, I do.

Therapist: O.K. Then, let's figure out where to start. I strongly
             recommend that we start with the emotional problems
             first, and then we can turn to dealing better with
             your husband. We might even bring him in. But, first,
             let's get your head together on this. What do you
             think?

EXAMPLE TWO—DIAGNOSIS AND GOAL SETTING

Wayne S. presented depression as a major problem when he
came to therapy. He traced the onset of his depression to an incident
that happened in his role as executor of his grandfather's will. Just
before his death, Wayne's grandfather redistributed his will such
that Wayne's mother received a disproportionately larger share of the
inheritance than her sisters. Wayne knew that he was somewhat
depressed, but he did not relate it to his grandfather's death until he
dreamed that he expressed anger at his grandfather for putting him in
the awkward position of mediating between his mother and her
sisters. When he related that he felt bad for arguing with his grandfather about the will, the following therapeutic interchange took
place.

Therapist: Tell me, Wayne, you said you were angry at your grand-
             father for changing his will the way he did.

Wayne: Yes, I guess I am.

Therapist: Ok. Now, what's so bad about being angry at him?

Wayne: Really nothing, I guess.

Therapist:	Yes, that's right. There is nothing really wrong with feeling angry. But I'm not convinced that you really believe that. Let yourself go for a minute. What do you think is so bad about being angry at your grandfather, whether it sounds silly or not?
Wayne:	I'm not sure what your're driving at. I don't know what you want me to say. Can you help me out?
Therapist:	Ok. I could be wrong, but it seems to me that you clearly have two problems. One, you have gotten yourself good and angry at your grandfather for doing something that you think he should not have done. That leads to your anger. But, secondly, you seem to be putting yourself down for getting angry—saying you should be above such petty things and really sticking it to yourself for being angry. That self put-down leads to the depression. Do you follow me?
Wayne:	Yes. It really fits. I am putting myself down.
Therapist:	You certainly seem to be. Now which problem do you want to tackle first. I would advise the second, the self-downing, but what do you think?
Wayne:	Yeah, I agree. Because I really am doing a job on myself.
Therapist:	Correct. And we can come back to the anger once we get you over this self-downing nonsense.

ROADBLOCKS TO RATIONAL-EMOTIVE PSYCHODIAGNOSIS AND GOAL SETTING

Readers should not assume that it is always easy to understand client problems and agree on therapy goals as in the second example. For clients *and* therapists sometimes fall prey to problems that prevent a smooth beginning of RET and delay the insight, working through, and reeducational processes that constitute the rest of RET. A few therapist and client problems, or roadblocks to RET progress, that can hamper and prohibit successful RET will be discussed in the following pages.

Therapist Roadblocks

Since the client is usually a naive, unsophisticated patron knowing little of the therapeutic adventure, the burden of conducting the early stages of RET falls on the shoulders of the therapist. What follows are some frequently found therapist mistakes that get in the way of successfully initiating RET.

Conceptual Confusions.   As mentioned earlier, it is rare for clients to present a coherent, organized story that clearly lays out their problems.   They frequently complain about a plethora of things, dispense their irrational ideas without knowing they are doing so, and passionately emote about all sorts of things.   Often all this is presented in a topsy-turvy order.

   This confusion requires the therapist to bring order out of chaos. The therapist must separate categories of problems, identify ABC sequences, and particularly tune into and identify the client's main irrational beliefs.   The possibilities for confusion are many and, without a thorough knowledge of rational-emotive theory and the skills presented in this chapter, psychodiagnostic errors are likely. The answer, of course, is for the therapist to become thoroughly familiar with RET through reading, attending workshops and lectures, and particularly through supervision of live therapy cases.

The Past History Trap.   Most systems of psychotherapy are enamored with exploring the client's past history.   Early childhood experiences are minutely investigated in order to first discover the presumed root of the present problem and then to abreact (and hence cure) all the bad feelings surrounding these experiences. In RET, exploration of the client's past history, while often enlightening and sometimes even interesting, is not crucial to the change process. Human emotional problems do not result from the experiences people have, whether these experiences are historical or current, but from the way people interpret and continue to interpret these experiences. When a person is emotionally disturbed, the disturbance results from a currently held way of thinking and believing. It is usually true that the client's irrational ideas have a learning history, but the crucial thing is for him or her to give up these currently held ideas so that tomorrow's existence can be better than yesterday's. In a sense, the person each day chooses to either hold onto disturbed beliefs or to give them up.

The rational-emotive therapist who persists in exploring past history is doing the client a disservice in at least two ways. One, the therapist inadvertently teaches the client that the problem, and hence the cure, lies in the past. Second, this endeavor simply wastes time that could be better spent in understanding how the client's current beliefs are causing problems and in determining how to move the client through the therapeutic process.

The Big Picture Trap. The big picture trap is a pitfall common to unsophisticated and unconfident therapists. These insist on obtaining a total picture of the client's past, present and future before beginning an intervention program. Unsophisticated therapists know no better and unconfident therapists believe they need to do this.

Obtaining a perfectly complete picture is neither necessary nor advisable. As discussed before, with the major "tools" being a thorough understanding of the ABC theory and the irrational beliefs behind the major emotional disturbances, it *is* usually surprisingly easy to understand the client's problems without obtaining a life history. If therapists remember, for instance, that guilt is invariably composed of two ideas—1. "I did something bad;" and 2. "because I did that bad thing, I'm bad."—they will quickly think of these themes in the client's current thinking when presented with a guilt concern without obsession about the past or the present.

The Myth of the Relationship. Like so many other concepts in psychology, the concept of "the psychotherapeutic relationship" has taken on magical properties. It has come to be seen as a real entity that, after its conception, exists in and of itself. Therapists who adopt this viewpoint consequently spend a great amount of time nurturing it—showing the client respect and unconditional positive regard, and attempting to display to the client accurate and empathic understanding. In RET, we think such a relationship is often sustained by therapists in order to meet their nurturance needs, and by suc-corant clients.

Contrary to the relationship myth, RET considers "the psychotherapeutic relationship" to be a construct that has no independent existence. It is a convenient way of thinking about the attitudes and feelings the therapist holds toward the client and, much more importantly, the attitudes and feelings the client holds toward the therapist. Attitudes that convey liking, respect, and trust toward the client are more facilitative than their opposite. Therefore, the task for RET therapists is to facilitate these attitudes in order to facilitate client change. Goldstein (1975) offers the following rather sensible overview of relationship enhancers and their results:

1. to increase therapist attractiveness, tell clients they will like their therapist, describe positive characteristics of the therapist and clarify for clients what to expect in therapy;
2. to increase therapist attractiveness, expose clients to people who like the therapist and who praise the therapist;
3. to increase respect for the therapist, behave in a relaxed, confident manner, converse in a lively fashion, make cryptic, to-the-point statements, move quickly to the heart of the problem and, among other things, display the trappings of expertness, such as diplomas and professional books;
4. to increase liking and trust for the therapist, behave in an empathic manner; and
5. to increase liking for the therapist, respond to clients in a warmer manner.

Client Roadblocks

The beginning stage of RET also provides clients an opportunity to undercut the therapy process. Fear of disclosure, tendencies to distrust strangers, confusion over the true nature of the problem, extreme upsetness that interferes with efficient problem solving, and a rigid view of the environment as the source of one's problems are some client problems that have been mentioned at various points in this chapter. These things are problems because they slow therapy and obfuscate the core issues, but more seriously, they often prompt premature termination.

Kempel (1973) defines premature terminators as clients who irrationally, irresponsibly, or unrealistically talk themselves out of returning for therapy. Nearly all clients question whether or not to return to therapy after the first, second, or third session, and the incidence of premature termination is reportedly very high (Bandura, 1969). Thus it is incumbent on the RET therapist to identify signs which are predictive of premature termination, and to openly deal with the client's ideas and feelings about terminating. We are not suggesting that the therapist coerce the client into remaining in therapy, but rather, our recommendation is that the client's reasons for leaving be examined to be sure they are rational. Sensible reasons are solid grounds for termination, but, if their reasons are not rational, these ideas should be treated as any other irrational B.

Three rather typical irrational reasons for terminating therapy are offered as an aide to therapists in identifying premature termination before it occurs. These reasons represent client pitfalls that can be fatal to therapy.

Approval Demands. A common client expectation is for the therapist to be gentle, passive, and paternal. Some with particularly high demands for approval consider the therapist's approval to be a requisite for life. These clients are prone to feel hurt and to engage in self-downing and/or to try to "look good" so the therapist will approve of their performance. Empathic techniques can help these clients ease into RET, but also needed is a persistent and gentle focus on *their* emotional responsibility and the ABC's. In particular, early attention to the demand for approval is advised.

The "Cathartic Cure" Myth. Clients who have suppressed the expression of their emotional upsets for a long time may feel an exhilarating sense of relief following their first therapy session. Thereupon they sometimes erroneously conclude that their problems are cured and that therapy can be terminated, when in reality they harbour the same irrational ideas they have always had and will continue in their disturbance.

During diagnosis and goal setting, the RET therapist can correct this misconception in a prophylactic manner and explain that disturbing emotions are likely to return as long as the beliefs which cause them remain intact. When clients emit messages indicating thoughts of having erred, a discussion of all this, with appropriate information given, is certainly in order.

Discouragement.   In contrast to the "cathartic cure" myth, some clients demand instant remedy and place on the therapist total responsibility for stopping their emotional upsets on an immediate basis. After one or two sessions, having given only token efforts, these clients decide that RET will not help them. To combat this, therapists should give ample attention, in the first session, to the setting of realistic goals and to a thorough explanation of the RET process. This information will correct the client's expectations for a quick and easy cure.

SUMMARY

A successful beginning to an RET case rests on the therapist's psychodiagnostic skills; that is, the skills of soliciting relevant diagnostic information from the client, accurately categorizing the problem(s), and most important, identifying the irrational ideas which precipitate the client's problem(s). These skills are necessarily based on the therapist's thorough understanding of RET theory, and a host of techniques which have been described.

Psychodiagnosis culminates in a diagnosis proper which will guide the therapist's efforts throughout the remainder of the RET process. The diagnosis proper is shared with the client, and contributes to the setting of therapy goals which are acceptable to the client and therapist.

Though psychodiagnosis is the first skill-area to be implemented when starting an RET case, it does overlap with the next one—rational-emotive insight. This overlapping will be true for the other skill areas to be covered in following chapters, and readers are encouraged to visualize RET as a smooth flowing process of interrelated skill areas and therapeutic stages.

3
Rational-Emotive Insight

Helping clients gain insight into their irrational thinking constitutes a second basic skill area in rational-emotive therapy. The reader would be mistaken in concluding, however, that the facilitation of insight necessarily follows rational-emotive psychodiagnosis. This process overlaps the diagnostic process and may indeed contribute to or constructively alter a previously established diagnosis.

Many approaches to psychotherapy recognize the importance of client insight to therapeutic progress. Indeed, some, like psychoanalysis and other Freudian-oriented therapies, believe that clients' understanding of their unconscious conflicts and motivations is the necessary and sufficient condition for successful change (Kutash, 1976; Mischel, 1976). In defense of this thesis, Henry Laughlin (1967) states that:

"The most valuable kind of psychotherapy has the increase of insight (that is, self-understanding) as its major goal. This means the uncovering of unconscious material, together with its acceptance, study and understanding . . . Symptoms represent a compromise way of dealing with the inner, threatening, hidden, and disowned urges. Symptoms can also provide the outward best disguised symbolic expression of elements of the conflict . . . When they become understood they become no longer essential. In other words, *insight is followed* by relief" (p. 26-27).

Gestalt therapists represent another camp that places tremendous emphasis on client insight. In fact, they discourage clients from going beyond insight or awareness, fearing that efforts at further learning or change may lead to the client being harmed. To wit:

"... it is much more useful to simply become deeply aware of yourself as you are now. Rather than try to change, stop, or avoid some things that you don't like in yourself, it is much more effective to stay with it and become more deeply aware of it. You can't improve on your own functioning; you can only interfere with it, distort it, and disguise it. When you really get in touch with your own experiencing, you will find that change takes place by itself, without your effort or planning" (Stevens, 1971, p. 2-3).

The quotations cited above suggest that some schools of psychotherapeutic thought have annointed client insight as the magic ingredient for successful psychotherapy: help clients gain insight and their troubles end. Yet RET, among other therapies (Watzlawick, Weakland, and Fisch, 1974), believes that the proposed magical insight is more myth than reality. "Quick Cures" following insight are rare; it is the rule rather than the exception that clients must engage in a sustained, energetic effort after they gain insight in order to change significantly. A close inspection of cases where insight alone seems to bring about significant change will usually show that these clients actually *work through* their emotional problems *after* gaining insight. Neither being a sufficient condition nor a necessary condition, insight is preliminary to a working through process.

Why is this so? Why is it usually necessary for clients to work long and hard to bring about real and sustained change in themselves after they gain insight? The most important reason is the irrational ideas that people hold, that constitute the heart of their disturbance, are usually so well engrained by the time they come to therapy that awareness is rarely enough for real change to take place. People typically come to therapy having fully believed their irrational ideas for years and having thought about and dealt with scores of situations consistent with these ideas. In effect, they have practiced thinking and reinforced believing what they do until the ideas have become "second nature." Imagine trying to change right handedness to left handedness simply by acknowledging that you are right handed and you will see what we mean. Changing anything so well learned requires repeated, energetic, and multimodel efforts.

We will return to this point in the next chapter when we discuss the rationale for and techniques of helping people give up their irrational beliefs. Suffice it to say at this point that client insight is, indeed, promoted in rational-emotive therapy, but it is a demythologized variety which is seen as a stepping stone to change rather than the ultimate change ingredient itself. With this in mind, the rest of this chapter will be devoted to defining rational-emotive insight, to describing several ways to promote it, and to alerting the reader to various client and therapist mistakes that inhibit insight.

RATIONAL-EMOTIVE INSIGHT DEFINED

The major goal of rational-emotive insight is to help clients clearly see and openly acknowledge the important ideational issues that lead to and perpetuate their disturbance and that require change if a different way of psychological functioning is to be realized. The rational-emotive therapist helps clients: (1) acknowledge their maladaptive or symptomatic feelings and behavior; (2) assume full responsibility for these as self-created and self-sustained; (3) accept themselves with their symptoms; and (4) look for and genuinely acknowledge the philosophic sources of their symptoms.

In reaching these goals, the rational-emotive therapist teaches five types of insights, all of which lay the groundwork for the crucial working-through and reeducational processes described in the next two chapters.

Insight Number One is simply that all behavior has antecedent causes. While this idea may seem simple and obvious to the reader, many clients assume that their emotional and behavioral reactions just happen and that the preceding and concurrent stream of environmental and self-generated events have absolutely no bearing on their reactions. Insight Number One teaches clients that events in the world operate on the basis of scientific cause and effect relationships, rather than by magic or chance, and that human behavioral events similarly do so.

Insight Number Two emphasizes the extremely important role that peoples' current ideas, beliefs, and philosophies play in causing their emotional and behavioral reactions. This, of course, represents the basic premise underlying rational-emotive therapy, which is that A, an activating event, does not really cause C, the emotional and behavioral consequences; rather B, the beliefs about A, directly causes C. This does not mean that past experiences are unrelated to present behavior, for most beliefs are learned in the context of past experiences. Rather, this insight stresses that it is beliefs held today, kept alive by repeatedly thinking and acting on them, that cause peoples' reactions.

This insight is particularly important. Many people are simply unaware of the precipitory thinking they do to cause their emotional-behavioral reactions. These people often fall under the rubric of the "It makes me" syndrome, as in: "He made me mad," or, "Making speeches makes me nervous." So, when a client says, "My spouse depressed me by not remembering my birthday," the therapist quickly introspects: "Slow down. He depressed you? Don't you really mean that *you caused yourself* to get depressed by *thinking* depressing thoughts—like how terrible such an oversight was and how terribly small you must be for him to forget?"

Other clients, while being aware of their thoughts and ideas, as phenomenological entities remain ignorant of the causal relationship between their thoughts and their feelings. They simply have no appreciation of the role their thoughts play, or they are what Maxie Maultsby (1974) calls "gut thinkers." Gut thinkers are people so enamored by their feelings that they tend to define reality with their feelings. Such a client might conclude: "I feel so bad and guilty that I *must* be worthless." This, of course, represents a magical thought contrary to reality and one that requires correction.

Insight Number Three is perhaps the most important, and the techniques which facilitate this insight come from the heart of this chapter. It represents a personal awareness and acknowledgement of the dynamics of one's own psychopathology. It consists of clearly recognizing one's own irrational ideas *and* appreciating the role they play in causing the symptoms in question. This insight represents a breakthrough in the therapy process for it fosters the client's awareness of the specific material to be dealt with in order to improve their psychological functioning. Additionally, this insight tends to undercut feelings of powerlessness and despair for clients discover, to paraphrase Raimy (1975), that they only suffer from a specific misconception or several related ones. It shows them that they are not helpless victims of outside forces or deeply buried unconscious processes, but they actually have control over them.

Insight three paves the way for insights four and five. By the time most people enter therapy, most clients are so propagandized by the ideas they hold, *and* they are so allergic to independent thinking that they blindly accept their beliefs as inherently true. Some, in fact, have been taught that it is wrong, even sinful to question the validity of their ideas. They rarely if ever question whether or not their ideas hold water.

Insight Number Four, then, is that any thought, particularly the ones in question, *may be* invalid and indeed *may be* challenged. The therapist helps the client see that any idea can be viewed as a proposition or hypothesis that can be empirically tested and logically explored to determine whether it is fact or fancy. This insight is often a revelation and provides a license for clients to freely, open-mindedly, and critically think about beliefs which for years they have blindly accepted as truth. We find this insight to be particularly dramatic for passive clients, very religious clients, and women and men who have succumbed to traditional sexual stereotypes.

Insight Number Five is that thoughts and beliefs can be given up if found invalid or self-defeating, and that better ones can be adopted to replace them. This is a particularly important insight for many people who do not really believe in their powers of self-determination. Clients who particularly find this insight valuable are those whom Julian Rotter (1954, 1966) calls externally locused, the depressed clients who feel hopeless about their circumstances (Beck, 1976), and those clients who have acquired a learned helplessness stance (Seligman, 1975). Regardless, clients are shown that they have the capacity to give up their self-defeating ways of functioning; that, if through the logical-empirical process, evidence can be found to support a hypothesis, they then can choose to keep it, but if no evidence can be found to support a hypothesis or if evidence is found to refute it, then they can give it up.

Benefits of Rational-Emotive Insight

The foregoing insights taught in rational-emotive therapy tend to have at least four significant benefits.

They Clarify Issues. By the time they come to therapy, most clients are very frustrated, and a good many are actually despondent and at their wit's end. They have ruminated and worried for countless hours about the roots of their problems; they have consulted with as many friends as would listen, they have read books and attended lectures, and they have attempted all sorts of things to make themselves feel better, all to little or no avail. The problem is that they have, at best, only a vague notion of what the problematic issues are; therefore, their various efforts at finding relief have been fruitless. Rational-emotive insight serves to teach clients the real loci of their problems and gives them a structure within which to separate environmental from emotional-behavior problems. It, thus, gives them an understanding of the issues and a direction for change efforts.

They Promote Hope/Facilitate Motivation. A major problem for many clients is their profound feelings of helplessness and hopelessness. They tend to believe that there is nothing they can do to bring about significant change in themselves or in their lives. This ideation leads to discouragement and tends to undercut their motivation to work in therapy.

One of the major benefits of rational-emotive insight is that it promotes a sense of hope and power, and produces an eagerness to participate in therapy. When clients come to understand that all behavior has antecedent causes, their interest usually increases; when they discover that their own feelings and behaviors are a logical consequence of the ideas they hold, they gain a sense of hope by realizing that they can be in control of their own lives. When clients really come to see that they can question their self-defeating ideas and give them up if they prove false, they are often enthusiastic and experience a profound sense of personal power and self-confidence. All of these insights are certainly therapeutic gains in and of themselves, but they also lead to increased motivation to continue the process of constructive change.

They Build Rapport. We could argue indefinitely about the relative merits of and necessity for the building of warmth and rapport with our clients. Rogers believes that a "good relationship" between the therapist and client is the necessary and sufficient condition for therapeutic gain.   Others, most notably Ellis (1977f) and more cognitive oriented therapists, question the supremacy of the rapport factor, at least as traditionally defined, and even claim that all sorts of harmful side effects can occur as a result of giving clients unconditioned warmth, support and caring.   We refer the reader to Ellis (1977e) for a more thoughtful discussion of this issue.

Nevertheless, if rapport is defined cognitively as the consequence of the ideas that the therapist and client hold about each other, we can quite nicely avoid the debate.   For if the client *believes* the therapist to be competent, efficient, professional and concerned with helping the client get better, then we can safely predict that the client will most likely trust the RET therapist, believe in what he or she says, and will generally cooperate with the treatment.

We have found that the facilitation of RET insight quite often serves to establish therapist credibility and promote excellent rapport between the therapist and client.   Clients often report they have never been listened to so well and never been understood with such depth, at least not so quickly as by their rational-emotive therapist.   Perhaps this phenomenon is due to the rational-emotive therapist listening to the most basic values and philosophies behind their feelings, rather than the more superficial material to which most other therapists attend.   Clearly, the client's sense of being immediately and profoundly understood enhances his/her receptivity to the RET therapist.

They Help RET Make Sense.   RET is not what most people bargain for when they first enter therapy.   Many clients expect the therapist to be a supportive, pipe-smoking father figure who sits back, listens, and lets them pour out their troubles.   Others think of their prospective therapist in the same mold as the family physician who briefly listens to complaints, pokes and probes for a few moments, and then writes a prescription that quickly alleviates symptoms. In contrast, the rational-emotive therapist is an active, directive, challenging individual who demands a great deal of effort from the client.

If client expectations conflict with what the therapist presents, there is a danger that clients will be turned off or scared off by what they encounter. We have found that helping clients gain insight early in the therapy process is a precaution against early termination, for these insights make the requirements of RET and the behavior of the therapist understandable and acceptable.

A Note on the Unconscious and RET Insight

One of the criticisms we often hear about RET is that it is too superficial. While clients rarely complain about the insights they acquire and rather find them quite impactful, our colleagues from other camps often advance the argument that RET only deals with surface dynamics and ignores the most important material that has been banished to the unconscious portion of the mind. Hence the insights gained in RET, they say, are relatively meaningless.

This of course implies that there is such a thing as *an unconscious,* and that what truly characterizes people is hidden in the sanctuary beyond their own reaches. The following quote is an example of this position:

The cornerstone of dynamic psychology is the concept of repression. As the psychic structure of the human personality develops in infancy and childhood, the primitive erotic and aggressive impulses come to be opposed by counter impulses deriving from the child's training and adaptive experiences. The chief counter impulse is repression, which banishes from consciousness . . . those impulses, some native and some stimulated by specific experiences, which the child discovers are condemned by specific experiences and forbidden expression by its upbringers . . . Topographically the unconscious is regarded as *the repository* of repressed impulses and forgotten memories, the preconscious as *that part* of the mind in which resides the rememberable but currently unattended to memories, and the conscious mind as the aware, focusing, thinking portion of the psychic structure." (Knight and Friedman, 1962, p. 54).

The RET answer to this is consistent with the social learning theory literature (Rotter, 1954; Kelley, 1955; Mischel, 1973). First, there is no such entity as *THE UNCONSCIOUS.* The notion of "an unconscious" is a construct that, like the constructs of id, ego and superego, has no basis in reality. It is a conceptual convenience rather than an actuality. Unfortunately such a concept most often serves to obfuscate the real data in question and leads the therapist into all sorts of roundabout and unnecessary behaviors—dream analysis, endless listening to free associations, reliance on the transference relationships and so on. The RET position asserts that there are indeed certain things—thoughts, beliefs, feelings—of which the person is unaware and hence are unconscious, but these experiences do not reside in any particular reservoir of the mind. They are entities in and of themselves, to which a person does not or cannot attend at a particular time. The task of the therapist is to determine what unconscious data are most relevant to the individual's problems and to directly help the client acknowledge them—to recognize and own their existence.

Second, RET questions the commonly-held assumption that the most important client data for therapy is the one held in the unconscious. Rational-emotive theory holds that the most important data, the client's ideas, beliefs and philosophies, are readily accessible to the client and that, with only a little digging, can be acknowledged. In fact, as we have already said, many clients are already aware of their irrational ideas before they come to therapy; they either believe them to be valid, or they do not appreciate the relationship between these ideas and the symptoms they are experiencing.

The techniques presented in this chapter rest on the assumption that the skilled RET therapist can rather quickly and easily help clients recognize and acknowledge their troublesome, self-disturbing dynamics. Since the relevant material is readily accessible, the therapist need not engage in rather convoluted, mystical and inefficient techniques like dream analysis and free association which characterize other less effective forms of psychotherapy.

FACILITATING CLIENT INSIGHT

As previously stated, the goals of rational-emotive insight are to help clients learn the five basic ideas, primary among them that philosophical and ideational issues are part and parcel of their disturbance. In other words, rational-emotive therapists try to teach clients ideas that will help them work through their psychopathology. They accomplish this goal through simple yet quite effective techniques. But, before describing them, we wish to first offer a few general guidelines in facilitating insight.

First, we again emphasize the importance of a thorough understanding and a comfortable acceptance of the rational-emotive theory of personality and psychopathology. The psychodiagnostic enterprise described in the previous chapter provides a simple, yet workable conceptual structure and a jumping off point for almost all the techniques to be described. Given an understanding of rational-emotive theory, the therapist can facilitate clients' insight by first seeing and hearing the basic irrational ideas as expressed vocally or through their emotional and behavioral reactions, and s/he can then help clients see and hear themselves.

A second suggestion is to be situationally specific. While it is crucial to attend to general beliefs or philosophies, the recommended procedure is to first explore the client's thinking concerning some specific event, and then relate it (then or at some strategic later point) to general beliefs or philosophies. It is often confusing and superficial in the early stages of therapy to deal on the level of major beliefs or philosophies, as per: "What is your general belief about people who fail in finding a job?" On the contrary, a therapist's lead should be more productive and naturally lead to the general belief: "What do you think about when you walk into a job interview?"

Third, make liberal use of visual aids. We find that clients are generally confused about their problems. They know they are upset, but do not know how to sort out their various distressing feelings. They often recognize the irrational thinking behind their feelings, but do not always clearly see which thoughts lead to which feelings. They get upset about being upset, but do not realize this compounding process; and so on. One of the best visual aids is to diagram the client's psychodynamics in terms of the ABC formula. This and other visual techniques often serve to clarify the situation and transform "frightening" issues into a logical problem solving venture.

Fourth, and finally, since some clients are so bound by their anxiety or are so rigid in their defenses, they have a difficult time attending to their irrational thinking. We think it wise for the well-rounded RET therapist to sometimes be willing to attend to clients' feelings at length. Accordingly, it is wise to be familiar with empathy techniques, relaxation exercises, and the various Gestalt techniques that help clients loosen up. We recommend that the therapist learn a set of these techniques and even keep a sourcebook of awareness exercises handy.

Having said all this, we can now describe the main techniques for facilitating rational-emotive insight. They include advancing hypotheses, leading techniques, confronting hidden ideas, and a didactic procedure developed by Maxie Maultsby.

Advancing Hypotheses

Advancing hypotheses goes contrary to the methods advocated by most forms of therapy. Some therapists want clients to struggle to acquire their own insights with the assumption that self-discovered insights are best.

Rational-Emotive therapists, however, believe that the most important insights are so readily available that waiting for self-discovery only wastes valuable time and perpetuates unnecessary pain and confusion. This is perhaps best communicated by Ellis (1971) in talking about one of his clients:

"Although I, as the therapist, know very little about the client, I size him up quickly and decide to take a chance, on the basis of RET theory, and to try to get to one of the main cores of his problem quickly: his terrible feelings of inadequacy or shithood . . . and I make an attempt to show the client, almost immediately, what he is doing to cause his central upsetness and what he presumably can do about understanding and changing himself . . . I know fully that I may be barking up the wrong tree, and am prepared to back down later if I turn out to be mistaken. But I know, on the basis of considerable prior evidence, that there is an excellent chance that I may be right; and I want, by taking that chance, to try to save the client a great deal of time and pain . . . I also try to show how human beings in general, easily think the way he does and how so many of them, no matter what their abilities and talents, wind up hating themselves because of this type of crooked thinking." (p. 106)

As a result of this reasoning, rational-emotive therapists quite frequently take the initiative in outlining for clients which issues are part and parcel of their emotional problems. This is particularly true in the early stages of therapy when clients are typically naive about their problems. It is also common procedure when dealing with the unintelligent, the very disturbed, and the quite confused client.

Exactly what hypotheses and how they are to be presented will of course be dependent upon what the clients present. Nevertheless, it is most common for rational-emotive therapists to advance hypotheses in one or both of two areas: (1) clarifying irrational ideas; (2) precisely defining terms.

Clarifying Irrational Ideas. Perhaps the most important arena for advancing hypotheses falls into the category of suggesting or interpreting irrational ideas. Most new clients are accutely aware of the events which preceded their emotional upsets and are quite cognizant of how miserable they feel. But, they rarely appreciate the important role that their ideas play in their disturbance, much less know precisely what particular ideas constitute the problem.

The simplest, most direct way of advancing hypotheses is to directly share with clients your understanding of their irrational thinking. Tentatively, yet authoritatively, point out what they are thinking to cause their distress. Suppose a client approached you about a public speaking anxiety. An exchange like the following might occur.

Therapist 1: O.K., Bob, I hear you telling yourself some pretty self-defeating things when you think about speaking in public that could only lead to anxiety.

Bob 1: Like what?

Therapist 2: Like you *have to* do well, and that the audience *must* like your speech or else it would be so *awful* that you *couldn't stand* to live another second. How does that sound?

Bob 2: Pretty close to what I do think.

Therapist 3: And, if that weren't enough, I hear you also thinking that your *ok-ness* depends on your getting their approval. Right?

Bob 3: Yes.

A slightly more complex variation on the theme is to show clients that they (and all people) concurrently hold *both* rational *and* irrational ideas that lead to qualitatively different emotional consequences. The following therapy vignette demonstrates how the therapist can clarify both sets of ideas for the client. Sally was a young woman who, among other things, felt very guilty and depressed about her four year affair with a married man, an affair that followed the typical path of promises to leave home that were never kept. Sally stayed in the relationship, refusing other relationships and more lucrative jobs in distant communities, until she began to realize that "I've been a fool." The following interchange took place during the first interview with her rational-emotive therapist.

Therapist 1:   So, Sally, from all this you've said, I certainly see that among other things, you really feel down on yourself.

Sally 1:   Really! I've been a fool. I've stayed with him for years and look what's it got me. I'm broke, I've suffered professionally and I'm not getting any younger.

Therapist 2:   But, I also hear you holding two ideas about yourself. One that is true and one that isn't. One leads to appropriate feelings, but the other leads to depression and self-downing.

Sally 2:   What do you mean?

Therapist 3:   Well, you've concluded that you've made some major mistakes in your relationship and, from what I've heard, I certainly agree that you have. But, you have also concluded a second thing that is patently false and that leads to all the guilt that you're carrying around. It's that you're *a fool, a real dunce* for doing foolish things.

Sally 3:   You're right. I am thinking all that. But, isn't it true?

Therapist 4:   No, not all of it is true. As I've said, you have done some foolish things and I'm not going to lie to you and tell you that your decisions have been sensible. They haven't! And, you had best evaluate those decisions. But, you've concluded that you—totally you, every bit of you—are a fool for doing foolish things. Now, that's where your guilt and feeling of self-downing comes from. I would feel down about me too if I called me a fool. Do you see what I mean?

Sally 4: Yes. But, I again ask you: Isn't that true?

Therapist 5: No. And thats what we need to explore. Whether that idea is true or not. If it is, then your feeling of worthlessness is appropriate, good and justified. But, if it isn't, and I'm sure that it isn't, then your bad feelings about yourself are unnecessary and self-defeating. So, let's think about your hypotheses: first, that you made some mistakes; but, secondly, that you are a fool, a real zero, for making foolish mistakes. OK?

Sally 5: O.K.

This example shows how the therapist simply and directly conceptualized the problem for the client. In his second remark, he pointed out to Sally that she concurrently holds two ideas and, in his third remark, he discriminates between her rational ideas about her poor behavior and her irrational ideas about her self-worth. Then, in response to her statement that she is a fool, he, in remark four, reiterates the difference between foolish acts and foolish people and he points out that feeling self-downed comes from the latter. Finally, in remark five, he again draws the distinction and takes the opportunity to tell her that she can question and give up the thinking that leads to the self-downing.

Precisely Defining Terms. One of the major ways that people disturb themselves is to think in vague, dramatic terms that exacerbate their emotional reactions. For example, they call themselves insecure, lonely, dependent, and a whole host of other things. Yet, except in a most general sense, they rarely understand what they are talking about, and they respond to the most emotionally electrifying connotation of the terms they use.

In this technique, the therapist helps clients precisely define terms so that the ideas behind the term are made explicit. June is a good example of a person who regularly upsets herself by using terms in a vague and sloppy fashion. Contending with the prospect of her husband leaving her, and being quite upset by believing herself to be worthless unless he loved her, she repeatedly expressed how insecure she had always been. After numerous incidences of describing herself thusly, the therapist showed her how her use of the term "insecurity" was an expression of her low self-worth. What she meant was that she found herself worthless unless cared for by another, for, she inappropriately believed she had to have other's unyielding esteem or else she was worthless.

Therapist 1:   June, you keep calling yourself insecure. Do you know what that really means.

June 1:   Well, I guess it means I have no self-confidence.

Therapist 2:   Yes. But, doesn't it really mean that you find yourself worthless and that you must have the approval of others in order to think you're o.k. Just like we've been talking in relation to your husband. Then, holding this idea—that you're only o.k. when somebody cares for you—you, by definition, worry about whether they will like you or continue to like you. That worrying is the feeling of insecurity, but insecurity is really the ideas behind the feeling.

June 2:   So, my insecurity is part of the larger problem we're talking about.

Therapist 3:   Exactly. And when you clearly acknowledge that your ideas are the problem with your husband and have been your "insecurity" problem for a long time, you can really begin to work on changing them.

June 3:   O.K.

Leading Techniques

Advancing hypotheses techniques are commonly used in the early stages of helping clients gain insight. But, they quickly give way to less directive methods, for in the last analysis, rational-emotive therapy wants to do two things: (1) "cure" clients of their irrational nonsense, *and* (2) teach them how to think scientifically for them- selves. In other words, RET wants to help clients give up their irrational ideas, while showing them how to be their own therapist when problems arise in the future.

To accomplish this, it is best for the rational-emotive therapist to do less telling and talking, and to require clients to do more of their own hypotheses advancing as time passes. When clients begin to do this, it indicates that they are indeed becoming aware of the irrational ideas that create and maintain their disturbances, and are beginning to think for themselves. Several methods lead clients to discover their own rational-emotive insights.

Use of the ABC Formula. The ABC formula is perhaps the simplest and best leading tool to help clients gain insight. This technique is employed by putting clients' concerns into the "A" and "C" portion of the formula and then asking them to supply the "B". To illustrate, here is the first session with Jane, who reacted with panic and anxiety when her boyfriend declared that he wanted to date others.

Therapist: Let's take a look at what's upsetting you so, Jane. I'm going to put it in terms of A, B, and C. At point A, Tommy said he wanted to date other women, and at point C you reacted with extreme fear and horror. Right?

Jane: Right.

Therapist: Now, we left out the B, which is what you think about or how you interpret A, Tommy's wish to date around. Now, what do you think, at point B, about Tommy doing this or wanting to do this?

Jane: Well, that I can't stand this. I need him.

Therapist: Correct! You believe you *must* have him and that you *cannot stand it* if you don't have his undying and total love. Now, do you see how this can only lead to panic and nothing else?

This brief interchange illustrates several points about the use of the ABC lead. First, it educates Jane on what causes disturbances in general and what causes her particular disturbance. When the therapist asked, "Now, do you see how this can only lead to panic and nothing else?", he dramatically underscored the importance of her thinking in causing her problems (and all problems, for that matter), and by implication deemphasized the importance of what her boyfriend did. This interchange also helped Jane separate and organize the myriad of things she is experiencing (the information from her boyfriend, her feelings, her thoughts) into some semblance of an understandable and manageable framework. She can now voice her feelings separate from her thoughts and both of these separate from the external events she encounters. And, third, this technique neatly and quickly set up the working through process which we will discuss in the next chapter.

Because the ABC theory is the heart of RET, therapists find this lead indispensable. They keep it in their heads as a structural aide both for psychodiagnosis and for guiding their various therapeutic efforts. Indeed, the ABC's may not even be referred to specifically, though it subtly underlies most general leads, such as: "Now, what did you think about in relation to what Tommy said to you that lead to your anxiety?"

Most clients have little difficulty discovering their thoughts when led in this manner, but the therapist should be prepared to assist the client who gives inaccurate responses. Jane, for example, could give an incomplete thought like, "I don't want him to go out with other women," and stop there. The therapist will confidently know that this thought, if that were all of it, would lead only to concern and not panic. The therapist would therefore confront Jane with this fact and nudge her to attend to the "shoulding" and the other irrational messages that lead to anxiety.

When clients fight the therapist's solicitation of irrational beliefs, after having been taught the ABC formula, it is relatively safe to conclude that they are exhibiting resistance. At these resistance points, encouragement to complete their thoughts often helps. For example, clients frequently exhort: "I can't think of what I was thinking" or "I don't know", to which the therapist can respond with something like, "Well, try!". The therapist then waits patiently as the pressure of the encouragement builds within the client, finally pushing him or her to exert the effort to think and discover the "B." The key dynamic in the "try" technique is the therapists powerful persistence.

A closing suggestion about the ABC lead is for therapists to use their knowledge of the basic irrational themes as a validity check on what the client reports. Clients can be expected to offer sometimes defensive and distorted reports to this level, and the therapist would be unwise to blindly accept such reports as valid. To illustrate we can turn once again to the example of Jane. She would not be afraid or panicky if she only concluded it was undesirable if Tommy dated others, nor would she be only concerned if she thought that it unbearable for Tommy to see other women. Feeling and behavioral consequences follow logically so that inconsistent B–C connections would be best noted and questioned by the therapist.

Use of Imagery. Even with the use of the ABC lead, some clients still find it difficult to identify their thoughts. Some even have a hard time getting in touch with their feelings. In such cases, we find it useful to employ imagery techniques in conjunction with the ABC formula. First the clients close their eyes and picture as vividly as they can the situation they find troublesome. Once they do this, we ask them to also picture how they felt at that time. While picturing these, we then ask them to determine what they are thinking. The use of imagery has all the benefits of the simple use of the ABC lead, plus it has the advantage of adding vividness and drama to the insight.

Contrasting Techniques. As Ellis (1962, 1977a) has frequently pointed out, people usually think both rationally and irrationally at the same time. They think the sane, sensible things and then pile on the insane things that lead to their emotional overreaction, to wit: "I don't like that *and* you *shouldn't* have done it." The techniques described here serve to help clients get in touch with both the rational and the irrational parts of their thoughts. They also allow clients to see the different emotional and behavioral consequences to their rational and their irrational thinking. And, they provide an immediate opportunity to help clients think through the validity of the irrational part of their thinking.

There are two variations to the contrasting technique. In variation one, the therapist first identifies the A, or activating event, and then asks the client to identify his or her rational thoughts about the event. Clients frequently give the wrong answer to this question, so it is often necessary to educate them about rational thoughts. Rational thoughts are always preferences or non-absolutes as in: "I *want* that;" or "I *desire* that;" or "I would find life *better* if I didn't have to contend with that." Thus, as a first step, help clients state their rational thoughts in these terms and then help them see the appropriate, yet often negative emotional and behavioral consequences (disappointment, frustration, sadness, sorrow, irritation, displeasure) that result from thinking these thoughts. Following this, ask them to identify the irrational thoughts they hold, which, following the theory, are always in the realm of absolute demands and absolute conclusions (i.e., musturbation, awfulizing, self-rating). Then, help them see the inappropriate emotional and behavioral consequences of thinking these thoughts (anger, anxiety, depression, guilt, low frustration tolerance).

A brief excerpt of a therapy session with a 17 year old youngster seen for performance anxiety, self-downing problems and very low frustration tolerance, illustrates this point.

Warren: I had a bad day at work Friday.

Therapist: What happened?

Warren: (He gives a lengthy description of being sent to the grocery store by the manager of a restaurant at which he worked to buy milk, buying too little milk, and being reprimanded by the manager.)

Therapist: And what did you feel at C?

Warren: Very angry. Frustrated.

Therapist: So you felt both angry and frustrated. Right? Do you want to work on these?

Warren: Yes. It's the same old problem.

Therapist: OK. So, let's find out what you were thinking that led you to feel like you did. First, let's look at what rational thoughts you had, because that will help you scientifically think about your irrational thoughts. What were your rational thoughts?

Warren: "I don't like that. He's making my day harder. I wish he would give me a break."

Therapist: Good.   Those are rational thoughts because they are your desires.   And, you are always entitled to your desires.   Now, do you see what feelings those would lead to, sticking only to those thoughts?

Warren: Irritation, disappointment.

Therapist: Correct.   Sticking to those thoughts you would have felt only irritation and disappointment at the worst. Now, what were your irrational thoughts?

Warren: That's easy (dramatically) "Here we go again. Why me? What right does he have to do that?"

Therapist: Correct again.   But, let's see if we can see a little more clearly the hidden message behind some of those thoughts.   Let's first take the self-talk, "Why me?" Turn that question mark into an exclamation mark and restate "Why me."

Warren: (pause) "It *shouldn't* happen to me."

Therapist: Right.   Do you see that that statement is a *demand* that life and people should be good and easy to you?

Warren: Yes.

Therapist: And do you see that that could only lead to frustration and anger?

Warren: Yes.

Therapist: OK.   We'll come back to some of the other ideas you had about what happened.   But, first, think about that notion.   Why should things be so easy and why shouldn't you get a little grief?

This excerpt demonstrates the use of version one of the contrasting technique.   In particular, it facilitated two important things. First, it helped Warren see that the responsibility for his emotional reactions was his own.   Second, it led naturally and smoothly into the working through process. Warren was prepared to think through or dispute his absolute assertion that life should be so good and easy to him; he had a sensible belief along with an irrational one, such that it would be difficult to not see the silliness of the irrational one. And, once this process was completed, he and the therapist went back, picked up another of his irrational ideas, especially the one directed at his manager that led more directly to anger, and then thought that one through.

Another variation of the contrasting technique is to first uncover the variety of emotional and behavioral reactions (the C's) that clients experience in particular situations and to separate the appropriate negative ones from the inappropriate negative ones. Following this, the therapist asks the client to identify the rational thinking that lead to the appropriate emotional reactions and the irrational ones that led to the inappropriate emotional reactions.

Once again, the client has a rational idea connected to an appropriate emotional response contrasted with an irrational idea connected to the inappropriate emotional response. And, a thinking through or working through process is ready to begin.

As before, the therapist would be advised to keep an eye on the congruity between the client's thoughts and the feelings. Clients often say they feel something like anger at point C, yet report thoughts as point B that are incongruous with angry feelings. These discrepancies should serve as a red flag to help the client correct either the B's or the C's. To do otherwise will lead to confusion on one or both parties' part and may very well represent a defensive attempt by the client to divert the therapist from the real issues.

Confronting Hidden Ideas

Thus far in this chapter two types of insight techniques have been presented—advancing hypotheses and leads. These two, while being directive and forthright, are not confrontive. Clients are *offered* a new way of looking at their problems and/or are *lead* into insightful discoveries. They are most frequently employed in response to clients presenting their tales of woe.

Clients also emit their irrational ideas in hidden ways, most notably through rhetorical questions, incomplete sentences or ideas, and slips of the tongue. We recommend watching for these and using them as opportunities to further help clients get in touch with their irrational thinking. Therapists must remember, however, that confrontation is not abrasive or aggressive, but rather assertive. Never should confrontation be used to subtly degrade or express anger toward the client.

Challenging Rhetorical Questions.   As discussed in the previous chapter, clients often display their irrational ideas—their musts, awfuls, I-can't-stand-its, and self-ratings—in the guise of rhetorical questions. It is not unusual, for instance, for people to say something like: "How could she do that!"; or "What kind of person would go around acting that way!" These statements, as we explained, are not real questions that ask for information, but rather statements that communicate a strongly held belief. The first rhetorical question, "How could she do that!", really says that "she *should* not do that." And, the message behind the second rehtorical question, "What kind of a person would go around acting that way!", is really "that person is a real *rat* for acting that way."

Because rhetorical questions usually represent strongly held beliefs, we advise being especially attentive to them. Furthermore, clients who express rhetorical questions are usually unaware of the real ideas behind them, ideas that precipitate so much of their disturbed emotional and behavioral responses. When presented with a rhetorical question, we advise the therapist to confront the client with it and assist him or her to see the underlying ideas. A simple way of doing this is illustrated below.

Jennie: . . .And my mother simply refused to cooperate. Again! How *could* she do that?

Therapist: Wow. You're really angry at her. But, do you want to get to the bottom of how you get yourself so angry at your mother?

Jennie: Yes.

Therapist: OK. You asked the question, "How could she not cooperate with you." Now, that sounded like a question asking for information; but my guess is that that was not a real question, but rather a rhetorical question. Do you know what a rhetorical question is?

Jennie: No.

Therapist: A rhetorical question is a strong statement of belief that is disguised as a question. Let me show you. Take that question of yours, "How could she do that? Change the question mark at the end to an exclamation point, and then with drama restate your ideas.

Jennie: (pauses and thinks) Well, that she *should* cooperate with me!

Therapist: That's right. The question of "how could she . . ." really is a statement of "she should . . ." And you probably add to it something like," the selfish bitch." And then you really set yourself off. Do you see how that line of thinking, disguised as it is, led to your anger?

Note the various components of this confrontation technique. The therapist first acknowledged Jennie's anger, indicated to her that she was responsible for her own anger, not her mother, and then asked her if she wanted to find out how she caused her anger. Next, he explained to her the concept of rhetorical questions. Then, he asked her to change her own "question" to a statement, which worked to uncover her "should," as it almost usually does. Finally, he connected Jennie's "should" to her feelings in order to help her clearly see how she indeed upset herself.

Completing Incomplete Sentences. As mentioned earlier, people think, or talk to themselves, in shorthand form. Some ideas, beliefs and philosophies come to be so well-accepted or believed that we think and act on them in very succinct form and in brief time frames. To say it differently, a whole host of discrete ideas and rather complex messages can get self-communicated in a very short, split-second period of time.

Unfortunately, clients are rarely aware of the incomplete nature of their thinking; they are also rarely aware of the complexity of the ideas or beliefs behind their thoughts. Thus, people report to the therapist what went through their minds, and it is quite often incomplete. In these cases the therapist may have to help clients get in touch with the rest of their thoughts and beliefs.

We have found several little challenges helpful in getting people to see and acknowledge the totality of these ideas. One is to repeat the sentence clients have already given and to simply ask them to finish it, adding a key word to what they reported, as for example: "So, she used your iron when you told her not to. Finish the sentence. 'She shouldn't use my iron because . . .'" Or, "So you think you might fail. Finish this sentence, 'I might fail, and if I do, then . . .'" A second method is to prompt clients to complete their thought by adding a word or two at a time until the idea is uncovered, as per: "Try to finish this. 'I might fail, and that would mean . . . that I . . . would be . . . (a failure).'" A third method is to ask the client to change the period at the end of the sentence into a comma (communicating that the thought is incomplete) to add the word "and," and then to wait for the client to complete the thought. For instance, the therapist might say: "she doesn't love me, comma, and . . ."

Emphasizing Key Words. Clients often express irrational thoughts without realizing their importance. For example, a client might say: "Damn it, that should never have happened."

In addition to all the other techniques described in this section, we find that simply attending to or emphasizing the most important word in the sentence can help the client to get in touch with the irrational idea. For instance, in response to the statement quoted above, the therapist might say: "That *shouldn't* have happened! Do you see the importance of that word, "shouldn't," that thought, in your frustration and anger?"

In Vivo Assignments. As will be discussed in some detail in the next chapter on working through strategies, rational-emotive therapy makes extensive use of behavioral homework assignments to help clients work through their irrational ideas. Yet, in vivo homework is also used to induce insights—to help clients get in touch with their irrational ideas and see both the extent and the importance of these ideas across the various arenas of their lives.

Accordingly, we find it a good idea to have clients engage in various activities outside therapy that are likely to cue them to their irrational ideas and hence to facilitate their awareness that they are thinking them. For instance, we might ask a man afraid of talking to women to approach three women within the next week and to simply observe (and later record) his thinking during those instances. This assignment serves to sensitize people to their thinking habits, and it often produces a quite dramatic experience which yields a great deal of additional information about basic beliefs and values.

Maultsby's Analogy Procedures

Maxie Maultsby has devised a somewhat standardized procedure for the first session of therapy to teach clients the five basic insights described earlier in this chapter. The steps are: (1) obtain a recent example of a situation when the client became upset (hopefully representing the core problem which brought the client to therapy); (2) relate an analogy that illustrates the first two insights—that all behavior has causes and that thoughts cause feelings and behavior— and didactically discussing these points; (3) relate a personal example or an example from another client that further illustrates the first two insights; (4) through an example obtained from the client, teach insight three—i.e. showing how the client's thinking led in this instance to the reaction that he or she had, and making the point that these thoughts, to the extent that they are typical, pro- duce the client's emotional disturbance; and (5) by the use of other analogies communicate insights four and five—that thoughts may not be valid and can be changed by engaging in rational-emotive activities.

Let us illustrate this process with a lengthy excerpt from the first session with Janice, a client who came to therapy to overcome severe feelings of inadequacy and guilt. The excerpt picks up about 20 minutes into the session and follows the client's presentation of the problem.

Therapist 1: OK. Let me teach you something. Let's take the situation at school that you were telling me about in which you felt guilty.

Janice 1: OK. The School Board passed this rule about vaca- tions and I thought it was really stupid. And I ran into this other teacher and she asked me how I felt about it and I said something like, "The goddamn bastards," and added all sorts of profanities. Then she looked at me kind of funny and quickly excused herself.

Therapist 2: And then you felt guilty.

Janice 2: Then I felt guilty.

Therapist 3: All right now. Where do you think that guilt came from? What caused you to feel guilty?

Janice 3: When I probably perceived my behavior as not a normal way to respond and it probably was bad.

Therapist 4: That is really beautiful. That is really a very good insight that you just had because it describes very accurately why you felt guilty. Now let me give you an analogy. OK? And then we will come back and look at what you just said and find out how right you were. Let's say that you have known me for a long time and learned to trust me. And you know that I am not going to BS you. Let's assume that we are having this conversation at the beach and I look under your chair and I all of a sudden say in a startled voice: "Jesus Christ! There's a snake under your chair." And you believed me. How would you react emotionally to that? How would you feel?

Janice 4: And there really was?

Therapist 5: Well, don't worry about that. What would you more than likely feel?

Janice 5: I'd probably get up and fly.

Therapist 6: Yeah. And your emotional reaction?

Janice 6: Panic.

Therapist 7: Right. That would be the natural thing to do. Now, what if I took a closer look and said: "There's no snake. If you will look carefully, you'll see that it's just a rubber hose. I'm sorry for the mistake." How do you think you would feel emotionally then, not toward me, but toward the snake? Would you still be panicky?

Janice 7: No, surely I wouldn't. I'd feel relieved.

Therapist 8: OK. So, within a thirty second span, you would feel on the one hand very upset, panicky, and then on the other hand you become angry at me, but that is another story. But, you wouldn't be panicky like you were in the first instance. Right?

Janice 8: Right.

Therapist 9: Yeah. Now, Janice, what is the difference between those two scenes that I just gave you?

Janice 9: The first time there was not a snake and the second time there really was a snake?

Therapist 10: No. Both times there was *no* snake. The first time I told you there was and the second time I told you there wasn't, but there was never a snake under your chair.

Janice 10: I'm not sure. One time I summed up the situation in one way and then I looked at the situation and summed it up differently.

Therapist 11: Exactly. The difference between the two was this: In the first instance you believed me and said to yourself: "Yes, there is a snake." And you probably then thought something like: "Snakes are very dangerous. I'd better get out of here." Nevertheless, you thought the kind of thoughts that lead to a strong emotional reaction, maybe even panic. That was your thought and then you felt panicky feelings. Now, in the second instance, you processed another bit of information in your brain.

Janice 11: "There is no snake."

Therapist 12: Right. "Therefore, I can just sit here and be comfortable."

Janice 12: Exactly, now I get you.

Therapist 13: And then you emotionally reacted to it. The point I am making is that the major difference between the situations that I just presented to you is the way you processed the information through your brain, the thoughts you had, right?

Janice 13: Right. So the thought goes through with the emotion being the result.

Authors Note. In this brief interchange the therapist shows the client how thoughts rather than events cause emotional reactions (Insight Number Two). In a rather didactic way he begins by telling Janice he is going to teach her something (Therapist 1) and professorily tests her pre-knowledge of the ABC formula by asking her why she thought she felt the way she did (Therapist 3). Despite the fact that she answers somewhat accurately that her *perception* of the inappropriateness of her behavior caused her guilt (Janice 3), the therapist was not confident that she understood the significance of this and launched into an analogy to illustrate the fact that thoughts are the things that cause feelings (Therapist 4 to 13).

Therapist 14: That's exactly right. And that is so important. Take the example that you gave of feeling guilty when you blurted out the obscene language to this other teacher and she looked at you with a funny look on her face. That doesn't automatically have any more capacity to make you feel guilty than the snake being there or not being there having the power of making you feel panicky. It is what you think about the thing you did that makes you feel guilty.

Janice 14: Right.

Therapist 15: The thoughts you have about it. No matter what you said, that does not have the capacity to make you feel anything. But you did get guilty so you had to say guilty things to yourself. What do you think they were?

Janice 15: "What an ass I am! How can anybody be as dumb as I am to do this!"

Therapist 16: Right. If you think those thoughts about your actions, those thoughts logically lead you to feeling the way that you feel. You say to yourself such things as: "How stupid of me for doing that! What kind of a fool would say that sort of thing in an elementary school! I must be the biggest, dumbest, person in existence." Now, I don't know if you say those particular words, but if you did, you'd feel guilty. But, what if I did something outrageous in public and said those kind of things to myself— "Oh, my god, what kind of dumb ass I am!" Now if I thought those sort of things, how do you think I would feel?

Janice 16: Guilty.

Therapist 17: I would feel guilty, inadequate, foolish. Right?

Janice 17: Right.

Therapist 18: OK. Now, what if I thought something like: "Here I go again. I made a mistake. What the hell, I'm a human being. I have a right to make mistakes. Not only do I have a right to make them, but it is inevitable that I am going to do dumb things. So, that's too bad. I'm still OK." Now, if I thought that instead of the things I said earlier, how do you think I'd feel?

Janice 18: Probably guiltless.

Therapist 19: Right. Now, let's get this back to you. Here you are saying obscenities to this other teacher and your typical way of thinking about what you do is to say: "What a dumb ass I am!" And you feel guilty, worthless. OK. What if you thought: "Well, I'm just a human being who makes mistakes. I've learned from my family to blurt things out and sometimes people find it offensive, but that's the way I am." Now if you really thought and believed that, how do you think you'd feel?

Janice 19: Better about it. I wouldn't have any guilt.

Therapist 20: OK. I think you're getting the idea. Can you try to sum up what we've been talking about?

Janice 20: Well, the way you think about yourself, you know, the preconception that you have or how you react to what you have done is the key. If you do something silly, or even act outrageous, and you chalk it up as "I made a mistake, da da da," then you have less chance of feeling guilty; or you wouldn't feel guilty at all if you say, "Gee, that's the way I am." If you look at yourself in those terms, instead of, "Gee, I'm less of a person," then you'd react quite differently than I do. Anyway that feeling of guilt comes from my thinking.

Therapist 21: Exactly. That's beautiful. You said it very well, but to summarize what I am saying is this: What you do to cause yourself to feel guilty, whether you blurt out obscenities or whatever, is the way you think about it. To put it into ABC terms, events at Point A, real things that happen which you do, do not make you react at Point C; it is what you think about at Point B, the way you evaluate A, that makes you react at C.

Janice 21: You know that is absolutely right. I can remember times in my past where at A, you know, I did mouth off or got mad in a particular situation where afterwards I felt nothing, absolutely nothing, no guilt. And I realized that people were upset but I took the attitude that this is just the way I am. I remember one particular incident on a weekend date when I was particularly obnoxious and the guy just took me home. He couldn't stand it, you know. And I just laughed. And afterwards I felt just great. You know, zero. I had no guilt about the way I reacted. But I can think of things just in the past year where it wasn't like that, where I just seemed to react with guilt. It is getting more and more frequent. And I do think that way about me now . . . and it's getting worse and I don't know where it came from.

Therapist 22: Well, you seem to have gotten to this point in your life where you have a very strong habit of thinking about yourself in shitty ways and putting yourself down. This doesn't mean that you are shitty by any means. We will get into this notion about shithood later. But what it means is that you have learned to think a set of thoughts that lead to you upsetting yourself—to make yourself feel guilty.

Janice 22: I guess that's right.

Authors Note. These interchanges illustrate how the therapist helps Janice acquire Insight Number Three—that *her* thoughts and beliefs cause her to feel guilty. First, he makes the connection between the ideas learned from the previous analogy to Janice's presenting problem (Therapist 14), diverts to a self-related example to further make the ABC Points (Therapist 16, 17 and 18), and then returns to her guilt problem (Therapist 19). He also shows her that different, more rational thoughts logically lead to more desirable emotional consequences just as her current thoughts logically lead to the guilt feeling that she currently experiences. Finally, the therapist asks Janice to sum up the ideas she has learned (Therapist 20) and then summarizes her summary in the ABC language (Therapist 21).

Therapist 23: That's right. OK, now the implications for therapy are very direct. The implications are that I want to help you to do three things. First, I want to help you become aware of what you think about yourself and say to yourself to cause you to feel so guilty. That is what we will dredge out and we already have talked about what the thoughts are. Second, I am going to help you analyze what you are saying to yourself and help you determine whether it is a rational, sensible thing to think or whether it is just a bunch of crap. Because what you think may or may not be true. And, I am going to teach you how to do that since I am already convinced that what you are thinking about yourself is nonsense. I am going to teach you criteria with which to evaluate your thoughts. After doing those things, I'm thirdly going to help you find more sensible ways to think about yourself that don't lead to guilt. And once you get to the point of thinking about yourself sensibly, in other words, get in the habit of thinking about yourself rationally...

Janice 23: Then you are making steps forward.

Therapist 24: You are not only making steps forward, but you are making steps to feel less and less guilty. You won't do it so frequently and, when you do make yourself guilty by thinking these thoughts, it won't be nearly so intense.

Janice 24: That would be great. I mean fantastic. It will be worth the cost of therapy.

Therapist 25: Time is almost up. We'll review all this next time. Do you have any questions before we stop?

Janice 25: I don't think so. But that is a very interesting undertaking. It's exciting.

Therapist 26: I should caution you that you will probably get discouraged at some point. People often get discouraged in therapy. And it will be hard work. And I am going to ask you to do a great deal of hard work. You've got this strong habit of putting yourself down and it will be hard work.

Janice 26: OK.

Authors Note. Rational-emotive therapy is above all a scientific method of hypothesis testing. Insights four and five speak directly to this point—that clients can view their beliefs as hypotheses that may or may not be valid, that they can be tested, and that, with repeated effort, they can be discarded if found invalid. In this section, the therapist directly and simply communicates these ideas (Therapist 23). Janice seems to have grasped all these new ideas and is now ready for the working through process as detailed in the next chapter.

These, then, are some of the techniques that we and others have found helpful in assisting clients to gain the types of rational-emotive insight previously discussed. Although these methods are not magical and will not always work, we believe they provide a requisite foundation for effective rational-emotive insight. The competent therapist will be proficient in using the techniques and be able to invent others as necessary to promote client insight.

ROADBLOCKS TO RATIONAL-EMOTIVE INSIGHT

It has been suggested throughout this chapter that rational-emotive therapy is hard work for both therapist and client, and that client change often does not occur easily. These are facts to be accepted. To demand that therapy be easy or that clients change quickly is obviously irrational.

Also contributory on occasion to slow and difficult client change, even for competent therapists, are therapist and client roadblocks. These, as noted in the previous chapter, are the typical and significant mistakes which can occur at any point in rational-emotive therapy, and which inhibit therapeutic progress at that time. In the final portion of this chapter we will discuss common therapist and client roadblocks that can inhibit or block rational-emotive insight.

Therapist Roadblocks

Many therapists block clients from acquiring rational-emotive insight by failing to accurately conceptualize the dynamics of the client's psychopathology or by failing to appropriately use the techniques described in this chapter. These represent lack of knowledge and skill, and call for remedial education in RET or intensive skill training. Sometimes personal issues prohibit appropriate therapist behavior and call for personal psychotherapy to overcome irrational problems.

The roadblocks represent special procedural mistakes that interfere with clients seeing and acknowledging the philosophic roots of their emotional disturbances.

Assuming Too Much. Because the ABC formula is so conceptually simple, and because the irrational ideas behind the various psychopathologies are so apparent to one familiar with RET, many therapists assume that clients are accurately aware of their emotions and irrational ideas. Believing this, the therapist then moves forward into a working through process and contributes to frustration and confusion for all.

As one might suspect, we find it advisable for the therapist to make sure that clients accurately perceive both their feelings and the ideas behind their feelings. We recommend that the therapist be particularly attentive to discrepancies in the client's verbal and non-verbal reports which indicate gaps in self-awareness; one being a discrepancy between verbal and non-verbal reports of feelings, and another being a discrepancy between their expressed idea and the feelings they report. For instance, a client might report frustration when the thoughts s/he has logically lead to guilt and feelings of self-downing. Regardless of the variety, be careful not to assume insight before insight exists.

Misuse of Questions.   Rational-emotive therapy makes maximal use of the logic-deductive method of scientific inquiry. As described in chapter four, a major and unique part of RET is to see to it that clients repeatedly question their irrational ideas until they are seen as faulty. While this is a primary tool for the working through process, questions at the insight stage often defeat the major goals of insight. Particularly the use of rhetorical questions ("What's getting you to feel anxious?"), multiple questions, and too many questions can serve to confuse clients and put them on the defensive. We advise the judicious use of questions and, more importantly, the maximal use of the insight techniques previously described.

Demand for Cooperation.   It is not uncommon for therapists to become impatient with or angry at their clients. In RET this often happens when clients will not "see" and acknowledge their irrational thinking. The therapist thinks that the client *should* be more cooperative, more involved, more enthusiastic, more perceptive, more astute, more courageous, more adept at learning, and so on.

These, "shoulds", of course, are forms of "musturbation" or demandingness on the therapist's part. Like all demands, they are irrational for they: (1) escalate what the therapist wants or what s/he thinks would be good for the client into a necessity; (2) grandiosely put the therapist at the center of the universe where s/he purportedly has the right to dictate peoples' behavior; (3) ignore the simple and obvious fact that the client is acting a particular way for some real reason, not capriciously; and (4) tend to undercut the therapist's effectiveness. In point of fact, a good argument could be made that clients should not be cooperative, involved, perceptive, and so on. After all, is it not logical to expect disturbed people to act in disturbed ways?

We think it quite important for therapists who find themselves angry at a client to work through the irrational basis of the anger. This, of course, involves a typical RET fashion: (1) the acknowledgement of the anger; (2) acceptance of the responsibility for the anger; (3) acknowledgement of the philosophic roots of the anger; (4) disputation of the validity of the philosophic premises behind the anger; and (5) replacement of the false anger-provoking premises with more valid ones that lead to client acceptance. To do otherwise would perpetuate undercurrents in the client-therapist relationship that could hardly be productive for either party.

Lecturing/Telling.   Although RET advocates a certain amount of directive, vigorous therapist activity, particularly in advancing hypotheses, a common therapist mistake is to do *too much* telling or lecturing. The result is that the client does very little work or, to put it differently, becomes an ineffective, passive learner.

We find that a lecturing/telling style occurs for several reasons. One has to do with therapists who are not sure of their abilities; lacking confidence, they often try to "make" the client understand and to change them with a barrage of verbiage. Another reason is misdirected attempts to model Albert Ellis' style. At first glance, it appears that Ellis simply tells clients how to think and feel, and that they just do so. A closer inspection reveals that he asks a great many questions and does a good many things that "force" clients to really think for themselves. The undiscerning observer often misses the latter and mistakenly mimics only the former. Another reason for too much lecturing/telling is the therapist being seduced by client resistance. Resistive clients often feign confusion, change the subject, or just out and out argue about points. Some therapists respond by trying to force insights on the client, which paradoxically serves to strengthen client resistance.

Regardless of the reason behind this posture, lecturing/telling tends to lead to a superficial solution to the client's problems. Clients are less likely to relate to insights when told about them than when they are thought through and they miss an opportunity to practice rigorous and deductive thinking. Our advice, then, is to do only as much lecturing/telling as necessary to induce clients to do their own thinking.

Client Roadblocks

Clients can throw up any number of roadblocks to impede the course of psychotherapy. In RET they share all the resistances and transference tendencies exhibited by those in other therapies. But, since RET is so uniquely focused on the client's philosophic system, there are some unique client roadblocks that particularly prohibit proper RET insights. We will now discuss some of these.

Focusing on Activating Events.   Rational-emotive therapy has the ultimate goal of changing people's basic beliefs and philosophies. To the contrary, a good many clients come to therapy with quite different ideas about what they want.   Some have a low tolerance for distress of any kind and simply want to relieve the pressure; others do suffer from very unfortunate circumstances that would best be changed; still others are caught in the "it makes me" trap and believe that external events cause them to feel as badly as they do.   Regardless of the particular problem, many clients will pressure the therapist to solve their external problems for them.

There is nothing in and of itself wrong with this. Most people's lives could be improved if some particular circumstance or other were changed.   The problem, however, is in cheating the client by primarily and/or exclusively focusing on changing undesirable circumstances.   That is, clients experience relief from no longer having to contend with that particular event in their lives, but they actually remain as disturbed as before, since the real problem is how they deal with or evaluate the event at Point B, rather than the event itself. The person no longer has to contend with something obnoxious, but still carries disturbed and upsetting ideas about dealing with such events. So, we have a temporarily happy or contented neurotic, but a neurotic nevertheless. Coincidentally, there is a danger that by removing the situational pressure, the therapist has indirectly lessened the client's pain and removed a motivation to continue in therapy.

We, as do others, strongly recommend that the therapist think twice before prematurely moving to alleviate external pressures. While this can often be therapeutically helpful and is sometimes important to do, we recommend that the therapist think through the following questions before doing so! Does the client see the external problem as *the* problem, while ignoring the internal one? Will the client want to terminate therapy and ignore personal change once the pressure is removed? Can the client independently solve the external problem either now or once the internal problem is solved? Is the external problem really that bad to begin with? If the answers to these questions are yes, then the therapist would be wise to avoid solving external problems and concentrate on the emotional problems about the external problems.

To help clients focus on the internal problem, it is useful to *persist* by showing them, through the techniques already described, how their thoughts (rather than events) primarily lead to their disturbed consequences. To repeat a cliche, "meet their resistance with persistence."

Another useful ploy is to remind clients of the differences between their environmental problems and emotional problems (see Chapter 2). Again, we will agree with them that the external event is bad, but that their real problem is an emotional problem about this environmental problem they have created. Most clients will recognize how this distinction applies to them, thus providing the therapist with an opportunity to explain how they will be able to solve their practical problems once they get over their emotional problems.

Focusing on Feelings. Abetted by popular and even professional literature, many people enter therapy wanting to focus on "getting in touch with" and exploring their feelings. They expect the therapist to sympathetically listen to their woes, commiserate with their suffering, and endlessly accept their complaints about life and their pain until the well runs dry. They might tolerate the therapist occasionally diverting to their thoughts or beliefs, but they will patiently or impatiently wait this out and then return to cataloging their miseries.

While some clients do indeed come to therapy so upset that they need to vent their feelings before they are able to really acknowledge and deal with the ideas behind their feeling, focusing for any length of time on client's feelings is usually unproductive and is often counterproductive. The venting of feelings is a highly cognitive activity in which irrational ideas that give rise to strong emotional reactions are rehashed. Giving vent to feelings thus serves to further habitate the ideas that cause the disturbance so that, in effect, the client actually practices being disturbed. As a result, s/he gets worse rather than better. Moreover, the temporary relief often experienced through venting feelings is pleasurable and serves as a reinforcement to continue the pernicious venting practice ad nauseum, both within and outside therapy.

We do not offer a magical solution for this client roadblock. But, we recommend that the therapist be cognizant of the problem and attempt again to show clients: (1) the real locus of their problems; (2) how their thoughts lead directly to their self-defeating emotional and/or behavioral problems; and (3) the necessity of cognitive change for emotional change. Without these primary insights, other insights and further therapeutic progress will be unlikely.

The Past History Trap. Mystiques in psychotherapy run deep. One that clients and therapists often share is a belief in the importance of exploring one's early childhood experiences. The idea is that uncovering unconscious conflicts spawned in early traumatic experiences and/or significant early relationships will bring about cure. Contrary to all this, RET focuses, as we have already said, on current issues and particularly on client's attitudes about these current issues.

We actually have not found the past history roadblock to be a particularly difficult problem except when confronting the psychologically sophisticated client. For most clients, therapist persistence in pointing out the relationship between thinking and emotional problems serves to win the day. For those stubborn few who have learned to delve into the past, we have found it helpful to ask them to suspend judgment for a week or two and to try to open-mindedly work within the RET framework with the idea that they have nothing to lose. This gives the therapist some grace time to get the therapeutic process started. It is of course essential to make maximum use of this time; we therefore recommend that the therapist immediately assign behavioral and/or written homework so that the client can quickly "experience" the benefits of RET. One incident of successfully using RET often captures the client's cooperation.

Fast and Unconscious Labeling. We have already discussed the fact that people often fail to attend to their thinking. When asked in therapy what they were thinking just prior to and during their emotional upset, many report that they had no thoughts at all. They vividly describe the events they encountered and the feelings they experienced, but go blank with regard to what went through their heads.

When clients claim that they had no thoughts when they became upset, we find it profitable to simply persist in our efforts to help them become aware of their ideas and beliefs. We suggest explaining the ideas contained in the preceding paragraph, show them through various examples and analogies how thoughts indeed cause feelings, and go back to one or more of the techniques described earlier in this chapter.

Sometimes clients actively resist admitting covert ideation. Rather than precipitate a therapist-client power struggle by trying to force an admission, we abandon the struggle and perform an "end run" by asking the client to freely "create" those thoughts and beliefs which would accurately reflect the feelings of another person experiencing similar emotional reactions. Nearly always these "created" thoughts represent the clients underlying irrational ideation. Without asking the client to openly admit ownership of these thoughts, the therapist can treat them as deeply held beliefs and proceed with therapy.

Feelings of Powerlessness. Whether we term it learned helplessness (Seligman, 1975), external locus of control (Rotter, 1966), or unrealistic beliefs about insurmountable life difficulties (Beck, 1976), some people think themselves so powerless, so much the helpless victims of circumstances, that they convince themselves they can make no positive impact on their lives. Consequently, they put little effort into getting in touch with and acknowledging their irrational ideas.

We view this client roadblock as a major personal problem in and of itself and recommend treating it first before undertaking other difficulties. We find putting the helplessness problem into the ABC formula quite helpful where "C" is simply the consequence of feeling helpless; we then help the client ferret out the "B's" behind the "C" using the techniques already discussed. Following Beck (1976), we also recommend inducing these individuals to engage in active, successful experiences in which they do indeed make some impact on the consequences of their own lives. We caution the therapist to orchestrate these efforts in such a way that successes are virtually guaranteed lest clients' belief in their helplessness becomes further entrenched. Once clients find that their efforts do indeed pay off, they then find it much easier to actively engage their thinking.

Self-Downing. A special type of roadblock in the insight process has to do with the clients who condemn themselves after they discover their ideational problems. As outlined in chapter two, they create emotional problems about their problems once they see them. These clients put themselves down for being so silly, petty or stupid for having the problems they discover in the insight process. Twenty-eight year old Frances is a good example. She was referred by her allergist after two years of unsuccessful attempts to medically treat her complexion problems. During this two year span, she shamefully refused to leave her house and virtually hid from everyone except members of her immediate family. Efforts at helping her get in touch with her awfulizing about her complexion and her self-downing were successful in the first session, but she came to the second session quite depressed and without having done her between-session homework assignments. What had happened was that she had determined that it was so silly to get so upset about something so trivial as her complexion that she condemned herself as worthless for doing this.

The tactic pursued in the case of Frances, and one we and most other RETers recommend for all such cases, is to deal first with the self-condemning before working back to the original problem. Clients who condemn themselves for making themselves disturbed will generally be unable to tackle their original problem until they are able to accept themselves as people who make mistakes.

SUMMARY

The five insights discussed in this chapter are necessary but insufficient ingredients for constructive personality change through rational-emotive therapy. These insights orient the client to rational-emotive theory, facilitate motivation for the hard work required in RET, and provide the conceptual tools with which the therapist helps the client to change.

Four therapeutic strategies provide the methodology for promoting rational-emotive insight: advancing hypotheses, leading techniques, confronting methods and a formal, didactic procedure devised by Maxie Maultsby, which capitalizes on the use of analogies. Rational-emotive insight is not easily gained by the client nor easily promoted by the therapist because of roadblocks which affect each party. Client roadblocks are those ideational distortions which block insight and produce a strong resistance to therapy, while therapist roadblocks are common blunders in performance which inadvertently inhibit the client from acquiring insight. Rational-emotive insight therefore depends on the clinician's skill in overcoming performance mistakes and in dealing effectively with client resistance.

Although insight is ordinarily acquired by clients throughout the therapeutic process, it is mandatory that some degree of insight be gained at an early stage, usually following an exploration of the client's problems and a psychodiagnostic formulation. This insight stage prepares the client for subsequent disputation of irrational beliefs in the working-through process, presented in the next chapter.

4

Rational-Emotive Working Through

Rational-emotive working through constitutes the heart of RET. Helping clients work through their problems—that is, systematically giving up their irrational ideas—is where most of the therapist's energy and time are directed and where longlasting change takes place. Successful working through leads to significant change, whereas unsuccessful working through leads to no gain or to superficial gain at best. It is as simple as that.

We emphatically state the necessity for working through for three reasons. First and perhaps the most important is that people vigorously cling to the irrational ideas they hold. They have typically believed these ideas for years and have thought about and dealt with scores of situations consistent with these ideas. They, in effect, have practiced believing irrational ideas until these ideas have become "second nature." It is therefore little wonder that awareness of or insight into the existence of irrational ideas is rarely enough to make clients give them up. Think for a minute of trying to change from being right handed to left handed by simply acknowledging that you are right handed, and you will see what we mean. Changing anything so well learned requires repeated, energetic efforts.

The fact that people, in general, tend to be allergic to thinking (Ellis, 1967) provides another reason why rational-emotive working through is so crucial. When we say allergic to thinking, we mean that people tend to be lazy. They tend to be intolerant of frustration and pain, wanting a facile, magical solution to their problems, a solution which requires little effort on their own part. Thus, they generally refuse or neglect to put energy into thinking about and assessing the validity of their ideas. Left with their insights, which they may even find interesting and perhaps even exciting, most people are likely to drift, goof and act upon their acknowledged irrational ideas even though they "know" better.

The third reason why rational-emotive working through is essential has to do with the nature of insight itself. Insight can be defined as the genuine acknowledgement and accurate expression (at least to oneself) of the thoughts and feelings which constitute the emotional disturbance. While certainly important, the process of gaining and dwelling on insights can have a distinctly counter-therapeutic effect, as this can constitute practice in thinking and feeling irrationally and can actually result in getting worse rather than better. Therapists who encourage such expression of insight as a primary therapeutic modality tend to make their clients more disturbed over time (Bandura, 1973; Ellis, 1967, 1977a).

We will now turn to discussing the nature of rational-emotive working through. After doing so, we will then present ways to facilitate rational-emotive working through and conclude by detailing both therapist and client roadblocks to its successful realization.

RATIONAL-EMOTIVE WORKING THROUGH DEFINED

Several kinds of working through are rarely if ever employed in RET, although they play a prominent role in many other therapies (Ellis, 1966).

1. As briefly stated above, RET does not encourage clients to dwell on, express, or abreact their feelings. RET therapists frequently help their clients fully acknowledge their feelings, especially those (such as embarrassment and rage) that they are likely to suppress or repress. But, as we have said, a considerable amount of psychological research and clinical practice has shown that the abreaction and catharsis of feelings such as anger is more likely to increase rather than decrease the negative affect, thereby doing more harm than good (Bandura, 1973; Berkowitz, 1970; Ellis, 1977a; Geen, 1976).

Although RET at times makes use of catharsis, especially in the course of its rational marathon encounters (Ellis, 1969a), it tends to do so cautiously and with a great deal of added cognitive analysis and disputing. One of its main goals is to show people how they unnecessarily create their own negative emotions, how harmful these feelings often are, and how they can effectively minimize or eliminate rather than express and "handle" them (Ellis, 1977a; Hauck, 1974). In this respect, RET distinctly differs from perhaps the majority of other major schools of psychotherapy.

2. RET greatly minimizes the significance of connections between present behavior and past experiences and relationships. While therapies such as psychoanalysis are highly cognitive in that they employ a great deal of interpretation into historical data, RET shows clients that they are disturbed today, that their present problems have little relationship to the past per se, and that how they interpret or view what happened to them in the past is the most important aspect of the problem. They are also shown that even though early influences such as their parents significantly helped them to create or adopt irrational beliefs, the main reason these beliefs persist is that clients still very actively and creatively carry them into the present. For parental- or culture-inculcated beliefs to effect them, *they* have to first *accept* such ideas and *they* have to keep carrying them on, or continue to *re*indoctrinate themselves with such beliefs. And, RET further shows clients that only by vigorous, hard-headed, persistent *work and practice* are they likely to surrender and keep surrendering such ideas and this kind of practice had better be in the cognitive, emotive, and behavioral realms.

3. RET also minimizes the working through of subtle and not so subtle factors in the therapist-client relationship. Clients' relationships with people in their everyday lives are typically far more important than the relationship with their therapists (Ellis, 1968), and client likes or dislikes for the therapist tend to be merely illustrative of personal difficulties rather directly the core of his or her basic problems.

4. And, RET largely ignores the working through of dreams, physical gestures and postures, and fantasies. While recognizing that these things often do have particular meaning for the client, and are not totally accidental, getting caught up in focusing on such data

proves time consuming and indirect at best. RETers believe that an analysis of clients' dreams and an exploration into the symbolism expressed in their gestures and the like, accomplishes far less than focusing on specific life events in their lives and particularly their responses to them.

These, then, are areas of working through that RET deemphasizes. Instead, RET emphasizes helping clients (1) clearly comprehend what thoughts and ideas lead to the inappropriate emotional and behavioral consequences they suffer, and (2) repeatedly see the falseness and foolhardiness of the ideas or philosophies that underpin their disturbances. To do this, the rational-emotive therapist acts as a nonsense-annihilating teacher who persuades, cajoles, encourages and teaches clients to suspend judgment, to consider each currently held irrational idea as a proposition or hypothesis to be tested, and to then think rigorously about the "trueness" of the proposition in question. If, through this process, evidence and logic can be found to validate an idea or belief, then clients are encouraged to keep it; but, if no supporting evidence can be found, then clients are encouraged to throw the idea out and find a more valid, self-enhancing one.

More specifically, in rational-emotive working through, the therapist largely employs the *logico-empirical method of repeated and persistent scientific experimentation.* Through a whole host of cognitive, and behavioral, and emotive strategies, the therapist helps clients do at least three things, all of which are designed to assist them in determining whether their ideas are valid or invalid (Ellis and Grieger, 1977). Clients are assisted in *debating* their irrational ideas. By raising rhetorical questions and devising behavioral and emotive experiences, and by seeing to it that clients do likewise, the therapist assists them to actively and vigorously engage in an internal debate about the tenableness of the idea in question. The therapist also helps clients *discriminate* between wants or preferences and needs or "musts," between undesirable and "awful" consequences, between bad, self-defeating behaviors or traits and supposedly bad people, between logical conclusions and nonsequiturs, and between possible or probable outcomes and absolute outcomes. And, the therapist helps clients clearly and precisely *define* their terms. Clients are helped to make finer and finer definitions of terms until overgeneralizations, black and white thinking, absolute predictions, and other such cognitive distortions are exposed as fallacious.

This, then, is what constitutes rational-emotive working through. Before discussing ways to specifically facilitate it, we think it helpful to make two critical distinctions: between elegant and inelegant goals in RET, and between intellectual insight and so-called "emotional insight."

Elegant and Inelegant RET Goals

RET makes a major distinction between elegant and inelegant goals. Inelegant goals consist largely of symptoms removal through *additional education.* In this, the therapist uses a variety of cognitive, behavioral, and emotive techniques to teach, condition, indoctrinate and even brainwash clients with more "rational beliefs, self-statements, and coping statements" that will help them behave more effectively and enjoyably (Ellis, 1977f, p. 77). The problem with additional education, however, is the irrational ideas that clients bring to therapy are left intact so that they continue to vie for prominence with newer rational ones. Furthermore, clients are not taught to think empirically for themselves, thus leaving them dependent on a slogan or two to feel good and function effectively.

Elegant RET goals consist of a *cognitive-behavioral-emotive re-education.* Reeducation "stresses the achievement of a profound cognitive or philosophic change in clients' basic assumptions, especially their absolutistic, demanding, musturbatory, irrational ways of viewing themselves, others, and the world" (Ellis, 1977f, pp. 74-75), rather than mere symptom removal. Elegant RET not only changes clients' existing problems, but it also gives them an anti-awfulizing, anti-musturbating attitude that will (1) help them cope with and eliminate their symptoms if and when they arise and (2) help them prophylatically ward off or minimize their chances of creating new emotional disturbances in the future.

While making this distinction, it is best to keep in mind that not all clients can achieve elegant psychotherapeutic goals. Some, like the retarded, the schizophrenic, or the young child, require inelegant solutions to their problems; and the RET therapist would be wise to set realistic, yet inelegant goals for them. In the main, however, people can achieve elegant solutions to their problems, and for the therapist to settle for less than this would do them a disservice.

In the elegant version of RET, then, or with the goal of cognitive-emotive-behavioral reeducation, the therapist tries to help clients give up their fundamental neurotic, self-defeating, disturbance-creating philosophies and to adapt, in their place, more healthy, goal-enhancing ones. At the same time, the rational-emotive therapist teaches clients how to think scientifically (logically and empirically) in order to deal creatively, comfortably, sensibly and appropriately with any difficulty that may arise in the future. When this goal is reached, then, clients hold new ideas or philosophies while having given up the old ones, and they have learned a way of thinking, or processing ideas, that can help them in the face of future difficulties.

Intellectual versus Emotional Working Through

One of the criticisms frequently voiced by therapists from other theoretical persuasions is that RET is too superficial and intellectual. RETers are accused of fostering both intellectualization and rationalization in their clients.

We sometimes also hear a similar thing from our clients. They will say, "I understand what you are driving at, but I don't feel it in my gut;" or, "I know you're right. I see that. But, I have only got that intellectually, not emotionally." They imply, as do our colleagues, that RET misses a deeper more profound kind of understanding and working through that is emotional in nature.

While this distinction sounds good on the surface, there is a fundamental error in its logic. The error is simply that there is no such thing as an emotional understanding that contrasts with an intellectual understanding; and intellectual understanding is really believing something only lightly and infrequently, while a so-called "emotional understanding" is believing something strongly, with conviction, and most of the time. To say it somewhat differently, to know something because you've read it or heard it is one thing, but to know something *because you believe it* is an entirely different matter.   In other words, there is only an intellectual kind of understanding: some things we believe lightly and some things we believe strongly.

In RET, then, we try to help people strongly believe the rational ideas, and give up or only lightly believe the irrational ones. We work toward what is often mistakenly called an emotional understanding, really a deep and strong intellectual understanding. We want clients to energetically and strongly endorse an idea, to really believe it, and to strongly act on it the majority of the time.

FACILITATING RATIONAL-EMOTIVE WORKING THROUGH

With this general introduction in mind, we will now present the "hows" and "whats" of rational-emotive working through. First, how, or in what manner, does the rational-emotive therapist go about this task? In all sorts of manners, for RET can be and is successfully done by people with all types of personality styles. Contrary to popular opinion, RET is not synonymous with the personality of Albert Ellis. A good many soft-spoken, low-key people from places other than New York City do RET quite effectively.

In the main, however, RET does advocate (though not demand) an energetic, forceful therapist manner. The reason for this is that most people actively perpetuate their own disturbances. They not only put energy into thinking and believing the crazy, disturbing things that they do, but they also lazily refuse to work at undoing or giving them up. In fact, they are unlikely to get better, or get better slowly and inefficiently, when dealt with in a namby-pamby way.

What then can we generally say about the rational-emotive therapist's style as he or she goes about the business of helping clients work through their irrational ideas? The following represent typical RET working through styles, as articulated by Ellis (1973).

1. The rational-emotive therapist is *active-directive* with most clients. S/he typically does a great deal of talking and explaining, particularly in the early stages of therapy, because clients rarely understand what bothers them or what is illogical about the ideas behind what bothers them. S/he also goes right to the heart of the matter by directly confronting clients with their problems because to do otherwise wastes a good deal of unnecessary time. And, s/he regularly exhorts, cajoles, persuades, and even sometimes argues clients into giving up their emotional disturbance because long-held, irrational ideas best respond to head-on approach.

2. The rational-emotive therapist is *vigorous* with most clients because they tenaciously cling to their irrational notions and because they have been reindoctrinating themselves with these notions for years. Without attractive, new ideas that are energetically presented, clients are likely to go on using their irrational ideation. Thus, RETers take a vigorous approach to first get clients to think and then to get them to reeducate themselves.

3. The rational-emotive therapist is *persistent* and *repetitive* with most clients. The RETer keeps hammering away at the irrational ideas underlying clients' emotional disturbances. Although s/he may indeed back off with some clients and patiently wait till anxieties diminish, s/he keeps after them knowing that frequent and repeated working through is required because most clients overlook their irrational ideas, push them out of their minds, rationalize them, and in general, repeat them over and over out of habit.

4. The rational-emotive therapist begins the working through process as quickly as possible, sometimes even during the first session and frequently before a "good relationship" develops with the client. He or she quickly appeals to clients' reasoning powers, rather than to their emotions, and believes that the obviousness of the material presented will generally be much or more seductive than "unconditional positive regard."

5. The rational-emotive therapist is unusually *didactic* and *philosophical*. The RETer continually explains to clients what underlies their problems, teaches them what is sane and insane about what they believe, and shows them what can be done to get better and how to go about doing this. Rather than being psychologically oriented, RETers introduce clients to the philosophic dynamics of their problems, that is, show them the philosophic attitudes and assumptions they have erroneously been making and why these are both erroneous and self-defeating.

All this represents *how* rational-emotive working through is conducted. *What* is done follows a comprehensive, multimodel approach. Although RET is most uniquely a cognitive therapy, it also makes considerable use of evocative and behavioral methods on theoretical grounds. Believing as it does, that people are transactionally and interactionally thinking, behaving, *and* feeling beings, it believes that maximum therapeutic growth is an integration of cognitive, behavioral *and* emotional change; and it agrees with Lazarus (1976) that the most significant change takes place in the context of a multimodel, cognitive-emotive-behavioral therapeutic effort (Ellis, 1962, 1963, 1975; Garcia, 1977).

Cognitive Methods

RET holds that there are many cognitive methods to help people acknowledge, challenge, and surrender their irrational beliefs. Indeed, Ellis (1977c, 1978b) has listed about a dozen major categories, each with ten to twenty subheadings, so that the list totals about two hundred altogether. Some of the main cognitive techniques for working through include the teaching of rational self-statements, the teaching of coping methods, focusing-distraction procedures, information-giving, persuading, philosophizing, semantic analysis, suggestion, and positive thinking. We will present the major ones that RETers most frequently use.

Disputing Irrational Beliefs. Among the most powerful of the cognitive methods, particularly for more bright and educated people, is the technique of disputing irrational beliefs. As Albert Ellis has already introduced in chapter one, disputing consists of questioning and challenging the validity of the ideas or hypotheses clients hold about themselves, others and the world. The rational-emotive therapist poses (and encourages the client to pose) rhetorical questions or challenging statements about the client's beliefs—*"where's* the evidence that . . .?" *"How* does that follow?" *"Where's* the proof?" *"Prove* your thesis!" *"What* would really happen if . . .?" *"Who* said?" "In *what* way is that true?" These are made in order to show, or help clients see, that their beliefs are both *theoretically untenable* (e.g., are unfactual or tautological, contain internal inconsistencies, are based on false premises, are non-sequiturial) and are *impractical* or *impossible* (e.g., lead to poor results, cannot be obtained or accomplished, result in short range gain at the expense of long range cost).

The RET therapist's role is to play the devil's advocate in first posing the questions, then challenging clients to think empirically about their irrational ideas, and eventually seeing to it that they arrive at the "correct" answer. The therapist acts as both a provocative *question raiser* and an authoritative *information and answer provider* until clients clearly comprehend the logic of the "correct" answer. And, through persistently and forcefully repeating this process, along with using many of the other techniques described in this chapter, the therapist leads them to believe the "correct" answers, and to therefore respond in new and healthier ways. Through all this, there is a conscious effort to teach clients to become their own devil's advocate in order to accomplish for themselves what the therapist intends. The end result of disputing, in cognitive terms, is that clients are functioning at a much fuller realization of their thought potential. Rather than simply giving up irrational ideas in response to the therapist's urging, clients have tested out these ideas, found them to be illogical and impractical, and then begun to formulate more rational beliefs. This last product of learning, how to think rationally on their own, without the therapist's help, is perhaps most important. We believe this self-generated rational thinking to be the highest goal of therapy, and disputing helps lead to this goal.

Perhaps the best way to give the reader a flavor of disputing is to present transcribed portions of two interviews with a twenty-six year old man afraid of becoming homosexual (Ellis, 1971). In the following interchange, from the first session, Albert Ellis has just helped the man see that his anxiety about homosexuality directly resulted from his belief that "becoming" homosexual would make him worthless. At the point we pick up the interview, Dr. Ellis is beginning to dispute this notion.

T: Now the problem is: How are you going to give up that crap?

C: (Pause) I mean, I-I sit there and I try to prove what a homosexual is. Then I try to prove what a heterosexual is. And then I try to prove what I am. And to try to prove what you are, as a person-

T: Yeah?

C: -is very hard to do.

T: Because there is no way of doing it—except by some definition: "that if I were completely heterosexual, or if I were a great supervising artist, or if I were an Adonis, then I'd be a good guy!"

That's the only way you can prove yourself: by some arbitrary definition of accomplishment.

C: Yeah, I kept, like—in the other therapy, I kept using the words abnormal and homosexual.

T: Meaning—but what you mean is, "If I were abnormal—if everybody is normal but me—I'm no good!" Is that what you mean?

C: Yeah, I do mean that.

T: But let's suppose that, now. Let's just suppose that. Let's suppose that ninety-nine out of one hundred guys are normal—which is not true, but we'll deliberately suppose it—and they all are screwing girls and having a ball and marrying and having children; and you're the one out of a hundred who can't do that, who really is homosexual. All you can do is go after boys, and you can't make it at all with girls. You're impotent; you just can't make it with girls. We'll deliberately assume that. Therefore, statistically you're abnormal. Right? 'Cause you're one out of a hundred, and they can do things that you can't do. Now, why would you be a no-goodnik? Not why would you be abnormal—we're just assuming that you would be; now, why would you be a no-goodnik if that were so; you were the one out of a hundred who couldn't make it heterosexually?

C: Well—maybe fear of loneliness.

T: That's why it would be inconvenient: because they'd get along with girls, and you wouldn't. So therefore you might be lonely. Though that's not true either: you might have a lot of homosexual guys. But let's suppose you're lonely. Now, why would you be a louse because you're lonely? Now why would you be failing? Because we're assuming you'd be failing. They're succeeding heterosexually; you're not. Now why would you be a louse?

C: For not falling in with what they're doing.

T: But that's a definition! Now let's suppose the opposite, incidentally—that ninety-nine out of one hundred guys just about made it with girls—they got a girl here and they got a girl there, and they sort of succeeded—but you were outstanding, and you really were very good-looking and bright and sexy, and girls just fell all over you. And you screwed one after another, and they kept calling you up, wanting more. Now that would be abnormal, statistically. Right?

C: (Pause) It would be.

T: Why wouldn't you be a shit then? You'd be one out of a hundred!

C: So I'm going by the use of a definition?

T: That's right! "That I have to be supergood. Then I'm okay. But if I'm superbad—one out of a hundred on the bad side—then I'm a louse!" That's your definition. See? Now is a definition —does a definition prove anything about a fact? Because it is a definition; and if you want to feel you're a shit, you can feel you're a shit. But does it really prove you are a shit?—if you can only get there by definition?

C: I dunno.

T: Because it can really get absurd. I, for example, could say: "I'm a tuba." And you say, "You're a tuba? Well, how did you become a tuba? Prove it!" And I say, "Well, I'm going around oomp-oomp-oomp-bah. Therefore I'm a tuba!" Now does that prove I'm a tuba?

C: No.

T: What does it prove? It does prove something. What?

C: That you're not one. You may want to be one-

T: Yes, that I think I am a tuba. That's what it proves. Because if I'm going to go around acting like a tuba, whether I am or not, I think I am a tuba. But it never proves I am, you see. Therefore, if you go around acting as if you are a shit, it doesn't prove you are one; but it does prove that you think you are. And that's the story of your life! "If I'm not at least as good as others, and preferably much better, I define myself as an utter lowlifer! A skunk!" Right?

C: Yes, that's true.

T: All right. Now, if that's so, how could you become a nonshit?

C: By recognizing what I have. Or what I am.

T: Recognizing—but let's suppose the worst; you recognize what you are. But we'll go back to the previous hypothesis; you really are the one out of a hundred who is homosexual, while the other ninety-nine are straight. Would you then be a shit?

C: (Long pause) Yeah.

T: Why would you be?

C: (Pause)

T: Not, why would you think you were? But why would you actually be a shit if you were the one out of one hundred who couldn't make it with girls and the other ninety-nine could?

C: (Long pause; silence)

T: You haven't proved it to me yet! Why would you be no good? Worthless?

C: (Long pause) Because I'm not.

T: You're not what?

C: I'm not part—of the ninety-nine.

T: "I'm not part and I should—"

C: I should be!

T: Why? Why should you be?

C: Because of what I am.

T: Look! If you really are homosexual, you are a homosexual. Now, why should you be nonhomosexual if you're really homosexual? That doesn't make sense!

C: (Long pause; silence)

T: See what a bind you're in?

C: Yeah.

T: You're taking the sane statement, "It would be desirable to be heterosexual, if I were gay," and you're translating it into, "Therefore, I should be." Isn't that what you're doing?

C: Yeah.

T: But does that make sense? It doesn't!

C: If I were the one out of ninety-nine percent—

T: Yeah; and we're assuming that's undesirable.

C: I should be heterosexual.

T: Why? You haven't given me any reason yet. "Because I'm abnormal, I should be normal." Now why?

C: Because homosexuality is described as being abnormal.

T: Granting that (1) it's abnormal, and (2) it's undesirable, we're assuming that. Now, why should you be normal and desirable? Not "Why is it nice to be?"

C: Because I want to be!

T: That doesn't equal should. You might want to have a million dollars. You might want to be the greatest supervising artist that ever lived. Most of us do. Now, does that mean you should be, because you want to be? No, you see you're saying, "I should get what I want. I should be most desirable!" But "I've got to be what I want to be!" Now, does that make sense?

C: In other words, I'm pushing up against it. I'm—I'm expressing my wants against what my desires, what my—

T: You're making your wants into necessities—not desires. Which they are! "I want a million dollars, therefore I should have it. And I don't have it; therefore I'm a shit" "I want to be straight. Right now I'm gay"—we're just assuming that you were. "Therefore, I'm a shit!" Now, do those things follow?

C: (Pause) No, they don't follow.

T: So, your shithood doesn't come from your desire. It comes from your demand: "I must be normal; I must do the right thing. I've got to!" And as long as you have any demands, you're going to be anxious. As I tell my clients all the time: if you demand that "I must have a dollar in my pocket, at least a dollar, at all times," what's going to happen when you don't have the dollar?

C: You're gonna feel all out of place without it.

T: You're gonna feel terribly anxious. Now suppose you do have the dollar. You're saying, "I've gotta absolutely have that dollar, at least a dollar at all times!" And you have it; you have exactly a dollar in your pocket. How are you then going to feel?

C: That you've gotta have more.

T: You'll still feel anxious. Because you'll need the guarantee that you'll always have a dollar; you can't have a guarantee. So even if you're 100 percent straight, and you're saying to yourself "I've got to be straight; I must be straight; it's necessary that I be straight," you'll be anxious. Because you have no guarantee that you'll always be straight. Twenty years from now, you might become gay!

C: That's what scares me.

T: "Because I've got to be!" Now suppose you were saying, "I'd like to have a dollar in my pocket at all times; I'd very much like to have it, but it's just a like." And you don't have a dollar; you've got ninety cents. How are you going to feel?

C: Well, ninety cents will have to suffice.

T: Yeah. "It's too bad I don't have a full dollar. I'll try to get ten cents more, since I'd like to have a dollar. But if I don't, I don't. And if I do have a dollar, and I'd like to have one, then I'll be pretty happy." Right? The like to have a dollar or like to be straight is vastly different from got to, isn't it?

C: One is a demand, and one is expressing a wish.

T: That's right. And you really don't have wishes. You translate all your major wishes into demands: "I've got to be a great supervising artist. I've got to be absolutely straight. I've got to do well in various other areas." Now, isn't that what you invariably do?

C: Yeah, I do, do that. I transform all my wishes into—into demands.

T: Now how can you be nonanxious, if you do that?

C: Yeah.

This lengthy interchange shows how rational-emotive therapists set up and persist in disputing an irrational idea. By questioning and structuring, rather than merely stating facts or pontificating slogans, Dr. Ellis showed this client that he created his own anxieties by believing the idea that he would be worthless unless heterosexual. Dr. Ellis gave him every opportunity to disagree with, argue about, or nit-pick with his questions, but he relentlessly set up and posed questions that were designed to illuminate the absurdity of this belief. When the client gave the wrong answer, or gave a superficial one, Dr. Ellis refined his questions to further box in the client; when the client gave the correct answer, he offered reinforcement and continued disputing.

What follows is part of the eighth session with this same man. He is beginning to let loose of his irrational idea. However, he shows that he has not completely done so and sometimes only pays lip service to his new-found rational notions. So, Dr. Ellis continues the disputation in order to continue the client's working through process.

T: Hi! What's doing?

C: I keep—I pretty much got it all sorted out.

T: Yeah? How have you got it sorted out?

C: Well, there just are no shits. There are just human beings who make mistakes.

T: All right. How, specifically, does that apply to you? Are you just a human being who can make mistakes?

C: I can make mistakes, just as anyone else can. That's it.

T: Right!

C: It's just whether I'm a better human being or not, if I correct them. That's all.

T: Right.

C: If I want to correct them—

T: And sometimes even if you want to correct them, some of them can't be corrected—it's too late. What about that?

C: Correct them too late?

T: Yeah. Let's suppose you make a mistake, and it can't be corrected any more; it's too late.

C: Fuck it, then! I gotta live with it that way then.

T: That's right. You're still a fallible human.

C: Um-hm. But there's nothing you can't correct.

T: Well, no; that's not quite true. If you buy a stock and it goes down, it goes down! And that's it! So don't say that.

C: Yeah.

T: Most things, however, you can correct.

C: Well, anything that has to do with feeling like shit, or anything else like that.

T: That you can always correct—right?

C: Yes, that can always be corrected.

T: You never have to feel like a shit, no matter what you've done poorly.

C: Yeah. You know, and I'm saying—anything physical, anything that you have control over like your own self, you can always correct.

T: You cannot do it again. If you went out and screwed a boy, you wouldn't have to keep screwing a boy.

C: No.

T: It would just be an error—

C: Yeah.

T: You could correct that error—

C: You could always correct it. As long as you have control over it yourself.

T: Which you do—if you don't blame yourself. Then you have the control.

C: Yeah. But otherwise, anything outside of you, you can always try to correct. Sometimes it's beyond correcting, so—but you're still not a shit!

T: You're never a shit!

C: No, you can never—you're just a human being who has made a mistake, and you've got the right to try again.

T: Right!

C: Because that's what a human being is. And I've been thinking about it more and more. Sometimes I pretty much hold onto

it, the idea of the whole thing. And I've thought it all out.
And sometimes, you know, a shit comes back to me—with
me.

T: "I did badly, or I thought badly, and therefore I'm no good!"

C: Yes, "and therefore I'm a shit!"

T: Yeah.

C: Yeah, that really hits me. Sometimes.

T: But then what do you do?

C: Well, then I remember that, you know—well, I try to think of
the classic case of—stereotyping. And, you know, they're just
human beings, who make mistakes. That's what hits me harder
than anything else—the stereotyping—which I'm slowly getting
rid of, though.

T: Yeah: that human beings shouldn't make mistakes; and that
they're lice when they do.

C: Yeah. But the stereotyping's there of the homosexual, the
one who goes prancing down the street—which is quite comical
now!

T: Yeah.

C: The stereotyping hits me harder than anything else does.

T: Because what do you think of when you think of that stereotyped "fairy"?

C: Oh, I think: "What a shit!"

T: He is?

C: He is. Or what a shit I could become.

T: But how is he a shit? Let's suppose that he's one of the few
homosexuals who is in that stereotyped "fairy"-like way.
Suppose that he's prancing down the street, showing off, etc.
Now, why is he a shit?

C: Well, I think he's a—the reason why I think he might be a shit,
even though there are no shits, there are no stereotypes, really—
is because he's made a fool of himself, number one—

T: That's why he's acting badly. And he's really not making a fool of himself. He's acting foolishly. You can't make a complete fool of yourself; you can just act foolishly. Because that same guy, in business or something else, might act very sanely.

C: Yeah.

T: So in that respect he's acting foolishly.

C: Yes, he's acting foolishly.

T: Now, let's suppose he is. Why is he a shit?

C: Well, because—suppose he's the type of guy who doesn't like to make mistakes. And therefore, you're not supposed to act foolish.

T: Well, you see, that's your nonsense: that you're not supposed to act foolishly; the human is at all times supposed to act well, sanely, properly. But where are these humans who always act well?

C: There are none, really. There's always—one aspect in each of us where we act foolishly, and some little quirk we have.

T: All right. But that's your worst stereotype: that a human is supposed to act non-foolishly.

C: Yeah.

Assuming the Worst.   Closely intertwined with the disputing of irrational beliefs, and with all working through methods for that matter, is the technique of assuming the worst. This technique is designed to counteract the tendency of many people to rationalize or explain away their problems with pollyanna thinking—i.e., by convincing themselves that their life circumstances or their personal flaws are in reality not so bad. By doing this, they preclude acknowledging and disputing the irrational "musts" and "awfuls" that make up their emotional problems. The therapist who encourages this— assuming the best—helps the client feel better, but actually perpetuates and even helps entrench the client's disturbance.

Twenty-four year old Karyn represented such a client. She experienced extreme social anxiety because she: (1) believed she *had to* do well socially and win approval for doing so; (2) believed that she lacked most all necessary social skills; and (3) thought it *awful* to have such deficits. In hearing this, Karyn's therapist mistakenly chose to challenge Karyn's notion that she indeed lacked social skills, implying that this was not true and also implying that her problems would end if she would only see how skilled she really was.

Since RET is primarily interested in getting clients to focus on their self-disturbing, irrational ideas, the RETer on principle has them assume the worst; s/he will sometimes even have them ignore reality by presuming that things are even worse than they really are. By doing this, we insure that the philosophies or ideologies that take bad circumstances into emotional disturbances are dealt with, and we continue the therapeutic endeavor in the direction of elegant change.

To briefly illustrate "the assume the worst technique," an interchange with Karyn might go like this:

Therapist: Kayrn, from what you've said, I hear you saying that you *must* get people's attention and approval in social situations, and that its a *terrible tragedy* when you are ignored or whatever.

Karyn: Yes. But, when I really look at it carefully I know that's silly, because I can handle myself ok. If I could only focus on the fact that I can do it, I'd be ok.

Therapist: Well, that's not really the issue. The issue is that you think you must do well and always get approval, not that you don't have the skills. *Assume the worst*—assume that you are sometimes inept and that you sometimes don't light up the room. Now, why must you? Why is it so awful when it doesn't happen?

Written Homework. The basic theory of RET holds that humans are easily and naturally disturbable, that virtually all of them explicitly or tacitly believe in some irrational shoulds, oughts, and musts, and that it is difficult for them to change their disturbance-creating "nature" and to largely and persistently surrender their crooked ways of thinking and dysfunctional ways of behaving. Theoretically, they can do so by merely making profound changes in their thinking processes, but actually they rarely if ever do so unless they work very hard and keep practicing new ways of cognizing, emoting, and behaving. This is particularly true when they have severe and long-standing emotional problems, such as serious phobias, compulsions, and states of depression, worthlessness, and low frustration tolerance.

A major way that RET encourages people to make profound changes is through written homework. Written homework directly extends the process of disputing irrational beliefs initiated by the therapist and it has the twin goals of (1) accelerating the process of abandoning irrational ideas and (2) teaching clients the disputation process for future use.

RET strongly advocates that clients do written homework on a daily basis. In fact, we make it a rule of thumb that no client is allowed to leave a session without being assigned written homework that will facilitate his or her working through process. To date, written homework has taken three forms: DIBS; the Institute's Homework Report; and Rational Self-Analysis.

DIBS. Disputing Irrational Beliefs (DIBS) (Ellis & Harper, 1975) is perhaps the simplest version of written homework. In a straight-forward way it consists of the client writing down and answering a standard set of questions that include: (1) What irrational beliefs do I want to dispute and surrender?; (2) Is this belief true or false?; (3) What evidence leads me to conclude that this belief is false (true)?; (4) What's the worst thing that could actually happen to me if I don't get (or do) what I think I must?; (5) What good things could happen if I don't get (or do) what I think I must?

The beauty of DIBS is that it is easily understandable. It has a relaxed, "conversational" quality to it that approximates what goes on in the therapist's office so that the negative connotations of doing homework is minimized. All in all, we have found that clients rarely resist doing it.

Homework Report. The Institute for Advanced Study in Rational Therapy has recently published a Homework Report (HR) that is quite comprehensive and detailed (see Figure 4-1). In filling it out, clients are instructed to first complete sections regarding undesirable emotional consequences (ueC) and undesirable behavior consequences

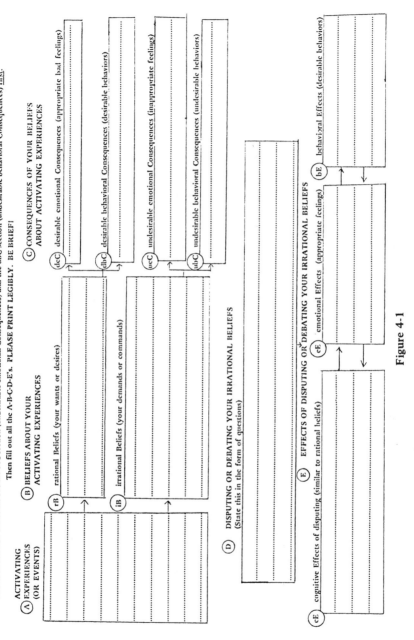

Figure 4-1

(ubC). Then, they are instructed to report on their activating experiences (A), both their rational beliefs (rB) and their irrational beliefs (iB) about the event, and their desirable emotional (deC) and their desirable behavior (dbC) consequences. Following this clients fill out the disputing section (D) by raising questions that challenge the irrational beliefs, and finally they provide the rational beliefs, appropriate feelings, and desirable behaviors that result from thinking rationally about the event (Section E of Figure 4-1).

The HR provides many positive features. It has the merit of helping clients see and appreciate the role their thoughts play in prompting their reactions; it helps them separate the desirable and undesirable emotional and behavioral consequences they experience; it facilitates their discriminating between their wants or preferences and their demands or "musts;" and it fosters their comprehending appropriate ways to think, feel, and behave as a result of disputing their irrational beliefs. The problems we have found with using the HR, however, is that clients often find it confusing and tedious so that they frequently refuse to do it or give up doing it after only a little effort.

Rational Self-analysis. The purpose of rational self-analysis (RSA) is the same as DIBS and HR. It is to provide a between-session forum for clients to question their habitual belief pattern in order to give them up. The format of RSA is roughly the same as HR (see Figure 4-2). Clients take a sheet of paper and first report the ABC's of their disturbance. Special care is given to listing as many irrational ideas as can be found. At the bottom the criteria for rational thinking is written. Then, clients become investigators, first checking the accuracy of their description of the event D or camera check and then challenging the validity of each of the irrational beliefs that are articulated (Db). Finally, at E, they write what they would feel if the rational beliefs uncovered in the disputing section were believed.

Rational self-analysis has its merits too. It is rather comprehensive; it helps clients see the total picture of their disturbance; it forces them to see the role their irrational thinking plays in their disturbance; and it is geared toward disputation. Yet, like the homework report, it is often found to be cumbersome and boring. Furthermore, the camera check section sometimes leads to inelegant or superficial

A. Event

B. Beliefs about the event
    1.
    2.
    3.
    4.
    X.

C. Emotional and Behavioral
    Consequence

Criteria for Rationality:
    1. Objective
    2. Life preserving
    3. Goal producing
    4. Interpersonally rewarding
    5. Emotionally rewarding

Da. Camera check (reality check) of

Db. Disputation of B's

E. Desirable Emotional Consequences

Figure 4-2 Rational Self-Analysis

solutions to problems. Clients often find their perception of the event to be invalid and, in seeing the event (A) more realistically, they often overlook or skim over the most important part of the RSA, which is the disputation of the irrational ideas.

Regardless of the format chosen, we think it essential to make written homework a regular feature of most everyone's therapy. In doing so, we have found the following guidelines critical in deriving maximum benefit from it. One, see to it that clients actually write it out.   The writing process slows down their thinking and prompts them to put more energy into thinking through. Some clients just look at the sheet of paper and mentally skim over it, thereby robbing the tool of most of its impact. Two, be sure to review the homework in the first session after it is assigned. This allows you to correct errors in procedure or thinking, it communicates to the client that you think it serious, and it provides them reinforcement for their efforts. If a client fails to do the written homework, it also provides an opportunity to discuss why and to reemphasize its importance. Finally, instruct clients to use operant conditioning or self-management methods; to reward themselves for doing the homework, and to punish themselves for not doing it. This often provides the extra incentive that makes the difference between avoiding or completing it.

Rational Role Reversal. Rational role reversal is a very simple technique for disputing irrational ideas that requires the therapist and client to change roles. The therapist has the client take the devil's advocate role and dispute his or her own irrational ideas as articulated by the therapist. This allows the client to aggressively dispute his or her own irrational ideas from another perspective.

A word of caution is in order here. The therapist better take pain not to be too good at defending the client's irrational positions, lest the client lose and become more entrenched in these ideas. I (R.G.) vividly remember asking a client to change roles with a second client in a group therapy setting only to have the second client argue the irrational position so convincingly and forcefully that the one with the problem left the session more disturbed than before.

Information Giving. The basic theory of RET holds that virtually all humans lack certain bits of information or do not know about or understand critical philosophic positions that could help them become less seriously emotionally disturbed. An integral part of the cognitive methodology of RET is to give clients a large amount of corrective information and ideas that help them become more adjusted (Ellis, 1962, 1975). Rational-emotive therapists regularly explain important self-help or self-management techniques to their clients, and they regularly discuss with or explain to clients such things as the philosophies of self-rating and self-acceptance, the nature of "awfulizing," and the drawbacks of demanding total approval from others.

A particularly effective information giving tool in RET is the use of analogies and stories. We often tell clients about other clients with similar problems (being sure to disguise identities) and willingly tell about incidents in our lives that illustrate important points. Sometimes when we are at a loss to think of a real person or incident, we may even fabricate a story or concoct an analogy to help clients learn something that will help them. Analogies abound in RET and we encourage the reader to develop his or her cadre to use when important points need to be made.

Following, as it does, a didactic, teaching-learning model of psychotherapy, RET also makes use of a wide range of educational opportunities. Clients are encouraged to listen to tape recordings, read books and pamphlets, and attend various lectures and workshops that deal with their particular problems and that will provide them with ideas and skills in living rationally. A regularly assigned sourcebook, in fact, is Ellis and Harper's *A New Guide to Rational Living* (1975). Clients are also often instructed to tape their therapy sessions and listen to them several times before returning. All in all, RET believes that unhealthy ideas can be unlearned and replaced by healthier ones in part with the acquisition of sane information.

Rational-emotive Imagery (REI). RET assumes that all people have a strong tendency to disturb themselves and, despite wanting to eliminate disturbed emotional or behavioral responses, tend to actively repropagandize themselves with the irrational nonsense that originally disturbed them. They regularly and persistently carry on self-defeating dialogues in their heads that are replete with vivid images and dramatic affect. The natural tendency thus is to practice (and actually succeed in) becoming more disturbed over time.

Take, for example, the case of Lynn as reported by Maxie Maultsby (1977b). Part of Lynn's problem was extreme anger at her mother-in-law, who incidentally was scheduled to visit soon. Lynn reported a great deal of anger about the up-coming visit; she in particular reported how she pictured her mother-in-law emerging from the airplane with a frown on her face and criticizing her. Just a little inquiry revealed that she also engaged in the typical anger litany: "She *shouldn't* gripe so much. Who the hell does she think she is! I don't know if *I can stand this.* The bitch!" What Lynn was doing was practicing becoming upset and thereby virtually assuring herself of increasingly intense anger at her mother-in-law.

Rational-emotive imagery (REI) is a special kind of cognitive technique, developed to help people counterpropagandize their irrational ideas. REI was originally developed by Maxie C. Maultsby, Jr. (1975) at the University of Kentucky and has become a main cognitive technique of RET (Maultsby and Ellis, 1974). The version described here, one of two that exist, is most appropriate for the working through process. The other version will be described in the next chapter.

I (R.G.) successfully employed REI with 26 year old Libby who came to therapy because of severe anxieties about graduate school. At the point where she came to therapy, she had seriously considered dropping out of school because her fears of failure and worthlessness virtually consumed her whole day. The following illustrates how the procedure is generally explained to clients and how it is used.

Therapist 1: Close your eyes, Libby, and get as comfortable as you can . . . OK, now, picture as vividly as you can yourself sitting in class getting ready to give a report . . . Can you do that?

Libby 1: . . . Yes.

Therapist 2: Good. Now picture yourself starting to give the presentation and the class members begin to look bored. They gaze out the window, yawn, and the works. It's a real bummer. Picture that scene just as dramatically as you can . . . Are you doing it?

Libby 2: . . . Yes.

Therapist 3: Good. Now, how do you feel? What's the feeling you get?

Libby 3: Awful. First I felt anxious and now I feel depressed, devastated. It's terrible.

Therapist 4: Right. That's how you normally feel. Now, change that feeling from depression or devastation to only disappointment and regret. Keep the picture in your mind, but only feel disappointment and regret. Do it . . . How are you doing? Did you do it?

Libby 4: It's hard. I don't know.

Therapist 5: You can do it. Keep trying.

Libby 5: . . . OK, I can do it. I feel just disappointment, not depression.

Therapist 6: Excellent. Now, how did you make youself feel that new way? What did you do to make yourself feel only regret and disappointment?

Libby 6: I guess I thought: "So they don't like what I'm doing. Cleveland hasn't crumbled. It's not the end of the world."

Therapist 7: What else?

Libby 7: "I'm not going to die no matter what they think."

Therapist 8:   Great. What you did was think rationally instead of a bunch of nonsense, and made yourself feel only regretful, not depressed. And you could also have gone on and remembered that you are not a terrible, worthless person regardless of how they like your talk and what they think of you. And you can feel OK, though not great, regardless of how they really feel about you.

Libby 8:   Sounds good.

Therapist 9:   Yes it does. And, if you practice doing this a minimum of ten minutes a day for several weeks, you very likely will find yourself feeling better and better about things. But, it's important to really practice. You see, you've been practicing being disturbed and I want you to practice being undisturbed. Make sense?

Libby 9:   Yes.

Therapist 10:   Now, what I will want you to do is do this every day, and I will give you some further instructions in a minute. For now lets run through this again now so you really learn how to do it.

This example clearly illustrates how to introduce REI to clients. The procedure is to first have them imagine the troublesome scene as vividly as possible (Therapist 1 and 2), making it as bad as it realistically can be, and then have the clients experience the inappropriate bad feelings that they do in these situations (Therapist 3). This helps them reproduce how they typically respond, both cognitively and emotively. The next step is to have them feel only appropriately bad (Therapist 4), and, once they do this, ask them how they did it (Therapist 6 and 7). Clients inevitably respond to this question by telling or implying that they changed their thoughts to some rational theme to make themselves feel differently. The therapist then critiques their thoughts, correcting good sounding but irrational ones, reinforces rational ones, and helps them fill out the picture with additional rational ones (Therapist 8). Finally, the therapist alerts them to the fact that regular practice in doing this is necessary, assigns them to do this, and repeats the process in order to further coach them (Therapist 9 and 10).

What we have just described is a procedure for doing rational-emotive imagery. We want to emphasize that REI is most effective when done daily. To facilitate clients doing it, we also advise the therapist to make use of operant conditioning or self-management principles: Teach clients to reward themselves with something pleasant (that is daily available to them) for doing their REI, and have them punish themselves with something unpleasant for failing to do their REI.

We will conclude our presentation of ratonal-emotive imagery by making one final point. Some therapists recommend introducing clients to REI by presenting them with mildly negative scenes, ones that they would have little difficulty thinking rationally about, and then presenting them with more and more unpleasant scenes as they get better at rational disputation. While this procedure might be necessary for the extremely anxious or depressed person, we find that most people can tolerate the upsetness of initially dealing with the "worst" scene and can successfully apply rational thinking to it. In so doing, they make a maximal impact on their own belief system and save a great deal of potentially wasted time. Thus, we strongly recommend that when teaching RET to clients, you present to them the worst, reasonable image and encourage them to do likewise in their REI practice.

Emotive Methods

Though RET has been a forerunner of and prime force for the cognitive-emotive-behavioral model of psychotherapy, a prevailing view among clinicians is that RET is a purely cognitive approach. We think this misconception stems from the strong cognitive intervention which is distinctive in RET writings and demonstrations, and because the emotive methods have not traditionally received nearly as much publicity as the cognitive methods.

Yet RET, like virtually all therapies, makes considerable use of emotive-evocative techniques. The crucial difference between RET and other therapies is the primary purpose for using them. The primary purpose for using such techniques in RET is to help people make basic ideational or philosophical changes in order to help them function in more satisfying and productive ways, not merely to help them "get in touch with" or abreact feelings. As Ellis and Harper

(1975) state, "we constantly employ but take care not to deify human emotions" (p. 210).

Empathy and Unconditional Acceptance. RET goes distinctly beyond the humanistic philosophy of Rogers (1961) by emphasizing unconditional acceptance rather than unconditional positive regard. As summarized by Ellis in chapter one and elsewhere (1972b), self-acceptance means never rating one's self or another's self, and realizing that: (1) people are too multifaceted and complex to accurately be summed up as total entities; (2) people are neither good nor bad, worthy or unworthy, but fallible and chronically mistake making; (3) no one good act or trait can ever generalize to mean someone is all good, and likewise no one bad act or trait means that someone is all bad; and (4) rating of selves typically leads to disturbed feelings and actions. In sum, self-acceptance means accepting the fact that flaw and frailties are the human lot and that no human equals his or her actions; self-acceptance means not rating one's own or another's self, while sometimes, when important, rating one's own or another's actions.

A major emotive method in RET is to provide clients with unconditional acceptance. This begins with understanding and accepting their distraught emotions and the value they place on their presenting problem (Garcia, 1977), and extends to accepting them no matter how foolishly or obnoxiously they behave (Ellis, 1974, 1975). It is actualized by never (or as rarely as humanly possible) getting angry or disgusted with clients, by giving people in great emotional pain the "space" to express their feelings before cognitively interrupting to change their irrational ideas, by communicating, both verbally and non-verbally, that you accept, even respect them as fallible human beings, while perhaps acting energetically to change their "bad" behaviors, by risking genuineness in the sensible expression of your own feelings and experiences, and by a multitude of other actions.

What are the benefits of all this? Is all this a necessary and sufficient condition for positive personal change? The answer to the latter question is no, but the benefits to the client are certainly substantial. The client learns a good many lessons or new ideas; that s/he can be accepted, and even respected and appreciated, despite his or her personal badness; that some people, in this instance, the therapist, do rather successfully live a life free from the hell of self-judgement; that some people (though not all) do not overreact to or catastrophize about bad actions or traits, and still associate with and even like people who do bad acts or have bad traits; that it is also important to please yourself, as well as sometimes pleasing others; that you can never please everyone, and that, while some people may be displeased with you, others may not be.

These lessons are by no means exhaustive, rather they are only illustrative of the rational ideas people can gain when shown unconditional acceptance. Still, two cautions are in order. One, we want to be careful to let clients know that not everything they do is acceptable—only that *they* are acceptable despite their doing non-acceptable things. To communicate otherwise leads to short range, egocentric gratification that is often just as bad as the neurotic anxiety that results from self-rating. Two, we want to take care not to allow clients to become dependent on us for their good or accepting feelings of themselves. Allowing this to happen does not alter their self-rating philosophy, but rather makes their self-acceptance dependent on the criteria of the therapist's approval.

Shame Exercises. It is probably true, as RET asserts, that shame is a most frequent and important part of most human disturbances. For shame results from self-downing, or the taking of one's negative qualities, traits, or performances and rating oneself as bad or shameful for them. RET therefore advocates that clients be given shame-attacking exercises, so that they can confront the irrational ideas behind their shame. In the course of doing these exercises, and then discussing them with an RET therapist, clients are shown how they create their own "shameful" feelings and how they can cease doing so. If they do the same or different shame-attacking exercises on several occasions, the theory of RET states that they will tend to make basic changes in their shame-creating ideas.

The assignment of shame-attacking exercises are only limited by the creativity and imagination of the therapist and client. Exercises can be selected that relate directly to presenting problems of the client, such as having a socially shameful person wear outlandish clothes or purposely make silly social errors; or the exercises can be one of the many funny, yet potentially embarrassing ones that Ellis mentioned in chapter one (e.g., yelling out stops in busses, elevators, subway trains; yelling out the time in a crowded store). One of the more creative ones we have heard was done by a woman who carried around midtown Manhattan a small tree decorated with condoms and sporting a sign that said "Rubber Tree" on it.

Before going on, we will make four points about the assignment of shame-attacking exercises. One, consider assigning these exercises regularly, particularly as soon after the client gains insight into his or her irrational ideas as possible; they are most impactful at this point. Two, stimulate their interest by having them generate the exercises themselves. Three, it is important to monitor their exercises so that clients do not do dangerous things (e.g., things that would cause them to lose a close friend) or countertherapeutic things (e.g., things that would flood them with inappropriate feelings, or that would serve to engrain their irrational ideas). And, fourth, be sure to ask them about whether or not they followed through with their exercises, as this underscores the importance of doing them and provides reinforcement to the client for engaging in them.

Humor. RET believes that human emotional disturbance largely consists of people taking themselves, others, and life events too seriously (Ellis, 1977d). Instead of merely wanting something and thereby feeling disgruntled or disappointed when thwarted, people disturb themselves by *demanding* that they get what they want—or solemnly insisting they must have or need something and view it as a catastrophe to be thwarted.

If this be true, what better way is there to undercut overseriousness than humor. Why not, as Ellis (1977d) rhetorically asks, "poke the blokes with jolly jokes"? RETers sometimes tell jokes to clients to help them see the absurdity of the ideas they hold; they use anti-pompous language in talking to clients about their problems, like R.P. (for rotten-person), and F.F.H.B. (for fucked up, fallible human being); they exaggerate clients' logic to the point of absurdity, thereby exposing its fallaciousness (e.g., "If you will only work for a day or two more you will indeed become perfect."); they use slang and obscene and evocative language in order to first get their clients' attention and then to show them that nothing is truly sacred; and they invent any sort of witticism that will help clients go beyond their overseriousness.

In this vein, Albert Ellis invented a special form of humorous psychotherapy and introduced it in a paper presented at a Symposium on Humor, Play and Absurdity in Psychotherapy at the American Psychological Association Annual Meeting in Washington on September 3, 1976—the use of rational humorous songs. These songs, composed to well-known tunes, are, at one and the same time, cognitive, emotive, and behavioral. Cognitively, they each present in satiric form a rational or an anti-irrational idea. Emotively, they bring mirth and intrude, dramatically and as esthetically, on gloom and inertia. Behaviorally, they tend (once learned by people with emotional problems) to automatically keep ringing in one's head, with the same insidious rational message, constituting and anti-anxiety activity in their own right and encouraging more effective behavior.

One of the rational humorous songs that has gone over most effectively with clients and members of the public is *Whine! Whine! Whine!,* with these lyrics sung to the tune of the famous Yale *Whiffenpoof* Song (which actually was composed by a Harvard man in the 1890's):

I cannot have all of my wishes filled—
Whine, whine, whine!
I cannot have every frustration tilled—
Whine, whine, whine!
Life really owes me the things I miss,
Fate has to grant me eternal bliss;
And if I must settle for less than this—
Whine, whine, whine!

(Ellis, 1977e)

Another popular rational humorous song is *Perfect Rationality,* sung to the tune of Luigi Denza's *Finiculi, Finicula:*

Some think the world must have a right direction—
　　And so do I, and so do I!
Some think that with the slightest imperfection
　　They can't get by—and so do I!
For I, I have to prove I'm superhuman,
　　And better far than people are;
To show I have miraculous acumen—
　　And always rate among the Great!

Perfect, perfect rationality
  Is, of course, the only thing for me!
How can I even think of being
  If I must live fallible?
Rationality must be a perfect thing for me!

(Ellis, 1977e)

Whatever forms it takes, humor is used to forcefully attack the disturbed ideas that people present. Remember, however, that we are poking fun at the ideas clients hold, not the clients. Humor is used in a kind, empathic manner that never loses sight of a total acceptance of the person who presents problems. Fun is never poked at people, only at their follies. Humor is never used to provide mirth to the therapist, only to strategically intercede in the client's on-going neurotic process.

Emotive Bibliotherapy. RET often has clients read highly dramatic pieces of literature that first arouse them and then stimulate them to think about the ideas contained therein. Plays and films are good sources of such stimulation, having the advantage of being both evocative and once removed from the viewer. Likewise, poetry provides a vehicle to explore concepts of rational and irrational, sensible and nonsensible human motivation, and the effects of demandingness in relationships. And biographies and fictional pieces of literature do much the same. We, as therapists are only limited by our own knowledge of these resources and the ingenuity we apply in selecting them for our clients.

Behavioral-Activity Methods

In this portion of the chapter we wish to emphasize and show that RET is truly a cognitive-emotive-behavioral approach to therapy, and that behavioral principles and techniques are utilized during the working through phase. The rationale behind behavioral methods lies in a recognition and appreciation for social learning theory. RET recognizes that most emotional-behavioral problems are *acquired* via behavioristic learning principles *as well as* through cognitive distortions and the adoption of irrational beliefs, ideas, and philosophies. Likewise, we know that these same learning principles can help people unlearn and overcome their irrational ideation and disordered behavior. Behavioral methods for working through are therefore employed as compliments to cognitive and emotive interventions.

Before describing some behavioral-activity methods for the working through process it is important to distinguish these from additional education techniques. In the next chapter on additional education, there are a number of behavioral techinques presented and the purpose of these is to give clients the skills needed to cope with their difficulties. For example, training in the use of assertive responses would be a behavioral method for additional education, as it would fill the client's skill deficit.

The behavioral-activity methods for working through do not focus on teaching new skills, though they might have this effect; instead, they are directed at (1) getting the client to behave in a way that contradicts and helps to eradicate irrational beliefs, and at (2) fostering behavior which requires rational ideation and emotional stability. Thus via overt behavior the client truly "works" through cognitive-emotional difficulties, and behavioral assignments offer the chance to practice rational thinking and emotional control.

Behavioral-activity assignments can be given and performed within the therapy session on occasion, but in vivo homework assignments are more typical. These assignments extend therapy into clients' everyday lives and lead them to actively and directively work through their emotion-behavioral problems. Clients are thus totally and continually involved in the therapeutic enterprise—a key to effective RET.

Stay-in-there. One of the most widely applied activity assignments in RET may be termed the "stay-in-there" assignment. This assignment is an anti-awfulizing, anti-avoidance method which consists of staying in rather than avoiding an aversive situation in order to work through the disturbed ideas and feelings about it. As Ellis (1977a) has noted, emotional disturbances result in large part from awfulizing about and hence avoiding some event. The stay-in-there assignment combats these pernicious neurotic ideas and helps clients learn that they can survive disturbing circumstances.

Stay-in-there assignments are done either implosively or via leading the client through a series of unpleasant situations which are encountered, one by one, on a graduated hierarchy. In the latter, the technique of desensitization is followed; easy assignments are encountered first and difficulty is progressive with each successive one.

Before asking clients to "stay-in-there," it is wise to prepare them to successfully handle the target situations. While they rarely find the in vivo encounters to be easy, diagnosis and insight processes, and particularly disputation, will ready them to respond in a cognitively "rational" manner. Thus, when clients enter the unpleasant situation, they will be able to respond in a constructive way—by identifying and disputing irrational ideas that pop up, by keeping a stream of rational thoughts flowing, and by enduring whatever emotional upsets arise.

Two final suggestions about staying-in-there are that acceptance of one's upset may be necessary before embarking on stay-in-there assignments, and that successful staying power is slowly developed. Clients have to stop awfulizing about their emotional upset before they are capable of staying-in-there and working through. Though it sounds contradictory, an acceptance of the problem is necessary before it can be assaulted.

Examples of staying-in-there assignments are maintaining contact with a spouse during a time of marital conflict, tolerating a visit from or to unpleasant relatives, sitting through a boring meeting, enduring a feared situation such as riding in an airplane, accepting unwanted criticism from a superior, and so on. In all these situations, the task is the same—to remain in a situation that is emotionally difficult to tolerate, while disputing the ideas that make a hassle seem awful.

Doing-It/Risk Exercises. Another behavioral-activity assignment similar to the stay-in-there method is "doing it." Humans tend to anxiously refuse to do the things they cannot do well. They particularly define such things as making mistakes and incurring the disapproval of others as horrible or awful and insist on condemning themselves if these outcomes occur. With these philosophies in mind, they avoid risks and thereby further engrain their irrational ideas.

In RET, we take the attitude that it is generally better to do than to do well. We, therefore strongly encourage clients to do it—to do the things they are afraid of doing. For example, I (R.G.) once insisted that a male client, afraid of being rejected by women, go to a disco and ask the five most attractive women to dance; I later encouraged him to ask three women for dates with the provision that he include in the trio two whom he thought would probably turn him down. As with shame-attacking exercises, risk exercises are best when they relate directly to client fears and are only limited by the ingenuity (and common sense) of the therapist and client.

Problems of non-assertiveness are another example: clients allow others to violate their rights, take advantage, and generally walk all over them. They usually want to act assertively and stand up for themselves, but anxiety stops them cold. As Lange and Jakubowski (1976) point out, self-talk such as the following creates a sense of inadequacy and an overall feeling of inhibition.

It would be awful if I hurt the other person.

I can't stop having these nervous feelings, I've always been this way.

But if I was assertive, the other person wouldn't like me. Nice people aren't assertive.

In order to overcome a lack of assertion, the client must eventually *act* assertively. Insight, skill training, REI's and other such therapeutic progress steps are only preliminary to the final task of performing an overt, assertive response in a difficult situation. When this point in RET is reached, a number of activity assignments, perhaps in a progressive hierarchy, force the client to implement the long-avoided behaviors. Once this step is taken the clients' non-assertive concerns begin to evaporate, particularly if therapeutic belief-changes are concurrently worked through.

Procrastination and a lack of self discipline is another instance where clients know how they would like to behave but have great difficulty "doing it." Ellis & Knaus (1977) have identified a host of irrational ideas which spawn procrastination, and these succumb to disputation. In addition, it is advisable to assign activity homework.

Through these assignments clients can take gradual steps toward self dicipline by doing those necessary but unpleasant things which lead to long range reward and welfare.

Self Management Techniques. There are two behavioral techniques which have been recommended (Ellis, 1977a; Ellis & Grieger, 1977) for client-managed use during the working through stage of RET: operant conditioning and desensitization.

Operant Conditioning is employed in conjunction with behavioral-activity assignments for the purpose of motivating clients to complete their assignments. Clients with emotional problems are not dependable performers, their emotional upsets interfere with task completion, and operant procedures can therefore be a valuable aide. When controlled by clients themselves, they promote a sense of responsibility.

Self managed operant procedures are based on reward and penalization. Clients reward themselves for the completion of activity assignments, and penalize themselves when they do not perform the activities. Both reward and penalties are contingent on whether or not an assignment is completed.

Rewards can be anything the client likes, but some thing not too extreme to give out each time an assignment is completed. Ellis (1977a) suggests choosing something that is not a commonly received pleasure, for such rewards are of low value. He also urges therapists to help clients choose penalties with reason ... those that are not too severe and are feasible to enforce. They can be one of three types: (1) withholding a reward, (2) depriving oneself of a daily pleasure, and (3) applying an aversive condition on oneself.

When self management techniques are instituted the therapist should be on the lookout for self downing and discouragement. Clients often blunder in their assignments, and then condemn themselves for being so weak and undisciplined. Rather than penalizing themselves per the self management procedures, they *punish* themselves with self blame. At these times, the therapist has an opportunity to help clients work through yet another emotional concern.

Self-managed Desensitization. Systematic desensitization is an effective means for overcoming the contingency between an event or stimulus and an emotional distressful reaction. When clients use the technique, it can be considered a behavioral-activity assignment and/or an additional education method.

We recommend self-managed desensitization as a potentially valuable adjunct to the working through stage of RET. It is an inelegant method, but helpful for those with debilitating emotional distress. Briefly, the method consists of the client first learning to relax deeply, and then alternating thoughts and images of an emotionally evocative event with rational sentences and relaxing cues and scenes. Gradually, through reciprocal inhibition, the client learns to remain calm while imagining the event.

By following a progressive hierarchy of events, clients can overcome quite stressful reactions. And, if the desensitization procedure is combined with rational-emotive imagery, a particularly impactful hybrid is created.

ROADBLOCKS TO RATIONAL-EMOTIVE WORKING THROUGH

Working through is perhaps the most demanding phase of RET for both client and therapist. The fun of unraveling problems is over, insights have been attained, and real effort usually has to be repeatedly expanded.

Special demands are indeed placed on clients during the working through process. For one, the responsibility for change is placed directly on their shoulders, a burden that is often difficult to carry. This burden is complicated by the frustrating fact that they are shown a straightforward method for solving problems before acquiring the full capacity to apply it. Furthermore, rational-emotive working through requires clients to exert a great deal of effort, both in and out of therapy, without necessarily receiving support from the therapist. Finally, working through encourages clients to immediately reflect upon strongly held beliefs that are often painful to confront.

When faced with these demands, some clients respond in a constructive manner. They conclude that it would be better for them to change and tolerate immediate distress as a necessary requisite for the long term goal of improved functioning. Other clients present simple resistances, such as a reluctance to self-disclosure or a mistaken expectation that the therapist's role is to "make me better." For still others, however, the burdens mentioned above precipitate thoughts and beliefs that represent serious roadblocks to a thorough working through of their problems. This ideation consists of significant cognitive distortions which are part and parcel of the clients' existing problems.

As will be seen by the large number of client roadblocks described in this chapter, there are many crises and challenges for the therapist to handle during the working through process. It is imperative that these be dwelt with directly and effectively, and therapists are often taxed to keep their clients afloat at this time. Successful beginnings to RET can dwindle away or clients can actually be lost if the therapist responds in a less than adequate manner.

We will now discuss some of the more common roadblocks to successful working through. We will first present some of the more serious client roadblocks and suggest strategic responses that have been found effective in undermining them. Then we will show some of the more common ways therapists block the working through process.

Client Roadblocks

Cognitive-emotive Dissonance. Most people's irrational ideas are so well ingrained by the time they come to therapy that they require repeated and sustained working through efforts before they really give them up. Because of this, many clients are prone to a special kind of discouragement called cognitive-emotive dissonance (Maultsby, 1974; 1977a). This dissonant state occurs at a point in RET when clients recognize their irrational ideas, understand the rational alternatives, but continue to think and feel the same negative ways. They see a better way, but cannot yet actualize it, so they conclude that they cannot possibly overcome their disturbance.

It is sufficient to explain to most clients that this is a common reaction, and to simply advise them to ignore their discouragement and continue working through their irrational ideations. Others, however, are particularly vulnerable to this and present a crisis of premature termination to the therapist (Grieger and Boyd, 1977). These include (1) people who see themselves as so inadequate and powerless that they feel helpless to change their well-engrained, maladaptive ways of thinking, and (2) people with such low frustration tolerance that they rebel against or are frightened by the effort required in working through.

The rational-emotive therapist can do several helpful things for clients to overcome their cognitive-emotive dissonance. A first can be prophylactic or crisis-oriented. It consists of warning clients' ahead of time, or reminding them later that they will probably become discouraged at some point in their therapy, and explaining to them that the process of giving up their irrational ideas will probably take both time and effort. A particularly effective way to do this is to equate their irrational idea with some other well-learned habit, such as using a pet gesture and showing them that their cognitive habit-breaking will take the same course as the breaking of that pet habit. Once they understand this concept, we show them the typical sequence of giving up, or working through, an irrational idea: (1) learning what their irrational beliefs are and learning how to challenge them; (2) learning to recognize when they think their irrational beliefs; (3) learning to effectively challenge their irrational beliefs when they occur; and (4) learning to think more rationally in their everyday lives.

In a similar vein, it is extremely useful to help clients set appropriate therapeutic goals. Many irrationally conclude that they must never feel upset again, mistakenly thinking that they are not healthy if they feel blue. In reality, all people become upset at times, and the "solution" is to minimize these feelings in terms of their frequency, intensity and duration, rather than to entirely eliminate them. In this light, it is best to help clients set their goals at coping rather than mastery. Meichenbaum (1976) defines mastery as the perfect attainment of a skill, while coping is the ability to deal effectively most of the time, but not necessarily always and perfectly with a problem when it arises. The goal of the therapist in this instance is to help clients set coping rather than mastery goals. From a coping stance, clients can attempt to maximize their rational thinking by using their negative feelings as cues to begin a rational problem solving process, rather than panicking and resorting to habits of irrational thought.

A final therapeutic response to cognitive-emotive dissonance is to confront and work through the irrational notions behind the cognitive dissonance. For instance with clients having low frustration tolerance, the therapist can take them through the irrational notions that make frustration tolerance overly difficult: "Why *should* you have it so easy?" "Why are you so special that you should not have to work through problems?" "What do you mean you can't stand it? You look unhappy, but you look like you're standing it." Such challenges are of course designed to force clients to work through their irrational ideas and represents the heart of RET.

The "I Won't Be Me" Syndrome. Most people believe they must be upset in the face of adversity (Ellis, 1962). Some even believe that not reacting strongly to negative circumstances is inappropriate, and doing otherwise is alien to their character. These notions are, of course, false for existing evidence strongly suggests that people almost always direct or cause their own emotional reactions by the ideas they hold, and they can choose to be upset or not when faced with difficulties. Conteracting these mistaken notions are often crucial to successful working through.

It is interesting to note that three specific irrational ideas often arise during rational-emotive working through that prompt the "I won't be me" syndrome. These include the fears of losing one's identity, becoming a phony, or becoming cold and machine-like.

"I'll Lose My Identity." After working through their emotional disturbance, many clients marvel at how different it feels to react calmly or mildly negative to situations in which they once went haywire. Surprisingly, however, some disturb themselves about this new way of feeling and react against getting better. This usually represents some metaphysical nonsense about a loss of their "inner essence," as per, "I've lost touch with who I am."

An interesting example of how this unfolds in psychotherapy is illustrated by the following therapeutic interchange.

Stan: It's really strange. I don't get upset the way I used to, and it's scary.

Therapist: How so? What's scary about that?

Stan: Well, I don't know. I've lost something and there's nothing to replace it.

Therapist: I'm not sure that makes sense. What have you lost?

Stan: The pain. The depression and anxiety.

Therapist: So what? What's the bad thing in that? That sounds like a good thing to me.

Stan: I know it doesn't make sense. Being depressed is being me. I've identified that with me. If I don't get depressed, I won't know myself.

Therapist: How so? How will you not know yourself? Will you look in the mirror and not recognize your face?

Stan: I just won't know myself anymore.

The most useful thing to do with this and with the other ideas behind the "I won't be me" syndrome is to reeducate clients about the ABC theory, emphasizing the fact that feelings are only logical consequences of ideas or thoughts, not mystical entities, and that new thought-feeling connections feel just as awkward at first as other new ways of responding. We find the right hand/left hand analogy particularly instructive to clients. We ask clients whether they would lose their identity if they were required to change from being right-handed to left-handed; then we show them that, although they would find it awkward for a period of time to switch hands, they would, with persistent effort use their left hand more often, more comfortably, and with more facility until it became "natural" to do so.

"I'll Be A Phony." It is not uncommon for clients, during working through, to worry that they will become a phony if they think and believe differently than they normally do. RETers often hear such comments as: "It's unnatural not to go with my true feelings;" or even more directly, 'I'll be a phony if I don't feel as I naturally do.' Clients who maintain such thoughts are prone to actively resist working through.

The distinction between brain thinkers and gut thinkers (Maultsby, 1974) is helpful in understanding this issue. Brain thinkers accurately realize that it is their thoughts that cause their feelings; gut thinkers believe that feelings are experiences that just happen or are caused by events.

In addition to reintegrating the ABC theory, helping clients see the difference between *pretending* and *practicing* is particularly helpful in this crisis. People are pretending, or acting in a phony fashion, when they do not have a sincere desire to bring about permanent change and only go through the motions of changing. People are *practicing,* or behaving genuinely, when they diligently try to learn something new with a sincere desire to change. Thus, sincerely and diligently practicing something is not phony.

"I'll Become A Machine." A final worry clients develop to prompt the "I won't be me" syndrome is that they will become mechanized, cold and unemotional if they give up their irrational ideas. We often hear such things as "I won't have feelings anymore," or, "I'll become a robot," or, "You're telling me that I shouldn't care at all." One guilt-ridden client said: "I'm not sure I really want to think differently; I'm more alive when I feel strongly about things even though my feelings are so painful." Other clients worry about becoming "contented cows" who will simply accept life as it is and who will let "people walk all over me."

Our advice is to respond to these clients as above by reinforcing the ABC theory. Another exceptionally important strategy to dispel this fear is to help them understand the difference between appropriate and inappropriate negative feelings (see chapter one), and that all sorts of appropriate negative feelings, such as irritation and regret, result from thinking rationally. For example, clients can rationally conclude that a particular setback in their love life is unfortunate and appropriately feel sad, or they can feel depressed by irrationally concluding that it is an *awful* thing that *should not* have happened. Furthermore, it is often useful for the therapist to point out that the minimization of neurotic feelings literally lend a great deal more time to devote to experiencing pleasure and joy. So, rather than becoming mechanized, clients who maximize rational thinking really have a chance to experience more frequent and more intensive positive feelings, as well as a whole host of appropriate negative ones, rather than no feelings at all.

Self-Hate. In addition to being the basis for most emotional disturbances, self-denigration will also sometimes lead to resistance during working through. Some clients block working through their belief in their worthlessness because they fear that their investigation will reveal that they are indeed worthless. Other clients are so thoroughly convinced of their worthlessness that they *insist* on suffering emotionally to punish themselves. A therapy session with a self-hating, overweight, middle-aged woman illustrates this problem.

Susan: Yesterday, I thought it was sort of a breakthrough, you know. I felt very good about the work I did here. And, uh, this has happened before. I felt really great and thought it was a breakthrough. I felt high, you know, and I couldn't sleep.

Therapist: You mean you felt so good you couldn't sleep?

Susan: Yeah. But, I'm now thinking that wasn't a breakthrough at all.

Therapist: You've changed your mind on that?

Susan: Yes. You see, now I'm doubting all the thinking I did yesterday. I'm doubting it because, you know, maybe it's really right. In other words, maybe I'm right and I am really worthless. And maybe I'm trying to keep the irrational ways of acting. I didn't have self-control so therefore I was punished or deserved the bad things that happened. So this means that the world is sort of, well, sort of made sense. The bad things that happened to me made some sense, because, maybe I deserved them for not having self-control.

Therapist: So you believe that something or someone is punishing you for not being . . .

Susan: I sort of deserved to suffer, yeah . . .

The therapeutic strategy for dealing with this roadblock is straightforward and consists of directly attacking the concept of worthlessness itself (Ellis, 1972). In typical RET fashion, the therapist vigorously assists the client to challenge these actions.

An interesting analogy to help the client see the illogicalness of ideas of worthlessness has been developed by Maxie Maultsby and his colleagues at the University of Kentucky. It first involves drawing a circle and placing within the circle a great many dots. The therapist communicates to the clients that a person's "self" is comprised of literally thousands of experiences, actions, and characteristics, each represented by a dot, and the therapist then asks the clients how many "dots" a person can reasonably remember. With the answer obviously being only a small percentage, the therapist then asks the clients to prove how reasonable it is to conclude that *all* their known "dots," much less all the dots in their total circle, are worthless because of one or several inadequate ones. The point is, of course, that total self-evaluation is a gross overgeneralization that is conceptually and pragmatically invalid.

Fear of Mediocrity. Clients with demands for perfection are prone to this roadblock during rational-emotive working through. Because they believe that they *must* obtain far-reaching success, they worry that they will lose their motivation and condemn themselves to mediocrity (or worse) if they give up their irrational "musts." Once they comprehend the relevancy of their perfectionistic ideas to their problems, these fears are often heightened to such an extent that quitting therapy is a danger.

We can illustrate how this often arises in RET with a brief excerpt from Mike S.'s tenth therapy session.

Mike: You know I'm really doing well. But you know, I had no dreams last week of conquering worlds. I found that sad.

Therapist: Thinking of imperfection led you to conclude that maybe your limits are not so far out there?

Mike: Yeah.

Therapist: What's so sad about that? Let's assume that your limits are short of becoming outstanding. OK? So what? What's horribly bad about that? There is a possibility you won't be super. Now, what's awful about that?

Mike: It shouldn't be that way. My impact is going to be limited.

Therapist: What does that mean?

Mike:	The impact of my creativity or skills on whatever.
Therapist:	That's true. If you don't have the skills of a Van Gogh, you won't paint the pictures of a Van Gogh. But, why is that so awful?
Mike:	It's disappointing. (long pause) It's just very sad.
Therapist:	Why?
Mike:	Um, OK, um, well, it's a loss. I'm not going to be able to do those things. I may never become dedicated or organized to, say, spend three or four years of my life to make an impact on the field, for instance.
Therapist:	But, let's say that you don't make an impact like you want. Now, that would be unfortunate for the field because they won't get the goodies of your efforts. But, why would that be sad for you personally? It seems to me that you find it sad for you, not for the rest of the world. Now, why is that sad for you?
Mike:	It's really a matter of finally letting go. To be wonderful is still very attractive.
Therapist:	I know. In a sense, this is one of the last vestiges, one of the latter hurdles in a therapy process, with people who have habitually demanded perfection of themselves. You have gotten to a point where you say, "Hey, I can give this up; I'm on the verge." But, when push comes to shove, you are saying, "Hey, wait a minute, I'll be mediocre if I give it up, and Jesus, that'll be horrible and terrible."
Mike:	Yeah, I can see that. I can see the process.
Therapist:	It's almost that if you can get over this last hurdle, you've got it made. You're to a point now where you can stay where you are and even go backward, or you can jump over this last hurdle. Because once you get over this notion that being mediocre is horrible and being not mediocre is wonderful, you're past your nuttiness.
Mike:	I've not felt nutty, just sad. And resistant.

Therapist:	It's just from this mourning process. The fear leads to resistance. Because you're telling yourself that this is my last chance to hold onto what I've always believed.
Mike:	Right. Yeah, I see. That's right.
Therapist:	So, you're at a crossroads.
Mike:	Yeah, the image I have is that I'm taking the last boat to Australia and, if I go, I'll live in Australia forever and I'm not sure I want to go there. Australia looks pretty bleak.
Therapist:	Be careful not to get discouraged.
Mike:	No, I'm not. Just resistant. It's going to take some work to get over this. But, it's giving up a magical notion.

Because we see this as a very critical roadblock in RET, we recommend that the therapist make a full and forceful response. What follows is a recommended sequence of action.

1. Explain to these clients the dynamics of the problem and relate it to their basic pathology. We find that this often places their anxieties into perspective.
2. Distinguish between concern and worry. Many clients believe that being rational means not being motivated at all. The opposite, of course, is true, for the person who thinks rationally will remain concerned about doing well and will then still be motivated to achieve; the person who thinks irrationally, on the other hand, will feel anxious, depressed and guilty, all of which tend to interfere with achievement.
3. Take the typical RET role of the logical-empirical scientist and challenge the irrational ideas of perfection: "Why is it so awful to not achieve perfection?" "Why are you so special and different from the rest of us?" "How can anyone, including you, achieve perfection?" "How is your self-worth diminished by a mediocre performance, or even doing poorly?" This process, of course, is the core of RET.
4. Add a few extra tidbits. We point out to these clients that they are ironically getting very little from their efforts and that they

rarely enjoy their achievements, much less the efforts. Furthermore, we point out that they have completely lost sight of the viable goals of happiness and enjoyment; and, after showing them how the goal of perfectionistic achievement blocks enjoyment, we challenge their mistaken notion that they cannot find life rewarding unless they achieve at an exceptionally high level in all endeavors. And last, we point that they can always readopt their neurotic notions at some later date if their fears of mediocrity are realized. They are really not, in other words, on the last boat to Australia.

Paying Lip Service. A particularly troublesome roadblock to successful working through is paying lip service to or parroting rational ideas without really putting in the time or energy to think through their rationale. Clients who do this sound good, for they know the right words to utter, but they insure themselves of little, if any, real gain.

The simplest and most workable reason for client parroting is because the client does not understand the concepts and/or does not understand the importance of the disputation process. S/he has latched onto some rational slogan, like "everybody is a fallible human being," and (perhaps successfully) repeats it in times of crisis with the mistaken notion that it is the best thing to do. Therapeutic intervention is directed in this case to an exploration of the ideas behind the slogan (e.g., "what is a fallible human being, Bill, and how does that apply to your case?"), and to an explanation of the importance of working through.

Other reasons for paying mere lip service to rational ideas are more complex and in fact represent emotional problems in and of themselves. One is to avoid the pain of truly acknowledging that a serious problem exists (most likely reflecting a threat to self-esteem, or ego anxiety), and/or to avoid the pain of taking the risk of acting on the rational ideas in real life (probably reflecting a fear of discomfort, or discomfort anxiety). These represent a defense against anxiety. By sloganizing, the client can appear to be correctly playing the RET game, but in reality s/he is avoiding discontent by hiding behind a facade and making little or no progress at all.

Another pathological reason for paying lip service is to placate the therapist. Clients who do this most likely suffer from approval anxiety, or believe they must have the approval of most everyone. They then transfer this to the therapist and ingratiate themselves in order to gain his or her approval.

Both of these instances of parroting require a direct and immediate therapeutic response, for to do otherwise would serve to reinforce the defense and stabilize the pathology. A confrontive way to respond is to simply say that you do not think they really mean what they say. A most helpful response, we think, is to interpret to these clients their defense; that is, to show them (using the insight techniques described in the previous chapter) the dynamics of the defense, where "C" represents the defense, "A" represents the emotional problem itself, and "B" represents the irrational idea that stimulates the "C" or the defense. Regardless, these instances of paying lip service cannot be allowed to continue.

Fighting the Therapist.   Clients fight with or resist their therapists for any number of reasons: for power or control, to increase their self-esteem, to avoid experiencing anxiety, to appear competent, and so on. Whatever the reason, a common way they resist is to debate the rightness or wrongness of a particular idea with the therapist. We ourselves recognize that this is happening when both we and our clients get into an alternating "yes, but" dialogue. At this point, we do something simple: we first comment on what we observe happening—that there is a debate going on; we then point out how foolish it is for the client to exert so much energy debating us when s/he is suffering and we ourselves are calm or indifferent about the particular issue; and we finally strongly make the point that s/he would be much better off debating his or her own ideas (with or without our help), for it is their problem, not ours. It is surprising how effective this strategy can be when undertaken in a non-defensive way.

Another way clients often fight the therapist is to see-saw (Harris, 1977). See-sawing is when the client jumps from one problem to another (e.g., from a self-esteem to a low frustration problem), or when the client helps changing the working hypotheses (e.g., from approval needs to fear of failure). In these instances, the therapist had better bring this to the client's attention and agree with the client the topics or issues to be discussed.

Boredom.   A final client roadblock to rational-emotive working through is boredom. This is not a particularly common problem in RET, yet it arises frequently enough to be alert for it. Boredom during the working through process can result from any number of things: low tolerance for the effort required for working through; distraction from other problems that are more pressing than the problem focus of RET; and a misdiagnosis of the problem so that the focus of the in-therapy discussions and extra-therapy assignments miss the point. Furthermore, rational-emotive working through can be a tedious endeavor in which the client goes over the same material time and time again.

There is no magic solution to this roadblock. What we generally recommend is that the therapist ascertain what is behind the boredom and work to alleviate that problem. This may entail focusing on the client's problem of low frustration tolerance, determining whether or not the client is sufficiently motivated at that particular time to work on emotional problems, restudying the data to determine if there is a more accurate problem definition, or assigning more relevant and dramatic in vivo exercises. Any or all of these may be necessary.

Therapist Roadblocks

Lecturing.   Therapist lecturing is as big a danger to working through as it is to the facilitating of insight. While verbal instruction of short duration can be quite helpful to the goal of getting clients to objectively think through some irrational idea, lengthy lecturing is often counter-productive to this. Lecturing puts clients into the position of passive learners, and the eradication of irrational ideas requires a disputation via energetic, active thinking. It is far better for the therapist to take the Socratic stance of asking provocative questions and succinctly making points that force the client to do a maximum of thinking.

Philosophizing.   A roadblock similar to lecturing through which therapists can fritter away their time is philosophizing. As noted by Harris (1977), therapists can easily get caught in the philosophical underpinnings of RET concepts and can slip into abstract (though brilliant) monologues. Such verbiage takes clients away from their core concerns, and does not help them dispute or rid themselves of irrational ideation. It is far better for the client if a therapy session consists of struggling to dispute their illogical and emotionally upsetting ideas, rather than to listen to the therapist's philosophical explanations of that idea.

Passivity. It is doubtful that any approach to psychotherapy can be effectively practiced by a passive therapist, and RET is no exception. Passivity or nonassertion stems from anxiety and these feelings are created by a host of illogical ideas and attitudes. Foremost among these is a demand for the client's approval, thus creating a fear of being properly assertive because the client might be offended. A common rationalization accompanying this approval-based passivity is that the client might be harmed if the therapist acts assertively and is wrong. In most cases, the actual chances are very slim of deleteriously harming the client by acting in a therapeutically asser-tive manner. If the therapist merely thinks through the real proba-bility of client harm, the issue fades away.

Overfocus on and Inattention to Feelings. In earlier chapters, the roadblock of too much attention on events and feelings was ex-plained, and it warrants mention again with regard to the working through phase. A particularly subtle form of overfocus on A and C is "neurotic agreement" (Harris, 1977) or sympathy for the client's predicament. The therapist agrees with the client that his/her problem is, indeed, awful! A blind spot of this magnitude can entirely thwart therapy progress, and therapists are urged to con-tinually assess their own feelings and appraisal toward the client and problems.

A contrary roadblock to overfocus is inattention to the client's upset feelings. In the therapist's eagerness to help the client change irrational B's and thereby the upset C's, the emotional pain and discomfort of the client may be overlooked. While RET does not advocate reinforcing pathology by focusing on feelings, we do recommend being supportive and empathic toward the client's dis-comfort. One's motivation to remain in therapy is stronger if you have an understanding therapist to work with.

Also of importance for the therapist's attention is clients' struggles in giving up long-held beliefs and behaviors. These personality components are considered by clients to be part of their core being and are often given up, as we said above, with great trepidation. While these ideas and fears about changing should be disputed by the therapist, it is also important for the therapist to be cognizant of their importance to the client and to show empathy to them during their struggles.

Unevocative Questioning.   At several points in this section of the chapter, we have urged therapists to avoid power struggles, lecturing, philosophizing, and other longwinded verbal expositions.   These errors do not promote clients' rational thinking. Another such error, even more difficult to see in the therapist's style, is unevocative questioning, i.e. asking questions which do not promote client thought.   Upon first glance the therapist seems to be doing well at questioning, but close inspection of the client's response or lack thereof shows that the questions are duds!

Harris (1977) has identified several ways that RET therapists can make this error, one being rhetorical questions for which no response is necessary.   A rapid-fire string of questions is another error, for it allows the client to answer the least threatening one.   A complete waste of time are questions which the therapist answers!

Unevocative questioning is a bad habit that slows the working through process, and therapists can improve their styles by replacing these errors with evocative, open-ended, and confrontive questions. Example: "are you feeling upset again?"–versus–"what ideas do you have behind those upset feelings?"

Failure to See Gains.   As clients improve their psychological functioning it is imperative that therapists recognize and reinforce these gains. This is especially crucial for very disturbed clients who make gains in small doses, and for other clients who simply do not evidence quick recoveries.   Clients are sometimes poor evaluators of their own progress, and if the therapist does not underscore even relatively small gains, the client may begin to think therapy is hopeless.

Success is accepting a failure or some other aversive event is another sign of growth, indicating a lack of demandingness and awfulizing. Still another improvement is movement from one emotion and idea to others. Self-condemnation and guilty depression is one of the most pernicious and debilitating forms of pathology, for example, and movement to almost any other state like anger is often a sign of progress. Depressed clients who become expressively angry, though perhaps a bit condemnatory, have nevertheless taken a step toward recovery.

SUMMARY

The working through phase of RET follows the therapist's formulation of a diagnosis and the facilitation of client insight. Together the therapist and client focus their efforts on target problems and a process of cognitive-emotional-behavioral disputation. As a result of this process the client gives up his/her irrational beliefs, and there is a consequent change in perception of self, others, and the surrounding world. The client becomes more accepting and less demanding of reality; there is a lowering of condemnation, the development of an anti-musting and anti-awfulizing attitude, and there is a heightened sense of frustration tolerance. These changes take place within the problems which the client brought to RET, and ideally they also extend on a general, philosophic level across the client's life.

Cognitive, emotive, and behavioral methods are employed by the RET therapist to help clients work through their problems. Techniques such as disputation, rational-emotive imagery, written and activity homework assignments, and shame exercises are integratively employed in the course of working through, as well as reeducation methods described in Chapter 5.

Because working through consumes more time than any other phase of RET, and also because it requires hard work and responsibility of the client, this segment of the RET process is filled with potential roadblocks for the therapist and client. For therapists, roadblocks arise from their own skill errors, and also from intricacies in the client-therapist relationship. Roadblocks for clients consist of a host of attitudinal and emotional reactions to RET and the therapist, reactions which are replications and extensions of their core problems. In a sense, clients play out their problems via their therapy performance.

If the working through phase of RET is successfully traversed the client will arrive at a point of near completion and be close to termination.   Before termination, RET further helps clients engrain rational ideas, and Chapter 5 will present some methods which can be employed to do this.

5

Rational-Emotive Reeducation

Rational-emotive reeducation is the fourth and final skill area in RET. It represents the end product of RET and directly leads to termination of therapy. Following rational-emotive insight and working through, rational-emotive reeducation serves to engrain or habituate in people new and rational ideas.

Having said this, a word of caution is in order. The process of moving clients from rational-emotive insight, through a working through process, and to a cognitive-emotive-behavioral reeducation is the ideal for clients who can attain the kind of elegant, philosophical change which is the preferred goal of RET. For these individuals we strongly recommend using the techniques described in this chapter *only after* helping them gain insight and *only after* facilitating a thorough working through. For those who cannot attain elegant change, such as the mentally limited, the schizophrenic, and the young child, it is probably more appropriate to minimize or even skip insight and working through, and move directly to reeducation.

Thus, the techniques described herein are useful when doing both elegant and inelegant RET. The issue is not whether to use them, but rather *when* to use them and with *what* clients. The major caution is to *always* ask the question: "Can this client attain elegant change?" It is crucial not to sell the client short by offering inelegant change, in which reeducation predominates, when elegant change is possible.

The focus of this relatively brief chapter is to present ways to help people ingrain rational ideas and to help them end up with a new philosophy of life. Like with previous chapters, we will first suggest ways to facilitate this, and then we will discuss client and therapist roadblocks to successful reeducation.

FACILITATING RATIONAL-EMOTIVE REEDUCATION

In thinking about rational-emotive reeducation, it should be emphasized that working through techniques do not end once reeducation ones begin. The process of and techniques for working through are used throughout RET and hopefully throughout life, at least with clients who pursue elegant goals. Accordingly, clients are induced to continue disputing their irrational ideas, and they are strongly encouraged to continue their written homework, their bibliotherapy, and their shame and risk exercises, for RET believes that people are disposed to think crookedly and will naturally do so unless they continue working through. Thus, working through techniques are used together with reeducation ones even though working through proper has ended.

Rational-emotive reeducation techniques include rational-emotive imagery, rational role reversal, rational proselytizing, reinforcing rational thinking, rational indoctrination, stress inoculation, and skill practice. We will discuss each in turn.

Rational-Emotive Imagery

This version of REI was developed by Maxie C. Maultsby, Jr. (1975, 1977b; Maultsby and Ellis, 1974) and is slightly different from the imagery method described in the previous chapter. We have found it best to use the previously described method during the working through process because it facilitates cognitive disputation. We recommend using the one described here for reeducation purposes because it is geared to the ingraining of rational ideas.

A prerequisite for doing reeducational REI is the successful disputation of the client's irrational ideas, and the construction of rational ideas to replace them, along with appropriate feelings that are consistent with the rational ideas. Once this is accomplished, clients are taught: (1) to relax through deep breathing; (2) while relaxed, to recreate the events of the troublesome situation as accurately as possible; (3) to picture themselves thinking *only* the rational ideas; and (4) to see themselves feeling emotionally consistent with their rational thoughts. After running them through this once or twice in session to make sure they understand how to do it, they are then instructed to do REI at home for at least ten minutes a day.

Maultsby (1977b) cautions us to be alert to the fact that clients sometimes become more, rather than less upset when they first do this type of REI. He suggests, and we concur, that this often means that the client's self-statements are really not rational but rather disguised irrational ones. To guard against this, it is best to think through, with them, the reasoning behind their REI thoughts to see if this is so. If the thoughts the client used in the REI are indeed rational, it probably means that they still are wedded to their old ideas and that they require further working through or disputation work as expounded in Chapter 4. The therapist would be wise at this point to retreat for a while and reintroduce working through techniques.

One other problem plagues some clients who attempt to use REI, and this is having vague, unclear, or unimpactful images and thoughts. Some people are good at evoking images, while others do it poorly. For those who do it poorly, we encourage clients to simply persist in their efforts and/or teach them how to imagine through a variety of awareness techniques (Stevens, 1971).

Rational Role Reversal

Some recent research indicates that rational-emotive therapists derive personal benefits from practicing RET. Maultsby (personal communication, 1976), for instance, notes that rational therapists involuntarily become more rational through doing RET, and Kassinove (1974) discovered that graduate students being trained in RET actually improved their own psychological adjustment. We ourselves have personally noticed that our calmest time during the work week frequently comes at the end of a long day of doing RET.

To capitalize on this phenomenon, Howard Kassinove and Raymond DiGiuseppe (1975) have developed the rational role reversal technique. The therapist assumes the role of a naive client, and the actual client takes the role of the rational therapist and explains to the "client" the rational concepts in question. The therapist asks clarifying questions and raises cogent points that allow the client to forcefully rehearse rational thinking. The therapist stays in the "naive" role, but continues to monitor and use the client's performance so that rational thinking takes place.

It is, of course, best for the therapist to only initiate rational role reversal after the client understands the rational ideas or philosophies behind his or her problems. Then, after successfully doing rational role reversal, the therapist can give the client rational proselytizing.

Rational Proselytizing

Rational proselytizing is a reeducation technique that follows rational role reversal. It derives from Bard's (1973) findings that college students who taught RET concepts to their friends became more rational themselves. Accordingly, it is often helpful in RET to give clients the assignment of proselytizing to their friends about the RET concepts in question.

Three cautions are in order when using rational proselytizing. One is to only assign rational proselytizing when you are sure the client understands the rational idea, otherwise s/he will teach nonsense to others and will also ingrain false ideas into themselves. Second, encourage clients to be selective in choosing people to proselytize to in order not to hurt another or lose a friend. Finally, it is wise to intermittently continue to roleplay with these clients in order to refresh their rational thinking and to reinforce their continued cognitive-emotive-behavioral reeducation efforts.

Reinforcing Rational Thinking

Another reeducation ploy designed to engrain rational thoughts and ideas is the reinforcement of rational thinking. As its name implies, the object is to use a variety of concrete, social, and activity reinforcers to reward clients for thinking rationally. The simplest and most obvious way is to socially reward the client in the therapy session. Most people relish praise, and clients who hear the therapist praise their rational thinking and behaving are more likely to continue these practices. Less controlled but equally effective is clients rewarding themselves for rational thinking and behaving. While the results of rational thinking are often rewarding enough in and of themselves, pleasuring themselves with something satisfying, or even with self-directed praise, is a real treat for many people.

As with many of the techniques mentioned in this chapter, we find it important to add a word of caution. Be conservative with the use of reinforcement until a thorough working through has been completed. Otherwise, the danger exists that clients pursuing elegant RET goals might be "conditioned" to superficial sloganizing rather than to truly thinking through their ideas.

Rational Indoctrination

Rational Indoctrination (RI) is a rational-emotive reeducation technique used to indoctrinate rational ideas into clients who, for whatever reasons, do not have or cannot summon the where-with-all to elegantly think through their ideas or philosophies. Basically, clients are encouraged to adopt and use rational ideas that will help them lead healthier, happier lives.

Forty-two year old James W. was a prospect for RI. His emotional problems began some 20 years before entering therapy for guilt problems—he was responsible for killing his parents in a car accident. In order to deal with the tremendous amount of guilt, depression, and feelings of worthlessness about this, he adopted the stance of the family patriarch. He tried to atone for his wrong doing and make himself feel valuable and responsible by seeing to it that the lives of each member of his extended family was prosperous and happy. All this worked relatively well for many years until two major things happened that shattered his defenses: his younger brother had a nervous breakdown and his 18 year old, unmarried daughter became pregnant. Upon discovering the latter, he lost control and began shooting up the house with a rifle, only becoming aware of what he was doing when he heard the sirens of the police car.

Some months later, James was referred to me (R.G.) after being released from the psychiatric in-patient ward of a local hospital.

He presented himself as an exceptionally depressed man; he walked with the gait and posture of a 90 year old, his face was virtually colorless, he dragged his left leg and hung his left arm in a semi-paralyzed fashion, and his facial muscles drooped. He found it impossible to dredge the motivation to work at his profession of carpentry; he could only sleep for a few hours at a time, and then only fitfully; he ate little, and he had virtually no interest in social activities.

Because of James' extreme lethargy, and because of only moderate intelligence at best, I determined that elegant change via a philosophic working through was impossible for him at this point. Accordingly, I skipped insight and working through work and immediately focused on rational-emotive reeducation by directly and forcefully indoctrinating him with rational ideas that I thought were antithetical to what was behind his depression: ideas of anti-perfectionism, self-acceptance, and forgiveness. I repeatedly hammered home the following message to him, replete with references to God in order to capitalize on his religious background:

"There's no question that you made a big mistake, James. But, that was 20 years ago. God has long ago forgiven you for that; He even knew you were going to make that mistake before it ever happened, and He forgave you. He knows you're not a terrible person, and you can forgive yourself too. Doesn't it make sense for you to forgive yourself if God does?

And, another thing, James. You're not God. Only God makes no mistakes. There's no way that you can possibly keep from making mistakes, even big ones, because you're not God. There's no way that you can be so perfect to make everything OK in everybody's life, because only God is that perfect. You're a man, not God, and that means you can't do everything. God knows that and accepts that, and you can too. It's OK to be human."

This captures the essence of rational indoctrination. The therapist repeatedly and authoritatively articulates a rational philosophy in order to undercut the client's opposite irrational ideation. To facilitate learning, the client is quickly encouraged to repeat the ideas in the session (much like a second grader learning the multiplication tables), and, once learned, the client is told to practice thinking these rational thoughts regularly between sessions. If possible, it is very helpful to have s/he do this while imaging himself in troublesome situations, particularly if s/he can avoid becoming too upset.

Stress Inoculation

Stress inoculation is a coping skills program developed by Donald Meichenbaum (1972, 1973, 1976a,b, 1977; Meichenbaum and Cameron, 1972). It is reeducational in nature because it emphasizes the teaching of a set of coping self-statements to deal with stressful events, rather than trying to alter ideas or philosophies that create the stress to begin with. To this date stress inoculation treatment packages have been applied to clients contending with physical pain (Turk, 1974), fears of flying (Girodo and Roehl, 1978), test anxiety (Meichenbaum, 1972), and anger problems (Novaco, 1976).

In its most formal structure, stress inoculation involves three phases. In the *educational phase,* the therapist tries to accomplish two things: (1) to teach clients that their coping poorly with stress is caused by their thoughts and that successful change would result from learning new thoughts that would help them when under stress; (2) to show clients that their stress reactions follow a series of four stages, rather than being one massive reaction, and that they could learn effective self-statements to counteract each stage. They could learn to prepare for a stressor; confront or handle a stressor; cope when overwhelmed by negative feelings; and reinforce themselves for coping.

In the second phase of stress inoculation, the *rehearsal phase,* clients are helped to develop a series of adaptive self-statements that would help them successfully mediate or cope at each of the four stages of the stress reaction. Self-statements are developed that help clients: (1) realistically assess the difficulties and stresses in a situation, and control negative thoughts and images about the stressor; (2) motivate themselves to cope and confront the stressor in a rational, problem-oriented way (rather than emotionally oriented); (3) cope with fears that arise during the experience of facing the stressful situation; and (4)   reinforce themselves for coping. Examples of self-statements for coping with fear and anger are presented in Table 5-1.

Table 5-1 Self-Statements for Dealing with Anger and Anxiety

I. Anger

A. Preparing for a Stressor

This is going to upset me, but I know how to deal with it.
What is it that I have to do?
I can work out a plan to handle this.
I can manage the situation. I know how to regulate my anger.
If I find myself getting upset, I'll know what to do.
There won't be any need for an argument.
Try not to take this too seriously.
This could be a testy situation, but I believe in myself.
Time for a few deep breaths of relaxation. Feel comfortable, relaxed, and at ease.
Easy does it. Remember to keep your sense of humor.

B. Confronting/Handling the Stressor

Stay calm. Just continue to relax.
As long as I keep my cool, I'm in control.
Just roll with the punches; don't get bent out of shape.
Think of what you want to get out of this.
You don't need to prove yourself.
There is no point in getting mad.
Don't make more out of this than you have to.
I'm not going to let him get to me.
Look for the positives. Don't assume the worst or jump to conclusions.
It's really a shame that she has to act like this.
For someone to be that irritable, he must be awfully unhappy.
If I start to get mad, I'll just be banging my head against the wall. So I might as well just relax.
There is no need to doubt myself. What he says doesn't matter.
I'm on top of this situation and it's under control.

C. Coping with Arousal

My muscles are starting to feel tight. Time to relax and slow things down.
Getting upset won't help.
It's just not worth it to get so angry.
I'll let him make a fool of himself.
I have a right to be annoyed, but let's keep the lid on.
Time to take a deep breath.
Let's take the issue point by point.
My anger is a signal of what I need to do. Time to instruct myself.
I'm not going to get pushed around, but I'm not going haywire either.

Try to reason it out. Treat each other with respect.

Let's try a cooperative approach. Maybe we are both right.

Negatives lead to more negatives. Work constructively.

He'd probably like me to get really angry. Well I'm going to disappoint him.

I can't expect people to act the way I want them to.

Take it easy, don't get pushy.

D. **When conflict is resolved or coping is successful**

I handled that one pretty well. It worked!

That wasn't as hard as I thought.

It could have been a lot worse.

I could have gotten more upset than it was worth.

I actually got through that without getting angry.

My pride can sure get me into trouble, but when I don't take things too seriously, I'm better off.

I guess I've been getting upset for too long when it wasn't even necessary.

I'm doing better at this all the time.

II. Anxiety

A. **Preparing for a Stressor**

What it is I have to do?

You can develop a plan to deal with it.

Just think about what I can do about it. That's better than getting anxious.

No negative self-statements; just think rationally.

Don't worry; worry won't help anything.

Maybe what I think is anxiety is eagerness to confront the stressor.

B. **Confronting/Handling the Stressor**

Just "psych" myself up—I can meet this challenge.

I can convince myself to do it. I can reason my fear away.

One step at a time; I can handle the situation.

Don't think about fear; just think about what I have to do. Stay relevant.

This anxiety is what the doctor said I would feel. It's a reminder to use my coping exercises.

This tenseness can be an ally; a cue to cope.

Relax; I'm in control. Take a slow, deep breath.

Ah, good.

C. **Coping with the Feeling of Being Overwhelmed**

When fear comes, just pause.

Keep the focus on the present; what is it I have to do? Label my fear from 0 to 10 and watch it change.

I should expect my fear to rise.
Don't try to eliminate fear totally; just keep it manageable.

D. **Reinforcing Oneself**

It worked; I did it.
Wait until I tell my therapist (or group) about this.
It wasn't as bad as I expected.
I made more out of my fear than it was worth.
My damn ideas—that's the problem. When I control them, I control
  my fear.
It's getting better each time I use the procedures.
I can be pleased with the progress I'm making.
I did it!

Application training is the third phase of stress inoculation. The therapist first has clients test out and practice their coping skills in stressful situations other than their troublesome ones. This amounts to a preparatory rehearsal. Following this, clients are instructed to confront the stressful event and employ their coping devices.

To sum, stress inoculation involves educating clients about the nature of stressful emotional reactions, developing and practicing coping skills, and applying these skills in actual stressful situations. Relaxation skills are also typically taught to clients to be used along with coping self-statements. Again, we want to emphasize that stress inoculation, while a powerful tool, is inelegant in the sense that it provides new, rational ideas while not necessarily undoing the irrational ones that already exist. It is therefore important for us to again remind the reader to only use stress inoculation after a working through process has been completed, or instead of a working through process if elegant goals are not appropriate.

Skill Training and Practice

As indicated before, RET places tremendous importance on getting clients to act contrary to their irrational ideas. Its theory holds that clients rarely change or give up their self-defeating ideas until they act against them. Consequently, RET therapists use a good many behavioral-activity assignments to foster a thorough cognitive-emotive-behavioral working through.

Consistent with the above, RET teaches skills in effective living, either concurrent with or following rational-emotive working through. When done concurrent with working through, a primary purpose is to make clients confront their irrational ideas and work to give them up. When skill training is done following working through, or as part of reeducation, its purposes are to both engrain rational ideas and to simply facilitate skill development itself. Regardless, a watchful eye is always kept on uncovering and undoing irrationality that prevents the proper use of the skills in question.

The list of effective living skills are endless. We shall briefly mention only three: assertive training, relaxation training, and problem solving.

Assertive Training. Assertive training has become one of the major behavior therapy treatments (Alberti and Emmons, 1974; Salter, 1949; Wolpe and Lazarus, 1966). Recently, assertive training has gone cognitive. That is, a good many assertive training approaches now combine behavioral skill training with cognitive training (Lange and Jakubowski, 1976; Lazarus, 1971), taking the stance that (1) changing people's ideas influences their assertive behavior, and (2) changing people's behavior leads to changes in their ideas (Lange, 1977).

It is beyond the scope of this book to outline cognitive-behavioral assertive training procedures. The reader is referred to Jakubowski-Specter (1973), Lange (1977), and Lange and Jakubowski (1976) for excellent presentations of such an approach. It is only noted at this point that cognitive-behavioral assertive training encompasses the teaching of the following cognitive and behavioral skills: (1) a set of beliefs which hold a high regard for one's and others' rights; (2) a set of beliefs which discriminate between assertive, agressive, and unassertive behavior; (3) rational ideas which facilitate assertive rather than aggressive or unassertive behavior; and (4) behaviors which are assertive in nature rather than aggressive or unassertive (Lange, 1977).

Relaxation Training. While being a palliative solution to dealing with various types of psychological stress, a considerable amount of data demonstrates that muscle relaxation reduces anxiety (Jacobson, 1929; Lang, Melamed, and Hart, 1970; Paul, 1969). We, as well as others, have also noted that relaxation is sometimes an important adjunct to many of the rational-emotive working through and re-education techniques mentioned in this text.

The methods for inducing relaxation are considerable and include anything from deep breathing to meditation and yoga exercises. The mechanics of relaxation training are so simple and straightforward that there is little reason why the skills are not a part of every clinician's repertoire. While cautioning that relaxation is a palliative solution to emotional problems, we refer the reader to an excellent discussion of the procedures and pitfalls of relaxation training by Goldfried and Davison (1976), and suggest Arnold Lazarus's (1976) audiotape of relaxation instructions as a perfect model for relaxation induction.

Problem Solving.   Despite RET's primary focus on irrational ideas and their relationship to emotional disturbance, it does recognize that people regularly find themselves confronted with difficult decisions and problems. It also recognizes that people vary greatly in their ability to successfully cope with problem situations and decisions, and that successful problem solving ability is closely related to emotional well-being (Goldfried & Davison, 1976).

Consequently, as a reeducation tool, it is recommended that the well-rounded rational-emotive therapist be an effective problem solving skill-trainer as well. Problem solving training programs are remarkably similar (D'Zurilla & Goldfried, 1971) and generally contain the following five stages: (1) a general orientation to problem solving; (2) a problem definition; (3) the generation of alternative strategies to solve the problem; (4) decision making; and (5) an assessment of the effectiveness of the strategy employed. We again refer the reader to Goldfried and Davison (1976) for an excellent presentation of how to teach problem solving skills.

These are a few of the more frequently taught skills in effective living that are presented during the phase of rational-emotive re-education. They hardly are exhaustive; others include communication training, social skill development, fair fight training, sexual skill training, male-female relating, effective study skills, and the like. The only cautions we again offer are two: be careful not to sell the client short by promoting inelegant solutions to their problems rather than elegant ones; and, always be alert to the potential for cognitive restructuring or the working through of irrational ideas as part of any skill training you are conducting.

TERMINATING RATIONAL-EMOTIVE THERAPY

How to terminate the therapist-client relationship is a much discussed issue. The literature abounds with treatises on preparing clients for termination, dependency and transference issues as therapy nears an end, and the like. We find that termination of RET is really a fairly smooth, uneventful time for most of our clients. It could be that they find us so aversive that leaving is a real treat. A more pleasing, and we think, more accurate explanation is that RET promotes client independence such that the severance of the on-going relationship with the therapist is in no way traumatic. In successful RET, clients learn that they are responsible for their own problems; they learn what their problems are and how to go about giving up both these and future ones; they free themselves from the tyranny of their "shoulds" and "awfuls"; learn to accept themselves without the necessity of doing well and being approved; they learn to accept existence with its injustices and discomforts; and they learn how to think scientifically and independently. Given all this, it is little wonder that termination usually goes smoothly and uneventfully.

An important termination item for the last therapy session is to review with clients the learnings and changes they attained during RET. As with other RET techniques, this review is best done by the client via the client's recall and thought processes. Termination is *not* the time for therapists to review *their* successes. Clients rarely articulate their gains as clearly as the therapist, and the therapist can of course help clients become aware of their progress. Beware of taking credit from clients, or of basking in their adulation. To do this would suggest that the client has been changed by an external agent (the therapist), rather than having made changes through one's own power.

By reviewing the client's RET gains a valuable lesson can be learned. The client can vividly see the source of his/her past difficulties, how s/he overcame these difficulties and which ones may remain to be conquered, and a planning for continued self-generated therapeutic growth can be done. A "life strategy" often develops from such a planning session. The client decides to face future emotional-behavioral difficulties and other life problems through the same steps that were followed in RET. Our clients frequently explain major alterations in their life goals during termination sessions. They have discovered and overcome neurotic strivings, thus enabling them to pursue healthier, happier pathways.

ROADBLOCKS TO RATIONAL-EMOTIVE REEDUCATION

Roadblocks to rational-emotive reeducation are few compared to those in the other rational-emotive skill areas. Indeed, client roadblocks to reeducation by and large represent many of those in rational-emotive working through, particularly the error of paying lip service to rational thinking. In paying lip service, it is likely that clients simply do not understand the concepts behind the rational philosophies, or, more seriously, that they are still fearfully hesitating to deal with their problems or they are still trying to please their therapist by spouting things designed to elicit approval. Suggested therapist responses to these have already been discussed.

A phenomenon that sometimes occurs as clients near the end of RET is a reactivation of their symptoms. Most typical among these are anxieties about disapproval and fears about losing the gains they have already made. In striking out on their own without the regular support of their therapist, they fear that they cannot maintain their rational gains.

This is not a phenomenon unique to RET, nor is it anything to become alarmed about. The most useful thing for the therapist to do when these fears arise is to simply help clients discover what they are telling themselves to become upset and to work these notions through—to anti-awfulize about disapproval and about future mistake making. Often behind these fears is the idea that a temporary slip into irrational thinking means an inevitable downhill slide that will only end when they again hit rock bottom. We recommend directly tackling this idea, showing clients that they fail to see both the variety of things they can do to intercept such a process and the many skills and strengths they have already acquired that substantially arms them against all this. Such a tactic usually undercuts their anxieties and furthers clients on the road to the completion of their RET.

Therapist Roadblocks

With regard to the therapist, there are indeed some roadblocks that can interfere with a successful rational-emotive reeducation and prevent a smooth termination of RET. The first of these was briefly mentioned in our earlier discussion of termination.

Therapist Grandeur. A very subtle therapist roadblock which can undo much of the significant gain accomplished in RET is therapist grandeur. This occurs when therapists smugly pat themselves on the back and take credit for the client's progress. Such a self aggrandizement is usually communicated to the client who unfortunately believes it, and attributes his/her therapeutic gains to the brilliant therapist! Another form of aggrandizement is for RET itself. Some clients adopt RET as though it were a life raft in the stormy seas of life. This reaction parallels the bizarre and mystical cultists who gain nationwide attention through demonstrable irrational behavior.

A rational perspective about the therapist and RET is an important goal to be attained during the final few therapy sessions. Achieving this, the therapist and RET will be viewed by clients as effective helpers who have assisted them in overcoming their irrational propensities. Self defeating cognitive habits have been restructured so that clients are, more than ever, in rational control of *themselves.*

Neglecting Elegant Goals. We have on several occasions already discussed the difference between elegant and inelegant goals in RET, and each time we have forcefully tried to make the point that RET therapists should be careful to pursue elegant goals for those who have the ability to attain them. We add this therapist roadblock to again underscore this point, since the reeducation phase probably represents the last opportunity for clients to obtain or complete a profound philosophic change before termination.

Failing to Accept Client Fallibility. A philosophic cornerstone of RET is that all people, being fallible, will make numerous and regular mistakes in the course of their lives. Indeed, RET therapists regularly try to get clients to understand and accept this fact and to cease demanding otherwise from themselves.

RET therapists on occasion also fall prey to demanding perfection from their clients. Sometimes it comes from their own perfectionistic needs where their self-worth has become wedded to their success with their clients; other times it comes from a failure to recognize that clients will be incompletely and imperfectly rational, just as they will be imperfect in all their other arenas. Regardless, therapists who demand perfect rationality from clients will keep hammering away at them to get better and better, and will in the process frustrate both themselves and the clients.

Again we emphasize the importance of the therapist accepting that clients will never achieve a perfectly rational existence and that they will have to cope with tendencies to think and behave irrationally throughout their lives. It is best to recognize this in order to gracefully accept the strides clients do make and to be able to help clients accept them.

Blindly Accepting Gains. A final therapist roadblock somewhat opposite to the previous one is assuming that clients apply what they say in therapy to their real lives. Two issues are involved here. One is whether or not clients actually make use of their rational thinking, and a second is whether or not clients apply rational thinking across various life situations as opposed to just one.

The danger for the therapist is to get seduced into thinking clients are both applying and generalizing rational ideas in their lives because they can articulate rational philosophies in conversations with their therapists. It is important to ask clients to bring to therapy examples applying to what they learned in therapy to their daily lives. It is also important to continually remind oneself to suggest to clients that they extend their new rational thinking into divergent arenas in their lives.

SUMMARY

So the full-term process of RET nears an end. Having progressed through the stages of diagnosis, insight, and working-through, the therapist employs reeducation techniques designed to engrain and habituate rational beliefs. Ideally, reeducation will build upon previous "elegant" gains which have produced a fundamental philosophical change in the client's ideation. But even if elegant gains were not possible, reeducation is an effective closure to inelegant RET.

Methods such as REI, role reversal, and proselytizing help clients build an even deeper rational belief system. For those unable to grasp the abstract principles of RET, the rote use of rational thoughts can be learned via indoctrination, reinforcement, and stress inoculation. Both elegant and inelegant gains in the cognitive domain can be enhanced, and comprehensive client changes completed, by the therapist's employment of skill-training methods.

The termination of RET is hopefully a time for the therapist and client to reflect upon significant client advances, and therapeutic gains are generalized to all areas of the client's present and future functioning. If RET has truly been effective it becomes obsolete as a formal entity, and the client begins a more fulfilling and independent life using the concepts and principles on his or her own.

6

Rational-Emotive Therapy
In Action

We have emphasized that RET is a craft composed of specific skills which fall into four groups: (1) psychodiagnostic and goal setting skills; (2) insight facilitation skills; (3) working through skills; and (4) reeducational skills. A reading of this text, without observational or experimental exposure to RET, might suggest that RET is an impersonal and mechanical process. We want to emphatically counteract such a misconception, for the effective RET therapist, in addition to having command of a rather sophisticated theory, continually maintains a flexible and highly dynamic interpersonal encounter with the client. As shown in this chapter, RET calls for skillful professional judgment and daring. The therapist's skills are integratively performed and combined into a creative experience for client change.

RET Case Presentation

The client is a twenty-seven year old female who is a graduate student at a large state university. She is doing quite well in her studies and is happily married to a man with whom she has an excellent relationship. Nonetheless, she is rather unhappy about a particular aspect of her life, her weight, which she proceeds to discuss.

T1: So, Jill, what brings you?

C1: Well, because I really can't deal with my weight problem anymore. For the past five years or so I feel like I've been constantly sabotaging myself. I gain weight and then lose it again. I'm presently on one of my many, many, many diets, but I'm getting discouraged, because I thought I was doing ok. The week of Thanksgiving I really blew it. I had intended to allow myself to eat on Thursday, but instead I ate the whole week and gained about six of the 10 pounds I'd recently lost. I've been really depressed about having to lose the same weight all over again. And I need help.

T2:   So, you're into getting on diets and blowing them. And you're in that up-and-down process right now *and* very upset about it. You said this last episode happened during Thanksgiving week. Tell me a little bit about that. What happened?

C2:   Well, I've been dieting really strictly for about four weeks. For me that means really strictly, because I do have a thyroid problem that makes it difficult, but not impossible for me to lose. I'd lost about 10 pounds in four weeks and I felt pretty good about how carefully I'd been keeping the diet. It's a very extreme kind of diet which I seem to need. I can't seem to make it on just eating less. I need to do things like completely eliminating kinds of food.

T3:   OK. And what happened for you to blow it.

C3:   I decided that it was ok to eat on Thanksgiving day and I was going to enjoy myself and then go right back to my diet. Instead of waiting for Thursday, I was at a dinner party on Monday and decided, "well, this is Thanksgiving too so I might as well eat." I ate and found that the food was pretty bad, but I ate it anyway. Then I started feeling pretty shitty about eating and not even enjoying myself. I ate and I didn't even like it and it was horrible. Because I was feeling so bad about eating that dinner, I couldn't seem to get it back together on Tuesday and this carried right on through. It took me a week to get out of that feeling bad syndrome of "what's the use."

T4:   So your feeling bad and your getting off your diet goes hand in hand. What begins as bad eating quickly turns into bad feelings.

C4:   Right.

T5:   Well, that sounds to me already, Jill, that you have two
      problems here, not one.   First, you have a problem with
      dieting—a thyroid problem, perhaps will power problems,
      bad eating habits, or something mechanical that prevents you
      from staying on a diet.   And, secondly, you get upset about
      eating badly and then eat when you don't want to eat.   So,
      you have a practical problem about dieting and you have an
      emotional problem about bad dieting—getting upset, depressed
      and discouraged, about dieting.   So far so good?

C5:   Yes.

Comment

This brief excerpt is a good example of how RET begins and how
quickly RET facilitates mutual problem definition.   Although the
first session has progressed only a few minutes, the therapist has
already begun the diagnostic task of separating problem categories in
his and the client's mind.   He immediately (T1) takes a problem-
focused stance by inviting the client to tell what troubles her.   In
response to this, Jill, as with most clients, tumbles out her story (C1
and C2) in a somewhat disorganized way, displaying practical problems of dieting with emotional problems of discouragement and
depression about dieting.   This is not at all unusual.   Most seasoned
RETers listen for a mixture of presenting problems from the minute
therapy begins.

The therapist in this case responds to Jill's presentation in typical
RET fashion.   Noting the dual concerns she presents, he first briefly
makes note of them (T2, T4) and then authoritatively sketches them
out for her (T5).   He does this in order to help her make sense out
of what she herself is concerned about, to allow her to discretely
focus on each problem, and to nudge her into making an appropriate
decision about which problem to tackle first.   As stated in Chapter 2,
we generally advise the therapist to first deal with emotional problems
about practical problems, because they often become manageable
once the excess baggage of emotional problems is lifted.

Before moving on, we want to stress the importance of making
sure the client understands what s/he has been told, as in T5.   Even

the most cogent and brilliant bit of information may be lost if the client is confused or unable for any reason to take it in.

T6: Now let's focus on this second problem— the emotional problem—for a few minutes. Here you were at the dinner party on Monday. The food wasn't good but you were eating anyway. And the next thing you knew you started feeling really bad. So, what was going through your head? What were you thinking as you were eating the food you didn't like that got you feeling so bad?

C6: That's easy. I felt like: "What the hell is wrong with me? Why am I sitting here eating this food that I don't even like when I suffered the past four weeks on this diet? It's bad enough to eat something and enjoy it, but to sit here and eat it and not enjoy it . . . I was feeling miserable. I think what I was thinking even affected my stomach. I had this terrible stomach ache by the end of the meal.

T7: So you were saying: "What's wrong with me! I don't like the food, I don't want to be eating it, but I'm eating it anyway."

C7: Yes.

T8: Now, all that sounds like you're asking a question, asking for information. But my experience tells me that when people ask themselves questions like that, they're not really asking questions; they're making some sort of a statement about themselves in question form. So, what is that statement you're making? Change that question to a declarative statement.

C8: That's easy too. "There *is* something wrong with me, that I'm sitting here doing this."

T9: Let's clarify that even further. "Because I'm doing something that I don't like, that I don't want to be doing, I'm . . . ," what . . . ?

C9: Shitty for doing it (very softly).

T10: Yes! Isn't that what you tell yourself?

C10: Yeah, I think I probably do. I feel so bad. In this case I felt so bad I had physical symptoms. I thought like: "Ooh, how can I eat this! It tastes terrible and my stomach is getting upset.

I'm uncomfortable doing it." And I talk to myself: "why am I doing this when it's getting me upset and I'm getting all this information that it's a stupid thing to do?" So I'm thinking I must be really stupid doing this when I know better. It's not that I don't know what's gonna happen. I know what's gonna happen.

T11: And, a person who engages in these behaviors who doesn't know better is ok; but a person who does things she doesn't like and knows they are bad for her is really stupid and really shit.

C11: Right!

T12: OK. Now, do you see how thinking those kinds of thoughts can only lead to feeling really bad and really bad about you?

C12: Yeah I do.

T13: Good. Because there's a real connection between calling yourself names like shitty and feeling really bad about you. If you said to yourself—"Hey, I'm sitting here doing something that's shitty, but who doesn't; I'm just like everybody else and that's ok."—you wouldn't have felt so bad, would you? But when you call yourself things like a really shitty person, how else could you feel besides bad? Right? See the connection? There's no other way you could feel and *that's* the basis for your emotional upset. You see that? (She nods) Then what do you do with that?

C13: Eat!

T14: You eat. And you eat because . . . .

C14: I'm upset and what's the use.

T15: Yeah. First you're upset and you baby yourself a little when you get upset by eating. Second, if you're really such a shitty person, what *is* the use. You think: "I'm so weak and shitty; and this is so huge that someone as shitty as I am can't possibly conquer such a huge problem. What's the use!" You then feel real helpless and hopeless. Right?

C15: Uh-huh. And then I start thinking I had it conquered and I blew it then. I was at a desirable weight and enjoyed being thin, but I went up again. So what's the use! I can't help my-self. Even if I get to where I'd like to be I won't stay there.

T16: Right. A shit like me will blow it again and again, so what's the use. So what we're saying then, in relation to this emotional problem, is that you really down yourself, you start calling yourself names. And then what happens is you get into feeling really rotten about you and really helpless and hopeless and small and ineffective and so forth in relation to eating. So you then give up and start eating, because how can someone so low do something so hard. So it has a circular effect upon eating.

C16: The helpless really hits home for me because I feel that way often when I *am* dieting and *don't* lose weight for several days, even when I know I haven't eaten anything. It doesn't make a difference what I do. I'm not in control here. My body is blowing it for me, so I might as well eat; because when I don't eat I don't lose weight anyway, and then I get into depression and helpless.

T17: You get into self downing and feelings of worthlessness, which gets into the helplessness and the hopelessness, which in turn causes you to overeat.

C17: But then I feel like a reasonably competent person in other areas. I feel like I'm successful in maintaining a pretty diffi-cult schedule at school and I'm extremely happy in my marriage. I do ok in other parts of my life so why can't I do ok here? It's not fair. Why can't I be incompetent in something else that doesn't mean as much to me?

Comment

This brief section demonstrates how rational-emotive psychodiagnosis and insight flows quickly and smoothly into each other. Although we are still only a few minutes into the first session, the therapist zeros in on what he considers to be Jill's major emotional problem—her self-downing. He knows on theoretical grounds that depression and discouragement most often result from people disparaging their self-worth because of their bad or inefficient behaviors. He also knows that the process of self-downing causes people to feel helpless and hopeless about tackling their problems. Like Jill, they will undercut their ability to solve practical problems like dieting. The therapist therefore focuses directly on the emotional problems about the dieting problem and helps Jill understand or gain insight into how she is making herself depressed and discouraged, and inefficient in eating.

Rather than simply telling Jill all this, the therapist chose to utilize leading and evocative rational-emotive insight techniques (see Chapter 3) to help her gain the necessary insights into her irrational ideas. As shown in this segment, he used the ABC lead (T6), the challenging of rhetorical questions (T7, T8), the completing of incomplete sentences (T9), and the contrasting technique (T13). Notice how they flow smoothly into each other. The therapist being well versed in the RET theory of psychopathology and well acquainted with these various insight techniques, goes smoothly from one to the other until Jill has a good grasp of her irrational ideation.

The use of these four insight techniques proved to be quite effective in relative short order. Not satisfied, however, that Jill appreciates the connection between her irrational ideas and her symptoms of depression, discouragement, and poor eating behavior, the therapist goes on in the latter part of this section to make the connection more explicit (T13, T14, T15, T16, T17). On too many occasions we have seen the benefits of well-developed insights lost because they are not clearly grounded to their consequences.

T18: OK, that's an interesting question. The eating obviously has a loading for you and it would be well worth our while to explore that at some point. And I also think it would be worth our while, in the near future, to talk about some behavioral management techniques of eating. No question about that. But I would really recommend, and I want you to tell me if you agree with this now, that we first focus on the self-downing that you do about your eating problem. Because so long as that's involved, it's going to be very difficult to put your energy into solving the eating problem. If you're always robbing your energy away from the eating problem by making yourself feel helpless, hopeless, downed, and worthless, you'll never get anywhere. Do you see that?

C18: Yeah, I really see that because in the course of five years I've tried them all and I could spout them off to you, and they didn't work and I think probably the self downing gets in the way.

T19: We can agree that's a goal.

C19: Yeah. The behavioral things I can handle on my own, I think, in terms of just planning out programs or diets or whatever. I've been the route. So whatever I do . . . .

T20: (interrupts) You know as much about that as I do, then.

C20: Probably more. What I don't know about is . . . .

T21: (interrupts) The stuff in your head that's making you not do the technical things that you know damn well know how to do. And do you appreciate that? Let me underscore this. Do you appreciate the role of your self downing? The idea that you have that "I am really shitty, I am really stupid for blowing it."

C21: Yes (emphatically). I think I probably do because I have a sense that there's almost something mystical interfering in my behavior and I've felt very often that if I could put my finger on it, I could stop it. I didn't understand to enough of a degree what's going on is me working against myself.

T22: Yeah, that's the self downing. I fully believe that if you get rid of the self-downing you will improve 90 percent of your eating problem. You won't improve completely because you have a thyroid problem and its gonna be tough to avoid delicious food because food is tempting, but you will be on top of it. I can almost guarantee that, if you're willing to put the effort into it. OK? That sound good?

C22: That sounds really good . . . .

Comment

The therapist has now rounded out the psychodiagnosis and insight stages of RET by helping Jill set therapeutic goals for herself. Knowing full well that he may have to return to insight and goal setting work again as she forgets what she has gained or loses sight of it in the process of disputation, the therapist forcefully pushes her to focus her attention on her self-downing problem. In T18 he directly tells her this and goes on to explain why. When she acknowledges that she can appreciate all this (C19), he more explicitly asks for her agreement (T19), checks out her understanding one last time (T21), and finally again underscores the B-C connection. Having gained the necessary insights and agreed to the goal of working on the self-downing, Jill is now ready to begin her working through process.

One other thing is worth highlighting in the previous interchanges. While the therapist basically uses less directive techniques to help Jill gain her rational-emotive insights, he nevertheless still takes an authoritative posture. He is in control of the flow of the interchanges, he professorily shows her the connections between her irrational ideas and her symptoms (T13, T15), he confidently sums up the insights he has elicited from her (T16), he unabashedly recommends the material she needs to focus on to conquer her problem (T18), and he confidently reassures her that she can expect to make significant inroads into her problem. All of this is typical of the RET therapist in his or her didactic, philosophic, directive posture.

C22: continued: . . . but, how do we do all this.

T23: By focusing on your ideas about yourself and seeing if they are true or not. Let's focus on your self-downing for a while. OK?

C23: OK.

T24: OK. Your hypothesis is: "Because I engage in this behavior that I know is stupid and self-defeating, I'm a real shitty person."

C24: And I get really ashamed. (softly)

T25: Yeah, because you're calling yourself a shitty person. Now, how does that make you shitty? Let's challenge that idea. How can you be a shitty person for doing these stupid things?

C25: Because if you're smart enough to know what you're doing to yourself, that you're doing something that's making you unhappy, then there's got to be something fundamentally wrong with me and that I'm doing it.

T26: But, how does that follow? Do you know any human beings who don't do stupid things? Stupid is defined as knowing better, but doing it anyway. Ignorance is not knowing better. Do you know anyone who doesn't act stupidly, ever in their lives?

C26: No.

T27: Is there something fundamentally wrong with them?

C27: I guess not. (softly)

T28: You said that meekly, Jill, which leads me to think you don't really believe it. Now, for instance, some people get lots of traffic tickets, some are perpetually late, some have a hard time getting along with members of the opposite sex, and on and on. Is there something fundamentally, totally wrong with these people, or is it just . . .

C28: A behavior (softly). But for me it's different?

T29: Why? Why is it different for you?

C29: I do it so continuously. I mean this has gone on for five years already. I've been pleased with my progress at some point, then I make myself so miserable by blowing it.

T30: (Interjects) Your thinking is getting circular right there. I want to intercept it, because the reason you get yourself so miserable is because you tell yourself, "I'm such a shitty person for blowing it," and we're attacking that fundamental belief. Your flaw is that you stupidly don't stick to diets; and I'm asking you to show me why you, as a totality, are a shitty person because you have that particular flaw or stupid habit.

C30: I guess because—this may sound circular too—I make myself so miserable and I don't like being miserable.

T31: That *is* being circular. Now why is that circular?

C31: Because I'm making myself miserable by saying I'm a shitty person.

T32: That's right. Do you know what a shitty person is, by the way?

C32: Someone who's always and only a shit.

T33: Yeah, right, that is totally—every cell in their body, every aspect of their personality and of their behavior is characterized by the essence of shithood. That's what a shitty person is. Does that describe you?

C33: No, but that makes me even worse, because I know I'm not a shitty person. I'm good at a lot of things and I see that I have good qualities and that I'm responsible and that I can do X, Y and Z, so it makes me feel incredibly frustrated that I can't do this. If I can be competent at other things, then why can I not be competent at something that means so much to me?

T34: But an equal and more powerful argument can be made that because you're so competent in so many areas it's likely you're going to screw up in some area; it *has* to give somewhere. You're bound and determined to put yourself down totally, Jill. You even use sensible arguments to put yourself down nonsensically. You say: "I clearly see that I'm not totally a rotten person; but because I'm not totally a rotten person, that *proves* that I'm totally a rotten person." You see how the logic on that is?

C34: Uh-huh.

T35: You don't call yourself a wonderful person because you're in graduate school, do you?

C35: No.

T36: But you could go totally in that direction. I'm not saying you should do that, but you could. You're saying a rational thing on the one hand and then finishing the sentence irrationally: "I have some very good qualities; but because I have good qualities, I don't have any good qualities." Now how much sense does that make?

C36: I can see it as making sense, as weird as that sounds. It's sort of like having something and not using it, which is a lot worse than not having something at all. For example, I know that I can lose weight because I've done it before. And I know that I can stay down for x time because I've done it before. So why not! That's where the shittiness comes in. I feel like I have the capacity to do it and then I don't. So I feel like somewhere along the way I'm choosing not to and I don't understand why.

T37: But, you *are* choosing not to. You are choosing to *behave* stupidly. I'll be the first person to agree it's not sensible to be overweight. But your contention is: "It's stupid for me to do these things; and because I'm choosing to do these stupid things, everything about me is stupid, or shitty." And that's when you start feeling so awfully rotten about yourself and start feeling helpless and stop trying to diet. What I want you to do is to really put some energy into seeing the difference between *THAT'S* stupid and *I'M* stupid for doing that stupid thing. That's where you're getting bollaxed up. OK?

C37: Yeah.

T38: Now, what I want you to do is think scientifically with me a minute. You're running through your litany of Jill irrationalities. Let's remove it once from you to a person out here. Person Sara behaves stupidly and her contention is, that stupid action, even though she knows better, makes everything about her stupid. What would you say to Sara? To show her that it's stupidity on her part?

C38: I would say that that's just a stupid thing that she's doing and she can't rate herself on one small aspect of her behavior.

T39: Also, she has so many other qualities, both good or bad, and no one quality equals her as a total person. What would you recommend she do?

C39: Tell her to stop rating herself as totally bad.

T40: Why would you recommend that for Sara?

C40: Because it doesn't make sense to rate yourself as totally bad for one stupid act because there's too many other things going on in her life and rating herself like that is just going to make her feel bad pointlessly.

T41: And what benefits come of it?

C41: None.

T42: And what disbenefits come out?

C42: She feels miserable.

T43: For no benefit. What else?

C43: It probably affects her actions so she gets caught up in a cycle of the stupid act.

T44: That's right! Feeling like she has no alternative. And if you had the power would you command Sara to stop that horseshit?

C44: I would.

T45: Now, Jill, still be a scientist and do it to you. What would you say to you. I don't want to hear Jill's litany of irrational nonsense. What would Jill, the scientist, say to Jill, the weight loser?

C45: It makes sense to me to say that, because I'm not a perfect dieter and a sensible eater all the time and because I've got problems in this area, that it doesn't make me a shitty person. Now I can buy all that . . .

T46: You're still a scientist!

C46: . . . That it's only one thing that I'm doing, one part of my life; that I have other things I do well, that would, well, not make me a good person, cause there's bad things I'm doing well; and there's good and bad things I do, and sabotaging myself with my dieting problem is a bad thing that I do.

T47: That's right. Now let me ask you one more question. Why not focus on thinking that way and training yourself to think that way rather than focus on training yourself to think the other, disturbing way? Because the other minute when you started being the scientist you almost jumped in and wanted to perpetuate the training of yourself to down yourself. Why not train yourself that way?

C47: There's no reason not to. I'm just so used to doing it the other way.

T48: Then, why not make a major commitment to stubbornly train yourself to only rate that behavior as stupid and to stubbornly refuse to rate self as stupid? If you really see that logic.

C48: I do see the logic.

T49: Why not do that then?

C49: There's no reason not to.

T50: Will you do it? Will you make the commitment?

C50: Yeah, I will!

T51: So the majority of the time, now that you have the commitment, is to tear apart the idea that "I *am* a shitty person for doing that thing," as opposed to spending most of your time focusing on the idea that you're a shitty person. See, you really spend a great deal of your time running through the irrational logic of: "Because I want to so bad, because I know it's so bad for me, and I still do this stupid thing, that proves that I'm a shitty and stupid person who doesn't deserve anything. I deserve nothing good and can never stick to anything because I'm so weak and hopeless and helpless." You spend so much time focusing on that line of logic that you are going to have to make a commitment to spend the energy and time tearing that down and focusing on the other line of logic. Now, will you do that?

C51: I will if you show me how.

Comment

This lengthy excerpt illustrates the rational-emotive working through process in the early stages of RET. In RET, we are primarily interested in helping people give up long held, strongly believed ideas that cause them both to suffer and to act inefficiently. Like the majority of clients, Jill is exceptionally committed to her ideas about her worthlessness and is very reluctant to give them up.

Impressed with the strength of Jill's belief, the therapist, in typical RET fashion, is highly vigorous, persistent, and directive in attempting to help her dispute it. After telling her in T23 that the way to give up her irrational belief about herself is to analyze it to determine its validity, he initiates a number of working through ploys. These include verbal disputation (T25, T28, T29, T30, T33), information giving and term defining (T26, T32, T33), and directly and powerfully showing her the illogicalness of her reasoning (T30, T34, T35). Each of these are spontaneously used depending on the various responses that Jill offers.

However, as with so many clients, all these efforts are to little avail.   Jill has aι her fingertips a whole litany of well-rehearsed arguments to support her irrational contention, which she readily offers to the therapist as "proof," as she regularly and energetically does to propagandize herself as well (C25, C29, C30, and C36). She has spent a great deal of time and expanded tremendous energy in believing her irrational idea about herself so that it comes "second nature" to her. By the time of this session, her belief in her worth-lessness is so strong that she almost reflexively slides into it (C45), despite the fact that she "knows" it to be illogical and self-defeating (C38 through C44).

Knowing that this is typical in the early stages of RET, the therapist is undaunted. Perhaps most striking in this working through process is the way he moves to intercept Jill's illogical reasoning process. Knowing that she is much better at this train of thinking than at a scientific, data-oriented one, in T30 and in T37 he interrupts her circular and illogical thinking process, and he does it again in T46 when she almost automatically reverts back to her illogical dogma. Then, he virtually forces her to focus on her irrational idea (T37), insists that she think logically about it (T37 through T44), and challenges her to commit herself to a scientific line of reasoning rather than a senseless one (T47 through T51). This type of therapist structuring and control is frequently necessary in the initial stages of RET when clients are rather weak in detecting and disputing their irrational ideas, while at the same time being quite adept at re-hashing what they already believe.

One other thing that we have mentioned throughout this book is prominent in this excerpt. While persistently challenging the content of Jill's ideation, the therapist also goes about the process of teaching her how to think. His goals at this point are twofold: (1) to begin Jill in the process of giving up her belief in her worthlessness, thereby reducing her depression and her poor eating behavior; and (2) to teach her to think objectively so she can become her own problem solving therapist in the future.

T52: I'll try, but will you? All I can give you is a few tools and pat you on the back and challenge you in the sessions, but you're going to have to make the commitment to do it yourself.

C52: I feel like I have to. I can't take much more of this. It's been so crazy. I can't afford to put the kind of energy into this problem that it's been demanding of me.

T53: OK. I'm going to give you three suggestions right away. These are not solutions. These are vehicles to the solutions and you can begin to make inroads, but you're going to have to work at it for a while. The primary prerequisite for doing these three things is to first and foremost recognize that when you spend most of your time telling yourself two things. One is, "That's stupid of me," which I agree with; the other is, "I'm a shitty person for doing the stupid things." You have to really recognize that that's what you put most of your effort into and you therefore, ingrain your irrational thinking. And the second thing is you have to make a commitment to stubbornly and energetically catch yourself thinking those thoughts, and challenging and destroying the idea. OK?

C53: OK. I do know in my head that it's a false idea. I just don't feel it in my gut.

T54: That's because you spend most of your time and energy ingraining this irrational stuff. That's why you have to make the commitment, and if you make the commitment and do what I tell you to do enough weeks in a row, I guarantee you that idea is going to start getting weaker. I can't guarantee it, but I really believe it'll start getting weaker. Take that commitment first. Are you willing?

C54: Yes.

T55: Then let me give you some suggestions. The first thing you can do is written homework on a nightly basis. And what I would suggest you do is to take a piece of paper. On the top of the piece of paper, write down your basic irrational idea: "Because I do this thing that's stupid, I'm a shitty person." OK? And you ask yourself three questions about it. One, "is it true or false?" Now, focus on tearing it apart, not supporting it. You've got a habit of supporting it. Is that true or not? Are you a shitty person?

C55: No. (meekly)

T56: You said that very meekly.

C56: I think I've just been believing it for so long.

T57: But is *it* true? This idea that you're a totally shitty person.

C57: It isn't!

T58: OK. You're taking the idea as an entity by itself. Is *it* true? We're talking science now. Secondly, you ask, "why is it not true?" And you really put effort into figuring out why it's not true. Not, as you've always done, simply believed it without thinking and running your crazy logic through your head. Now, why is that objective idea realistically not true? Then the third thing you ask is: "If I continue to behave in this stupid way which is undesirable, what's the worst thing that's going to happen to me?"

C58: I'm going to continue to be miserable.

T59: No, no, no. You're only going to continue to be miserable if you believe that idea at the top. If you tell yourself you're a shitty person.

C59: Can't I just be plain old miserable about being fat?

T60: I doubt if you'd be miserable. You'd be sorry, but not miserable. But, if you really stop to think what's the worst thing that could happen to you, . . .

C60: I'll continue to be fat. (sadly)

T61: That's right. And you'll have some practical difficulties like clothes not fitting. You weren't really asking the question of what could happen *to* you. You've got to answer that question. Now, those are the three questions. If you would ask those, and be very careful to focus on challenging that idea in order to destroy it, instead of focusing on the ideas you previously had in your head, just letting them flow out like you had no control over them, you'd give the idea up, be less upset, and probably diet better. Now, really be a scientist and do that. Will you do that every night?

C61: OK.

T62: Now do we need to give you an incentive?

C62: I will do it, I've got enough incentive.

T63: You don't need a little operant conditioning here—a punishment, reinforcement paradigm?

C63: No, I *will* do it. Its important enough to do it.

T64: Let's find out.

C64: OK. I'll do it.

Comment

The therapist recognizes that Jill is not yet ready or able to give up the belief of her own worthlessness. Realizing that she will need to put forth a great deal more effort to do so, he belabors the point that a huge commitment on her part is necessary (T52, T53, T54). This is one of the main cores of RET—irrational ideas require frequent, persistent, and energetic counterattacks before they diminish in strength, and clients had better see the logic of this to motivate themselves to undertake such a major effort.

The important role of written homework is illustrated in the remainder of this excerpt. Continuing with the premise that Jill must do a great deal of self-directed disputation in order to get better, the therapist next shows her how to do between-session, written homework. While doing this (T55, T56, T57, T58), he again forcefully emphasizes that she must focus her mind on logically tearing down her belief, not just using it as an opportunity to further ingrain her disturbance-producing idea (T55, T58). He again recognizes that Jill, like so many clients, is so wedded to her irrational idea that she will have to consciously and purposely focus on disputing her belief, or else she will just rehearse her same old nonsense and end up more disturbed than before.

Finally, in the excerpt, the therapist took the opportunity to have Jill actually dispute her irrational idea by answering the three questions she will pose to herself as part of her written homework. At the end he probably made a mistake in not insisting that Jill impose reward-punishment consequences on herself for doing or not doing her homework, given the fact that her irrational idea is so strong and given the fact that many people are too lazy to do it regularly. But, he leaves the door open by indicating (T64) that he will wait for her efforts and perhaps give consequences to her later.

T65: Now, the second thing I want you to do is find five overweight people. I don't mean necessarily gargantuan people, which you're not by the way, but just overweight people. And I'd like for you to ask the same three questions about them that you ask about yourself. And assume that these people stupidly overreact. Now ask the same questions—are they totally stupid or worthless?

C65: Except I don't think I'm totally shitty and totally worthless from just plain being fat.

T66: But they know better than to eat badly too. We're talking about people who have a brain in their head. They've read the studies.

C66: But, I'm sure there are people who are heavy who have accepted that they're heavy and they've decided that they're willing to be heavy and its ok for them. It's not ok for me and that's where the shit comes in. I've decided I won't accept being heavy. I just won't.

T67: Well, you don't know anything about these people, so we can make any assumptions we want about them. Let's assume they're just like you. They don't like being heavy, they would prefer to be thin, and so on. And they're still really over-weight anyway. Ask the same three questions about them, and answer them, stubbornly sticking with rationality, not with Jill's whole litany, cause you're focusing in on reality, not on your habit. OK? (she nods) Now, the third thing I want you to do is an imagery exercise. I'm gonna run you through it once right now. What I want you to do is picture yourself in your mind's eye. Right now you're at the table at this dinner party on Monday. You're sitting at the table and you really don't want to eat but you're eating anyway. Can you picture that? (She nods) And you're starting to feel really bad about you. OK? (She nods) Now, make yourself feel only sorry, only regretful, not shitty about you. Make yourself feel only those things. . . . OK? (She nods) Now, how did you do it?

C67: I practiced the questions. Why does this make me shitty? It's a stupid thing to do, but you'll get over it. You're not a stupid person and you can deal with it. That's an important part that gets me over the hump.

T68: I realize that this is not totally me, it's only an aspect of me. It's only a problem that I have. It's one part of me that's problematic. If you focus on that, you'll first stop feeling like a heel; second, it won't seem so overwhelming; and third, you can focus on the problem itself.

C68: That's a point that's real important. It seems *so overwhelming.*

T69: Right. Because if you believe you're a total shit, what strong, good things could you, a total shit, do? The answer is, little if anything. All a shit can do is hopeless and shitty things. Instead of that, focus on: "I am acceptable. I have this one unacceptable feature and it's a problem." That reduces it to manageable size. You may not be perfect at it, but you can tackle it, undercut it when you don't put yourself down so. . . . You know what happens when you take the shithood out of it? You stop focusing on all of you and the problem becomes only a *part* of you, a dysfunctional behavior, a bad habit. Jill, I want you to do that once a day for about 20 minutes, too. Now, I sense that's going to be harder for you to do than the written homework, because it looks to me like you get into doing it and start getting upset. So it's something that would be easy to avoid. Right?

C69: Right.

T70: We need to give you some incentive for that, I think. Because this is the hardest, it's probably the thing you should do most. So what I'd like to do is give you something as a reward that you have available to you to pleasure yourself on, on a daily basis.

C70: I could read something that I want to read that's not school related. I haven't done that in years.

T71: OK. If you do this imagery exercise, you get one half hour of pleasureable reading. And the other side of it is—what do you have to punish yourself with that's unpleasant, painful?

C71: I guess housecleaning.

T72: What's the most unpleasant part of that?

C72: The bathroom. The toilet bowl, scrubbing the floor.

T73: OK, if you don't do your 20 minutes of REI by 10:00 p.m., you have to completely clean the bathroom before you go to bed. You have to do it.

C73: We'll have the cleanest bathroom in town.

T74: But the point is you don't ever have to do it if you do your REI. . . . So, Jill, we see what the problem is. A major component of your dietary problem has been self-downing. It makes you feel rotten, hopeless, and helpless. And what we're suggesting is that it comes from the idea that, because I'm doing this stupid thing and I know better, then I am a real shitty person. And even though you know some of the time that that's not true, you most of the time believe it to be true and do not see all of your other qualities, and you rate yourself like that.

C74: I think what I am is my own worst enemy. I know I've done something bad, and so I condemn myself. I get into that self-downing you talk about.

T75: You're exactly right. And, I'm confident you can make significant inroads into all that. Now, the last thing I want you to do before the next session is to listen to the tape of this session two times. OK?

C75: OK.

T76: I've given you a lot of work, but that's what changing is all about. OK. See you next week.

Comment

This first session comes to a close with the therapist giving Jill two major homework assignments, one of them being rational-emotive imagery (see Chapter 4). The reason he gives her so much to do is to inundate her with exercises that will facilitate the sort of rational thinking that she is poor at doing, while undercutting her tendency to engage in her too well-learned irrational thinking processes. After doing this the therapist again summarizes the problem for Jill

(T74) and reiterates his belief that she can get better (T75). As a final item, he assigns her the task of listening to the tape of the session, the rationale being again that the more consciously she attends to her irrational thinking and becomes aware of its illogicalness, the more able she will be to intercept it and eventually give it up.

Jill is by no means cured by the end of this first session. As she notes in C74, she is her own worst enemy. She no doubt will need to relearn her insights, readopt her new goals, and repeat her working through efforts over and over. The therapist knows this and will be ready to help her do so again in the next session. But, for the first time, she has clearly seen how she defeats herself and has acknowledged that she applies special rules to herself that do not apply to other human beings. And, perhaps most importantly, she has had her first taste of rational thinking and the positive feelings that go with it. She undoubtedly needs a good deal more RET, but with continued effort, will make significant inroads into her difficulties.

7

Skills-Based Training and Supervision for Rational-Emotive Therapists

The purpose of this chapter is to offer guidance to those who will implement our skills-based model in the training and supervision of RET therapists. Clinical preparation takes place in diverse settings such as university courses, practicums and internships, inservice activities, workshops, and advanced training programs such as those offered by the Institute for Rational-Emotive Therapy. In all of these and other such settings, we believe our skills-based model will prove helpful, for the main goal of clinical preparation remains the same—to impart and foster the development and competent performance of therapy skills.

Before explaining how the skills-based model can be employed, it seems appropriate to review the model and make it as explicit as possible. An understanding of the skills and stages of RET, as displayed in the model, is a requisite for the supervisor and instructor, and we have also found the model to be a foundational learning for beginning therapists. Thus the following figure is an important teaching/learning tool.

As shown in Figure 7-1 and presented in Chapters 2 through 6, the effective practice of RET entails four distinct but overlapping stages. Each stage has its own set of objectives and skills to meet these objectives. Therapists may differ in their particular "styles" of doing RET, and their therapy behavior may appropriately differ from one client to the next so as to respond to clients' unique

Psychodiagnosis	Insight	Working-Through	Re-Education
Establish a Working Relationship and Explore the Client's Concerns	Advancing Hypotheses: Clarifying Irrational Ideas Precisely Defining Terms	Cognitive Methods: Disputation Written Homework Rational Role Reversal Information Giving Rational-Emotive Imagery	Rational-Emotive Imagery
Categorize Client Concerns: Career Concerns Practical Problems Emotional-Behavioral Problems Problems about Problems	Leading Techniques: Using ABC Formula Imagery Contrasting Technique	Emotive Methods: Empathy & Acceptance Shame Exercises Humor Emotive Bibliotherapy	Rational Role Reversal Rational Proselytizing Reinforcing Rational Thinking Rational Indoctrination
Pursue the ABC's Through: Discriminative Listening Pointed Leads Reflective-Clarifying Responses	Confronting Hidden Ideas: Challenging Rhetorical Questions Completing Incomplete Sentences Emphasizing Key Words In-Vivo Assignments	Behavioral-Activity Methods Stay-in-there Assignments Doing It/Risk Exercises Self Managed Rewards and Penalties Self Managed Desensitization	Stress Innoculation Skill Training: Assertion Relaxation
Psychodiagnosis Proper Goal Setting	Maultsby's Analogy Procedure		

Figure 7-1. Rational-Emotive Psychotherapy. Skills-based model.

person-problem characteristics. But the four stages transcend such differences, and the skills within the stages remain the essentials of RET.

Inside each of the four RET stages are therapist skills and methods which determine *if* and *how well* therapy progresses. These competencies are the nuts and bolts of effective RET. When they are performed at a satisfactory level of competence, the RET process flows forth and clients make constructive changes in their cognitive-emotional-behavioral realms. When competency performance is at a low level of quality, the RET process breaks down. Thus, one must have competencies in each of the four stages, and perform these capably, in order to complete the entire RET process.

We should also mention at the outset of this chapter that we make a distinction between training and supervision. As liberally defined here, training is the teaching and imparting of knowledge and skills, and the application and practice of these learnings via simulation and other instructional exercises. Training precedes and makes possible the actual practice of RET.

Supervision is a companion to training, but remains a different function because it follows training and consists of overseeing the actual practice of RET. The supervisor helps therapists employ in psychotherapy those skills they have learned in training.

With the foregoing preface in mind, we can now address ourselves to the topic of training in RET. Specifically, what kind or form of training will most accountably give therapists the skills of RET as outlined in our skills-based model?

SKILLS–BASED TRAINING

One of the great ironies in psychotherapy is that therapists make such limited use of their knowledge and skills outside their profession. An example of this is the therapist who encounters personal problems but uses no self-help techniques to resolve the difficulties. Another irony, more pertinent to this chapter, is the lack of transfer from therapy to training. That is—aren't there some teaching/training methods used in therapy which could also be employed in the preparation of therapists? If RET is a straightforward learning-based approach to therapy, can it contribute something to the training (and supervision) of rational-emotive therapists?   We believe the answer is a resounding *yes*.   Further, we think RET trainers can capitalize upon the entire field of learning, particularly skill learning, and find valuable training principles and techniques.

In a recent book by the second author (Boyd, 1978), a review of training and supervision for psychotherapists was completed.   From this source, and from observations of and experiences in therapy, training, and supervision, we have developed the training guidelines and methods offered here.   These will first be presented, and then synthesized into a recommended training model.

Experiential Learning

A most powerful modality which we strongly recommend for use early in RET training is experiential learning.   This modality takes the form of experiencing and participating in the application of RET to one's own personal life.

Experiential learning has many merits for RET training.   It seems to penetrate the resistance and lazy thinking that often characterizes trainees who have developed such tendencies through umpteen years of boring "education" and degree pursuit.   Such trainees, when given a traditional didactic presentation of RET, may turn off or severely screen the message.   The opposite is often true, however, if trainees can "experience" RET.   At the very least, they will understand the basics (e.g., ABC's) of RET as applied to their personal concerns, and if this application is even a little bit helpful, they will see value in the approach and become enthusiastic about studying it further.

In addition to the motivational merits of experiential learning it also has profound educational value.   That is, trainees can learn how to use RET with others by having it applied to their concerns.   For example, if a trainee is engaged by the instructor in a personal disputation, and successfully thinks his/her way out of an irrational idea, s/he will experientially understand what it's like to dispute as well as having vicariously learned how to help others dispute.

Probably the best experiential learning activity for trainees is to participate in individual sessions of RET; second best would be group RET.   In both activities, the trainee will have the opportunity to experience all four stages of the RET process.

When it is not feasible to offer RET to trainees, there are other experiential learning activities which can be devised. These activities are usually more limited than actual RET in the range of experiential learnings offered, but even a single experience is worth the time and effort expended by the instructor because it can start off training in a positive direction. The intent of these experiential activities is insight—helping people gain as many RET insights as possible. (see Chapter 3) Several of the experiential activities we have found valuable will be briefly described, along with their intended effect. These techniques are merely examples, and trainers are encouraged to develop their own.

Rational Belief Inventories.   Naive audiences and trainees are most susceptible to this technique, and thus it should be used prior to introducing RET. If trainees have studied RET and are familiar with irrational beliefs, the instructor is advised to use another technique.

Experiential learning occurs when trainees complete a rational belief inventory (of which there are numerous versions) and discover, through interpretation of the results, that they did endorse some of the irrational beliefs on the inventory. Usually the interpreter must help trainees understand and then dispute the irrational belief if a true understanding is to accrue. When this is accomplished, trainees will have gained the insight that they are capable of irrational thinking, but that rational thinking can be achieved through disputation.

Rational Self Analysis (RSA).   An RSA exercise leads participants through the ABC's of RET. They are asked to identify and describe in affective detail a recent emotional upset from their personal lives; then they are requested to clearly describe the activating event they were upset about; last they are assisted in finding and disputing the irrational ideas that led to the emotional upset. This final step can be done by asking the following four questions and challenging the answers.

What do I see as being awful or horrible?
How am I saying I can't stand it, it's intolerable?
What "should" or "must" am I saying about this situation?
Who or what am I condemning?

Another tact is to have participants examine lists of irrational beliefs and find those that seem to hit the meaning behind their upset feelings. In both methods, the objective is to help participants understand the ABC paradigm, and in particular to recognize their B's.

Imagery Exercise. We first discovered this imagery technique while doing a research project in which subjects were asked to alternate imagined scenes of pleasant experiences and those of social rejection (e.g., being stood up for a date). They were to record their post-scene feelings on an affect adjective checklist, and as expected, results showed that the subjects experienced marked changes in their feelings from one scene to the next. Pleasant scenes evoked pleasant emotions, and visions of social rejection produced anxiety, anger, depression, and so forth.

Subjects were amazed at the influence their images had on their feelings—they could see their emotions recorded on the checklist and thus could not escape admitting them. Many subjects freely voiced the thoughts that accompanied their images and feelings, and not surprisingly, irrational ideation was linked to negative emotions and scenes of social rejection.

From the above research study, we found an experiential technique for insight. We now use these steps to lead trainees into discovering the contingency between images, thoughts, and feelings. Moreover, by fostering free discussion and exploration of participant's internal monologues, they express irrational ideas that they would normally suppress. At this point in the exercise, the trainer can introduce RET concepts and help trainees understand their experience.

Audio-Video Recordings. Recalcitrant and highly defensive clients can sometimes gain RET insights by watching/listening to video and audio recordings of their therapy sessions. They can hear and see irrational beliefs in their voice and behavior, they become aware of their defensiveness toward the therapist's hypotheses, and so on. Insight is most likely when they openly deny a thought, feeling, or behavior, and then are immediately confronted with the recording in the therapy session.

Trainees can find insights in the same way. By imagining a recent emotional upset, and "putting words to their feeling" while being recorded, they produce a record of irrational meanings and ideas which are undeniable. The record can be used to analyze beliefs and find out exactly how trainees disturbed themselves.

These four experiential exercises can be altered and combined to the trainer's desire, and new exercises are easily developed. Whatever the technique, the goal remains RET insight, the same discoveries clients get in therapy as described in Chapter 3.

Didactic Instruction

Of the instructional/learning dimensions to be mentioned in regard to RET training, the didactic dimension is the most traditional and well known. Didactic instruction consists of reading, lecture and discussion—mainstays of pedagogy. But any good thing can be overdone, and this is certainly true for didactic instruction. If employed to the neglect of other types of instruction, the didactic method can deteriorate training.

We believe didactic instruction is particularly important in the beginning of RET training. At this time, it can give trainees a description of the RET approach, and then a thorough explanation of RET theory. Our reason for advocating such a didactic start to training is that RET is first and foremost a theory (Chapter 1) and second a methodological approach to psychotherapy. Learning to perform RET is therefore a process of developing an understanding of RET propositions about human personality and psychotherapeutic change, and subsequently utilizing this knowledge via RET skills (Chapters 2 through 5).

Once trainees have studied the RET theory and therapy approach, they are ready to learn the skills-based model—the skills, techniques, and methods of performing RET. They do not abandon theory and substitute skills, rather, both become areas of study as skills are related to theoretical propositions. Didactic instruction in RET skills is most helpful when it helps students link *skills* (i.e., the therapist's behavioral acts) to their *intended effects* (i.e., how the skills influence clients) and to the *theoretical propositions* upon which the skill-effect bond is based.

In closing the topic of didactic instruction, we want to encourage instructors to force trainees to *think*. Group discussions, frequent quizzes, and other teaching methods can be used to help trainees ask and seek answers to theoretically and clinically relevant questions. The ability to make clinical judgements begins in this manner rather than through rote learning.

Before going further with our training guidelines, we should say that trainees are assumed to have completed or be in the process of finishing a comprehensive program of preparation in a help-giving discipline. Skills-based training in RET can be a major part of such preparation or an addition to it, but we are not suggesting that it substitute or replace an academic degree program in psychology, social work, psychiatry, or the like.

Modeling/Observational Learning

Accompanying experiential learning and didactic instruction as a recommended modality for RET training is observational learning. A substantive body of research studies (Boyd, 1978) have shown the efficacy of modeling for the teaching of psychotherapeutic skills, and it is unlikely that a quality training program could be designed without modeling instruction being a prominent part. We believe this is particularly true for our skills-based model of RET, and we are presently developing a series of videotapes for the observational learning of RET skills as outlined in Chapters 2 through 5.

Observational learning is used for RET training by showing skill-demonstrations to trainees. These models can be written, such as therapy typescripts or excerpts therefrom illustrating focal skills, and/or they can be live or video- and audio-recordings of RET. We have found live demonstrations in class to be particularly stimulating for students. Whatever the form, these models can provide an impressive learning impact upon trainees *if* they are used properly by the instructor, and Albert Bandura's (1969, 1976) writings and research are the basis for the straightforward guidelines which we now pass on.

Gross to Specific. The modeling effects from observational learning range from *gross to specific.* Gross effects are global learnings which ordinarily precede specifics. They require less didactic preparation than specific skill learnings, and they are not likely to produce skill performance in the trainee. Through the observation of an RET session, some examples of gross modeling effects are noticing that the therapist was active and directive, that the therapist asked a lot of questions, and that the client was calmer at the end of the session than in the beginning.

Specific modeling effects, in contrast to gross effects, may require a didactic preface which teaches observational cues. They are predominantly behavioral, though informational and attitudinal content may also be gained. In regard to our skills-based model, the specific modeling effects we target are the acquisition of those therapist skill-behaviors which comprise the four stages of RET. However, we recommend starting at the gross level and progressively moving toward specifics.

Preparation and Attending. Two more interrelated guidelines for observational learning concern the need to prepare trainees for modeling so they will attend to focal skills. We have frequently seen these two guidelines violated when instructors show an RET demonstration to a naive and unappreciative audience. The audience watches the demonstration, and then proceeds to make comments about details of the demonstration which are extraneous to the therapist's skills and effect. Their responses indicate that even gross learnings were missed!

Ineffectual outcomes such as these are usually avoided if instructors precede modeling, even gross modeling, with didactic instruction which prepares the trainee for the intended effect. An introductory film on RET can be prefaced with readings and a discussion about RET. An advanced group of trainees can read our description of disputation (Chapter 4), for instance, before watching a demonstration of the skill. And so forth.

Given such didactic preparation, trainees will attend to focal skills and ignore irrelevant material in modeling demonstrations. They will "acquire" skills in their imagination, gaining the capacity to see the model in their mind's eye. This kind of acquisition is necessary if the skill is to be translated into actual performance—the goal of RET training.

A final note on preparation and attending is that it also counteracts the aversive reactions trainees can have toward RET models. Some trainees react to RET demonstrations by feeling overwhelmed with the complexity of the model. There are so many techniques which are not understood that trainees conclude they can never learn RET. Moreover, if RET conflicts with some of their attitudes about therapy (e.g., "be quiet and let the client determine what to discuss") they defensively and impulsively conclude that "RET is not for me." Again, preparation and attending can stop-gap these unfortunate reactions.

Incentive, Length, and Discrimination. Among the many things that could serve as guidelines for the use of observational learning in the training of therapists is incentive, length, and discrimination. In practical terms these three terms mean that:

1. Observers attend to modeled skills more closely if they have an incentive to do so. For example, if a quiz follows the modeling exposure, or if modeling is part of an exercise where observers are expected to learn and then respond, they will concentrate more closely than if there is no incentive.
2. Brief modeling exposures, with a minimum of irrelevant stimuli, are more effective in producing the acquisition of skill-behavior than long modeling exposure with an abundance of irrelevant material.
3. Modeled skills with distinctive properties are acquired more easily than vague models. And, according to Robert Carkhuff (1969), the exercise of simply discriminating one skill from another, and assessing different levels of skill fidelity, is an important learning step toward eventual skill performance. Later in the chapter we will describe a "skill discrimination exercise."

Skill Practice and Shaping

The last major training dimension we will mention for the preparation of RET therapists is a three step sequence of skill practice, performance feedback, and repeated skill practice. This sequence, found in many skill-training programs and having special prominence in microcounseling (Ivey, 1976), is really a behavioral shaping procedure. Trainees attempt to perform, within simulation exercises, those focal skills which they have learned experientially, didactically and through modeling. As part of the exercise, trainees receive feedback on their performance from the instructor, peer trainees, or self-critique. Following feedback, trainees try to improve their performance in a second trial by further shaping and refining the focal skill-behaviors. The three step sequence can be repeated as many times as necessary until a satisfactory level of skill-performance is demonstrated.

Exercises for skill practice and shaping are easily developed and the greater the variety, the more pleasing to trainees. We will describe several different kinds that have been successful in our training.

Discriminative Listening Exercises. The listening skills of RET therapists are usually overlooked by laypeople and trainees who observe, instead, verbal responses. Opponents of RET go so far as to say that RETers *do not* listen to clients. Both the overlookers and opponents are wrong, for RET therapists do listen very closely to clients—but they listen for things which other therapy approaches ignore—in particular, the ideas, philosophies, and attitudes which precipitate emotional-behavioral problems.

Trainees do not easily acquire RET listening skills, for the development of this competency requires much instruction, practice, and actual therapy experience. Listening skills begin by didactically learning what RETers listen for, watching them do this, and then practicing the skill of discriminative listening. Skill-practice can be gained by listening and/or watching the recordings of clients in therapy. Instructors can erase or edit out the therapists' responses, allowing trainees to listen only to clients. Guidelines such as these can help focus trainees' listening.

- Listen to this client and identify the activating event in his/her problem.
- Now, sort out the client's emotions. What are the predominant ones you hear being expressed?
- Having identified the client's A's and C's, let's now try to target beliefs, attitudes, and philosophies. Find the B's.

- In this segment there are several problems expressed; identify and categorize them.
- No one has yet spotted an emotional problem about an emotional problem. There is one in this segment, and we've just read and discussed this type of problem category, so let's look at the tape again and try to find it.
- Listen for disguised expressions of irrational ideas—rhetorical questions, incomplete sentences, and key words.

Because listening is an integral part of many skill-practice exercises not directed at listening, trainees generally receive ample listening practice. But we encourage instructors to give separate attention to listening skills, for skill deficiency in this area sabotages the entire training process by prohibiting other skills from developing.

Skill Discrimination Exercises. When trainees have gained an understanding of RET skills through didactic instruction and have seen these skills in action, they can begin to identify and discriminate among them. This discrimination ability is a prelude to actually performing RET skills, and it is enhanced by listening to or watching recorded therapy sessions and pointing out the skills. Gradually trainees move beyond simple identification to questions of higher order discrimination: Was the skill performed poorly, adequately, or expertly? Should the skill have been used in this instance? What skill (if any) would have been more appropriate in this instance? When trainees ask and accurately answer these questions they can provide critique and supervision to their peers.

Verbal Response Exercises. Perhaps the most formidable skill area for RET trainees to tackle is "knowing what to say and how to say it." Experienced therapists are rarely lost for words, while trainees are frequently stopped cold by unexpected client responses. Our article entitled "Psychotherapeutic Responses to Some Critical Incidents in RET" (Grieger and Boyd, 1977) addresses this issue.

A direct assault on trainees' verbal deficits can be mounted through verbal response exercises. These skill practice exercises, instituted after trainees have received didactic and modeling instruction in the verbal techniques of RET, systematically teach trainees to use verbal techniques from the skills-based model (see Figure 7-1). Paper and pencil exercises can present trainees with client statements to which they respond in writing with selected verbal techniques (pointed leads, clarifications, advance hypotheses, etc.). Instructors can use video- and audio-recordings of clients in therapy to offer trainees an opportunity to play the role of therapist and practice verbal techniques. Roleplaying exercises similarly present trainees with life-like therapy situations which call for responding skills. In all of these instructional methods the goal is to practice the essential RET verbal techniques in authentic therapy situations.

Case Study Exercise.   The case study exercise is one that can be used early in training to practice skills from all four stages of the RET process. Trainees read a detailed and clear case study, perhaps one from the instructor's clinical experience, and then proceed to answer a list of questions. The questions are those that RET therapists ask themselves during a case, and the trainee's skills are both developed and tested by the questions.

1. After reading the case study, analyze the client's concerns and place them into the appropriate categories: career concerns, practical problems, emotional-behavioral problems, emotional problems about other problems.
2. Identify the ABC's in those emotional-behavioral problems identified in question 1.
3. Write a brief psychodiagnosis proper in the words you would use when sharing it with the client.
4. What are the goals you would recommend for therapy, based on the diagnosis proper?
5. Complete a Rational Self Help Form for one of the client's troublesome ABC sequences.
6. Design an in vivo homework assignment that would promote client insight into a troublesome ABC sequence.
7. Write an analogy a la Maultsby which would reflect a problematic ABC sequence.
8. Write a rational-emotive imagery assignment to help the client work-through one of his/her emotional-behavioral problems.

9. Write a shame exercise for the client.
10. Write a behavioral-activity assignment for the client that would help him/her work-through one of his/her emotional-behavioral problems.
11. Describe how you would use a reeducation technique with this client, assuming a successful RET process was nearing an end.

Triad Roleplay Exercise.   Roleplaying is a training technique with enormous utility because it can tap so many learning avenues. By playing a client's role, trainees get closer to client dynamics, diagnostic understanding of the client is enhanced by acting out the ABC's. When playing the therapist's role the objective of roleplaying is skill practice. Trainees can perform newly learned skills in a lifelike but non-threatening situation.

A particularly powerful roleplay technique, borrowed from Spice and Spice (1976), is a triad exercise using three trainees. One plays the therapist role, a second is the client, and the third trainee is called the supervisor. The instructor can direct the triad exercise toward specific skills by assigning a role to the client, asking the therapist to practice a particular skill(s), and making the supervisor responsible for critique and feedback. By carrying out this exercise three times, and rotating roles, each participant will gain experience with skill practice, playing client dynamics, and supervision.

Instructors can put more flexibility into the exercise by allowing trainees to use their own personal concerns in the client role, and by permitting therapists to perform those skills they think are appropriate for the therapy situation. This way of using the triad roleplay exercise is desirable when trainees are adept at basic skills; then they are ready to practice the choosing, integrating, and performance of multiple skills as is done in actual RET sessions.

Skill-Training Guidelines

An extensive treatise on the training of psychotherapists is not possible in this brief chapter, and we have limited our remarks to the four major instructional/learning dimensions of training. But before the chapter enters a discussion of supervision we wish to offer the following guidelines for skills-based training in RET.

Getting Started.   Skills-based training is best begun with the didactic study of RET theory, a thorough and descriptive look at the RET method, and finally an overview of the skills-based model. Additional experiential learning is desirable, preferably via therapy for trainees and/or through periodic experiential exercises at the beginning and spread throughout training is another alternative.   This kind of solid beginning prepares trainees to be adroit skill learners.

Using the Model.   When trainees have gained an understanding of RET from their introductory study, training can be turned toward skills. Starting at the beginning of the skills-based model, and using the instructional/learning dimensions previously described, instructors can focus training on discrete skills and skill-sets as they lead trainees through the model.

Performance Objectives.   We suggest that instructors set performance objectives as evaluative criteria for training and trainees. For each skill in the skills-based model, the performance objective would be the competent demonstration of the skill within simulation exercises. Certainly training would be accountable and trainees competent if such objective were used and met.

SKILLS–BASED SUPERVISION

The questions to which we address this part of the chapter are: what kind or form of supervision will most accountably promote the competent performance of RET? As supervisors, how can we help supervisees put the skills-based model of RET into action? To answer these questions we first overview supervision, suggest an approach to RET supervision that has been effective in our work, and then go on to discuss the operations, techniques, and problems that characterize RET supervision.

Supervision Overview

In this chapter's introduction we defined supervision as the function of monitoring the actual practice of RET and helping supervisees employ the skills they developed in training. While this is an accurate definition, two main points deserve further explanation. Of first note is that as a function, supervision consists of *multiple activities.* Authorities on supervision have settled on four activities which comprise the supervision function: consultation, training, therapy, and evaluation (Boyd, 1978). If we closely observed supervisors as they interact with supervisees, we would probably see them moving from one activity to another. They would offer consultative assistance, for example, in regard to diagnosing a client or constructing a viable homework assignment. When supervisees encountered skill problems the supervisors would do some training, perhaps by modeling and skill practice within the supervision session or by giving the supervisee some self-instructional homework assignments. If supervisees encountered emotional concerns which disrupted their learning, supervisors would offer short-term therapeutic assistance. And, throughout supervision, supervisors would provide evaluative feedback. To summarize, supervision is not a rigid and narrow role but a rather broad one having four activities among which the supervisor is continually moving.

A second aspect of our supervision definition deserving clarification is the implied ideal that skills-based RET training should precede supervision. While this is certainly an ideal worthy of pursuit, it does not reflect reality. Training does not always precede supervision (for various not-so-good reasons), and supervisees do not always have a fully developed repertoire of RET skills when they enter supervision. So, realistically speaking, the RET supervisor had better be prepared to deal with supervisees having a range (bad to excellent) of training backgrounds and skill proficiencies.

A final overview comment regards the supervisor's approach, that is, the theoretical/methodological thrust that guides and characterizes the supervisor's activities. Over the years there has emerged two basic approaches to therapist supervision—the psychotherapeutic and behavioral approaches. Even if the RET supervisor is not familiar with these two, s/he may unintentionally fall into one or the other because they are universal orientations.

The psychotherapeutic approach to supervision is similar to therapy; supervisors provide a therapeutic relationship to their supervisees in which the dynamics of psychotherapy can be explored and constructively altered. Together they examine the interaction or interpersonal dynamics between therapist and client, as well as the intrapersonal dynamics (e.g., thoughts, feelings, images) within each party. The purpose of this examination is to uncover dynamic patterns which are inhibiting therapy progress. If and when such patterns are discovered, the supervisor employs psychotherapy techniques to help the supervisee change the troublesome dynamics. For example, if a therapist and client were aggressively sparring back and forth, the supervisor would help the therapist to resolve his/her anger and to respond in a more therapeutic manner toward the client.

Psychotherapeutic supervision does not restrict itself to the dynamics in therapy, but also attends to dynamics within supervision. Supervisee emotions and defensiveness toward the supervisor may be investigated, and supervisors themselves may share and discuss their own dynamics. The overriding objective of psychotherapeutic supervision is to teach therapists to be a monitor of their own dynamics and to use these dynamics therapeutically.

Behavioral supervision contrasts the psychotherapeutic approach in its focus on skills rather than dynamics. The purpose of behavioral supervision is to help supervisees eliminate inappropriate social behaviors and ineffective therapy techniques from their psychotherapy style, and to promote the development and practice of effective therapy skills. To do this supervisors enter a consultative/training stance and follow these steps (Boyd, 1978):

1. A skill analysis and assessment of the therapist's psychotherapy style is conducted.
2. Skill-based supervision goals are set.
3. Supervision strategies, based on skill-learning principles and techniques, are constructed and implemented. Strategies preferably include both supervisee and supervisor responsibilities.
4. The supervisee's progress is evaluated and skill gains are generalized.

The behavioral approach sounds quite formal and structured when described, but in practice it flows smoothly via the supervisor-supervisee working alliance and regular meetings. Steps one through four are repeated again and again as the supervisee's therapy goes through the stages of the skills-based model, and as the supervisee progressively gains proficiency in all the skills of the model.

Both the behavioral and psychotherapeutic approaches to supervision are widely accepted and practiced, and each one has received empirical support (Boyd, 1978). The RET supervisor is thus left with a choice—which approach will be most effective in fostering the competent practice of RET?

RET Supervision: A Psychobehavioral Approach

Our experiences in supervising RET therapists has led us to refuse choosing between the psychotherapeutic and behavioral approaches. We believe that each approach has strengths, and that by integrating the two, a psychobehavioral hybrid is created which is superior to either of the major approaches alone. Further, we have concluded that supervisees can benefit from both kinds of supervision because of the nature of their supervision difficulties.

There are three kinds of targets which supervisees offer the RET supervisor: (1) emotional concerns, (2) skill problems, and (3) emotional/skill problems. The emotional concerns of supervisees come from three sources—their private lives, therapy-based upsets, and supervision-based upsets. Private life concerns are things such as a relationship going sour, financial difficulties, and the death of a loved one. Examples of emotional upsets about therapy are anger toward the client, feelings of incompetence in the therapist's role, and frustration over one's imperfect therapy performance. Supervision-based concerns include a demand of the supervisor's approval, fearing disapproval and refusing to play therapy tapes, etc. Each of these three types of emotional upset hinders supervisee performance and thus become the province of supervision. The psychotherapeutic approach to supervision (using RET) is well suited for these emotional concerns.

Supervisee skill problems are a second target for supervisors, and these consist of *skill deficits* and/or *performance difficulties.* When supervisees have minor skill deficits, the supervisor institutes remedial training; major deficits indicate the supervisee is unprepared for supervision and would best be referred to a skills-training program. Performance difficulties, in contrast to skill-deficits, are to be expected.

Even trainees who have completed skills-based preparation may perform clumsily and need the supervisor's help with skill refinement. They will be unsure of themselves and want technical assistance in constructing and following a course of action. Though they have acquired RET skills, under the pressure of actual therapy they will sometimes forget *when* and *how* to use them. For these and other skill problems we recommend following the skills-based model and using training techniques from the behavioral approach to supervision.

A third target for supervision is emotional/skill problems. These combine the two prior problems and are particularly difficult for supervisors because the supervisee is emotionally upset *and* performing inadequately in therapy. In these dual problems, the psychobehavioral method proves itself because neither of the major approaches is sufficient for problem resolution. The next few paragraphs will explain this point further.

The Psychobehavioral Method. Essentially, the psychobehavioral method consists of remaining alert to the three kinds of supervisee problems, and treating these problems with RET, training techniques, or both. As supervision goes on the supervisor alternates between RET and training, but when an emotional/skill problem is confronted a truly integrative response is in order. First, the supervisor delves into the emotional part of the problem with RET. This part is approached first because as emphasized in earlier chapters, emotional distress disrupts behavioral performance, and by resolving the supervisee's emotional concerns skill performance may improve.

Supervisees' Emotional Concerns. Emotional concerns from supervisees' private lives will not be discussed here because they are the same as those for clients, and Chapters 1 through 5 have touched many of these. We would be remiss, however, not to mention that supervisors have a responsibility to remove seriously distressed supervisees from RET practice. The disturbed party can be referred to an RET therapist and resume supervised practice when the emotional problem is resolved.

Emotional concerns from therapy and supervision deserve special mention, for they are almost inevitable. It is our hypothesis, as well as others' (Kell and Burow, 1970; Kell and Mueller, 1966), that the experience of supervised psychotherapy practice elicits the supervisee's ideational and emotional problems. Without going into detailed explanation, a list of the most common concerns is offered.

- *Impatience:* Supervisees sometimes demand that the route to RET proficiency be quick and easy. They become frustrated at the slowness of their skill progress, and the more frustrated they become, the more they inhibit their learning.
- *Perfectionism:* Another road to LFT, and anxiety, is setting unrealistically high standards for your therapy performance, and then fearing that you will make an error. Upon making mistakes, supervisees compound the problem by self downing and feeling depressed.
- *Resistance and anger:* Some supervisees are resistant and angry. They cannot use constructive criticism because they demand total approval, and when they don't get it, they condemn the supervisor.
- *Dependency:* Supervisees who constantly seek the supervisor's advice fear making mistakes, and condemn themselves as weak and powerless, are dependent to the extreme of being unable to learn by their own initiative. Their emotional dependency completely blocks supervision.
- *Upsets with clients:* There are many kinds of emotional upsets supervisees can have with clients. They can get angry at clients, feel sympathy for them, become frustrated over their lack of improvement, condemn and dislike them, etc. These emotional problems stem from therapists over-personalizing their relationships with clients and imbuing the interaction with the relationship problems that are characteristic to their personalities.

The RET supervisor deals directly with supervisee problems of this type, practicing short-term therapy with the supervisee as client. But supervision should not become therapy; excursions into therapy are relatively brief, and we encourage supervisors to keep the main focus of supervision on RET skills. Even when emotional concerns require a majority of the supervision session at least one fourth can be reserved for skill work. It follows, then, that the second step in supervising an emotional/skill problem from the psychobehavioral method is to return the focus of supervision to RET skill performance.

Supervisory Skill-training Techniques. When RET supervision focuses on the supervisee's therapy performance the skills-based model (see Figure 7-1) becomes a central ingredient. Skill focus begins by asking: where in the RET process is this supervisee's therapy—to what stage has therapy progressed? Answering this question helps to orient the supervisor and supervisee, and tells them which therapy objectives and skills are timely. If the supervisee has reached a certain stage but has performed poorly and missed objectives in earlier stages it is best to backtrack. Illustratively, difficulties with the working-through stage may indicate that the client has not been afforded rational-emotive insight. A quick check by the supervisor into prior therapy sessions will offer evidence, and if insight was not accomplished the supervisee can be guided in this direction.

Backtracking is not necessarily a sign of ineffective RET; experienced RETers have the knack of monitoring the therapy process and the client's reactions, and finding things they missed in earlier sessions. So it is good training for supervisees to continually assess their locus in the four stage process, and to review past sessions for overlooked skills and objectives.

Once supervision has settled on the proper RET stage to focus on, an analysis and assessment of skills can be done. Again the skills-based model (Figure 7-1) becomes a tool by showing the skills to look for and evaluate. The supervisor reinforces skill proficiencies in the supervisee's therapy performance, and skill deficiencies and performance difficulties are targeted as supervision goals. Next, supervision becomes a skill-training endeavor in pursuit of skill-goals.

An extensive review of skill-training techniques appropriate for RET supervision is available from the following references: Boyd (1978), Delaney (1972), Kaslow (1977), Krumboltz (1967), and Levine and Tilker (1974). From these sources five basic techniques will be listed here and annotated.

- *Roleplaying:* Within the supervision session a most valuable training technique is roleplaying. The supervisor models the focal skill performance as the supervisee plays the client role. They then rotate roles, and the supervisee practices the focal skill. Feedback and more practice can follow.

- *Co-Therapy:* A fine technique for helping supervisees make the shift from training to actual practice is co-therapy. By working with an experienced therapist (supervisor) the supervisee models skills, learns what the RET process is all about, and accepts increasing amounts of responsibility for conducting therapy sessions.

- *Peer supervision:* Supervisees can learn much by listening to and critiquing each others' therapy tapes. If they have a grounding in the skills-based model and know how to use it for critique purposes, they can promote skill development and refinement. However, peer supervision can flounder if participants are not first trained in a method and structure to follow.

- *Self-instructional homework:* Just as RET asks clients to work on their problems between therapy sessions, RET supervision helps supervisees set up self-instructional homework assignments. Examples are reading a skill manual or therapy transcript, watching a modeling tape and recording the incidences of a focal skill, performing and recording a skill-practice exercise, critiquing one's own therapy tape with an eye on certain skills or inappropriate behaviors, and skill training modules which could include many of these assignments.

- *Supervisory critique:* Supervisees with a solid training background, and few skill deficiencies, can improve their therapy performance by supervisory critique. Together the supervisor and supervisee review a therapy tape and critique it, perhaps with the aid of an RET Skill Rating Form (see Appendix). The supervisee receives reinforcement and instruction concerning skills, and gradually a skill shaping process occurs. Though critiquing is a supervision staple, it loses its power and becomes monotonous if not interspersed with other training techniques.

Summary—Psychobehavioral Method. We have proposed a psychobehavioral method for RET supervision—an awareness of emotional and skill problems in supervisees, and the supervisory treatment of these problems with an integration of therapeutic and skill-training techniques. The psychobehavioral perspective and method is perhaps most clearly displayed when treating emotional/skill problems because within each supervision session an integrative methodology is displayed. In these instances, the supervisor practices RET and teaches its skills.

The psychobehavioral method weaves its way through RET supervision and maintains an order and consistency to the supervisor's efforts. But there is much more to the practice of RET supervision, and in the final part of this chapter we will discuss practical aspects.

Practicing RET Supervision

Supervisory Relationship. One of the disputed topics in therapy supervision is what to make of the supervisor – supervisee relationship. Should it be warm and caring, or cool and aloof? And what if the supervisee has feelings toward the supervisor—affection, anger, anxiety, etc.?

In RET supervision, we place less emphasis on the warmth and closeness of the supervisory relationship than the psychotherapeutic approach. A cordial and empathic relationship is highly desirable for an easy going professional association, but we do not see the need for interpersonal closeness. We think interpersonal relationships are a playground for neurosis (as well as a pleasurable and stimulating experience,) and that close, intimate relationships are more emotionally provocative than less intimate ones. For supervision we choose the latter, knowing that sooner or later there will be some tense and confrontive moments between the two parties, and that in a professional relationship these incidences are easier to handle than if the two are close friends.

Further, we find that supervisees bring enough affective dynamics to supervision to keep us busy, as described earlier in "emotional concerns of supervisees." If we supervisors bring a like set of intrapersonal dynamics to supervision the process will be doomed. As supervisors, we had better have our emotional state in order so we can give therapeutic assistance to supervisees.

Finally, we find that supervisees experientially learn much from interacting with a rational supervisor in a healthy professional relationship. They are often relieved that the relationship is not threatening or blameful, that they are free to openly express themselves without having to soothe the supervisor's wounded ego, and they appreciate the supervisor's frank feedback and efficient use of time. There is, of course, wide latitude in what kind of a supervisory relationship to establish with an RET supervisee, but the preceding comments are characteristic of what we have observed across many RET supervisors.

Conducting the Session. An RET supervision session has the same efficiency as therapy. The supervisor does not rush, but proceeds calmly and surely, following a definite set of procedures and operations.

1. Supervision is done through regularly scheduled meetings.
2. Supervisees record their RET performances on audio or video tape and bring these tapes to supervision.
3. Supervisees are asked to review their therapy tapes before coming to supervision, and to choose portions of the tapes to work on in the supervision session.
4. A brief report of each therapy session is required by some supervisors. By reading this at the beginning of the session, the supervisor is oriented to the case, and information gathering time is reduced. Report writing also helps supervisees collect their thoughts.
5. Supervision sessions usually begin by discussing the supervisee's completion of homework assignments, then attention is given to the supervisee's recent cases.
6. The skills-based model of RET is used when reviewing therapy tapes. Questions are asked by the supervisor such as:
   At what stage of RET is this session?
   What are your objectives, and what skills are you using to reach them?
7. Much of the supervision session is devoted to skill critiquing and a discussion of the client's reactions to therapy. The supervisor offers assistance from a consultant stance.
8. When skill deficiencies or performance difficulties are found, the supervisor utilizes skill-training methods and assigns homework that continues skill training outside the supervision session.

9. A particular skill deficiency may receive continuing attention in supervision although the skill is not germane to the supervisee's immediate therapy cases. Homework assignments and training techniques are continued until the supervisee exhibits skill proficiency.
10. When supervisee emotional concerns are encountered, the supervisor becomes a therapist and administers short-term RET.
11. An RET supervision session is closed by summarizing its content and, with the supervisee's aid, constructing homework assignments by which the supervisee can continue to work through emotional concerns or skill problems.

Individual Therapy Styles. Skills-based RET supervision does not attempt to force supervisees to replicate the therapy style of the supervisor, Albert Ellis, or any other therapist. Though we consider the skills in our model to be essential to the effective practice of RET, we likewise recognize that individual differences are an inevitability, and indeed desirable. As Hogan (1964) has suggested, inexperienced therapists tend to dependently conform to a therapy method, but as supervision and experience are gained, they gradually adapt the therapy method to their personality. Eventually they arrive at some creative techniques of their own. From this perspective, we encourage RET supervisors to facilitate the development of personalistic therapy styles, but without compromising essential RET skills.

Group Supervision. The techniques and methods described in this chapter apply to group supervision as well as sessions with individuals, and the advantages of the group method make it highly desirable. In group supervision all participants learn in two ways. Their skill discrimination and clinical judgment are enhanced as they offer critique feedback to whoever is presenting a case or tape, and each member receives a wide variety of comments and suggestions from group members about his/her therapy performance.

A valuable group method we learned from Bill Knaus (1976), former co-director of training at the Institute for Rational-Emotive Therapy, consists of these steps. Each group member presents, one at a time, a therapy tape to the group and asks for supervisory assistance with a certain segment and its skills. This first step puts goal setting responsibility on the supervisee. Next, the group spends an allotted length of time critiquing the supervisee's taped performance, and each group member is asked by the supervisor to offer feedback.

In the third step the supervisor summarizes the critique, clarifying and condensing content so the supervisee is better able to understand and learn from the group's feedback. The supervisor then comments on each group member's performance, reinforcing those critique points that were helpful and those that went astray. This step has a shaping effect on group performance and produces better group supervision. Last, the supervisor adds his/her final comments, and asks the supervisee to summarize the salient aspects of the session.

Supervisee Roadblocks. In Chapters 2 through 5, we have identified roadblocks and pitfalls that supervisees typically struggle with during RET, and we encourage supervisors to become familiar with them. A significant portion of the supervisor's time is spent helping supervisees work through these hurdles, for roadblocks are indigenous to the learning of RET. If they are not resolved in supervision, they can become permanent weaknesses in the RET therapist's style.

Our supervisory approach to roadblocks is the psychobehavioral method, described earlier in this chapter. To illustrate how this method is applied to roadblocks, we will explain our strategy for dealing with a supervisee's "demand for cooperation" (see Chapter 3), a roadblock from the insight stage of RET. Let's assume our supervisee is dealing with an argumentative client who resists insight. A scenario is repeated in therapy wherein the supervisee attempts to impart insight by clarifying the client's irrational ideas and the client responds by stubbornly refusing to listen and by changing the topic. Subsequent to such incidents the supervisee makes a few angry remarks and then becomes passive, allowing the client to dominate the remainder of the session with whining, demanding, and awfulizing ramblings.

Supervision would intervene into this roadblock by first focusing on the supervisee's feelings of anger and frustration toward the client. The ABC's of the scenario would be revealed, and the irrational beliefs behind the emotions would be disputed. Here is an excerpt from a supervision session with one of our supervisees (therapist) who was demanding cooperation.

Supervisor: Don, this sounds like a difficult client for you.

Therapist: That's an understatement, this guy refuses to participate, he dominates! And he doesn't listen to anything I say!

Supervisor: And you are getting frustrated . . .

Therapist: Yeah, (sigh)

Supervisor: and angry.

Therapist: Well, I don't think I'm angry, it's that he is so frustrating to work with.

Supervisor: I'm not going to argue about whether it's anger or not, but if you listen to your tape again I think you will hear some rather terse and angry remarks from yourself. This leads me to hypothesize anger. But even if it's not anger, just frustration, it would be a good idea for us to look at how you are creating it, because I think it's beginning to interfere with your therapy. Think about it, Don, what are you telling yourself to create that frustration and perhaps anger?

Therapist: Hmm . . . (pause) . . . maybe I'm saying this client is impossible, that I can't get through to him.

Supervisor: And to complete that sentence: "He shouldn't be this way, he ought to cooperate. After all, he asked for RET and now he's resisting, I shouldn't have to put up with this!"

Therapist: (Smile) Yes . . . yes . . . that does sound like what I'm feeling and thinking.

Supervisor: And I also hear an "I can't stand it" in there, and maybe the beginnings of a self put-down. Like, "I must be a lousy therapist if I can't get through to this client quickly and efficiently."

Therapist: (Sigh) . . . yes, I am questioning my abilities.

Supervisor: O.K. Now, can you dispute these notions, and lower that frustration and anger?

Therapist: I guess . . . (thinking) . . . there's no reason why the client should behave the way I want, but it sure would be better if he did . . . better for him.

Supervisor: Good, what else?

Therapist: I guess it's realistic to expect difficulty from some clients, particularly since I'm a beginner.

Supervisor: Yes, you seem to have a foothold on disputing your "shoulds", but what about another LFT idea? Let's assume, and get this picture in your mind, that this guy will always ignore your input and try to change the topic. See yourself sitting there trying valiantly but unsuccessfully to penetrate his resistance, how are you likely to feel?

Therapist: Frustrated, exasperated, ugh!

Supervisor: Why do you feel this way?

Therapist: Because . . . I know the right answer . . . it's the B's . . . I'm saying I can't stand it. But . . . (sigh)

Supervisor: But you really don't believe this . . . you know the answer, but don't believe it.

Therapist: I guess so, it's just that I hate the idea of sitting there calmly and having no therapeutic influence on the client . . . what good will that do? So I'm calm and rational, but being of no help!

Supervisor: O.K., I know what you're saying. You want more skills, some other techniques, and we'll work on this, but what if you learn all the skills . . . you're the best RETer in the universe; still the client doesn't cooperate and all your great skills are not having an effect? Imagine that . . . now what . . . how would you feel?

Therapist: Frustrated!

Supervisor: Right, *highly* frustrated, because why?

Therapist: . . . I can't stand it.

Supervisor: And how could you dispute that?

Therapist: . . . it's not true, I could stand it, even though it would be difficult, not fun, unpleasant . . . Yes, I see.

Later In The Supervision Session

Supervisor: Awhile ago, Don, you mentioned wanting to be able to do more with this client, and I agree that there is more you could do. At those places where your RET doesn't work I have rated your performance on this skill sheet and see that you are trying to clarify the client's B's, but he ignores you.

Therapist: You can say that again! He doesn't hear anything!

Supervisor: No, that's an exaggeration, he does hear some things, but they are irrelevant to the core of his concerns.

Therapist: Well . . . yes.

Supervisor: You advance hypotheses and clarifications, but he doesn't respond, yet you continue to use that technique. What are some other techniques you could use to get through?

Therapist: Well . . . uh . . .

Supervisor: Let me make a suggestion, because we don't have much time left in this session. Re-read your class notes on insight techniques, and then rate your tape using the insight section of this skill rating form. This will show you exactly what skills you are using, and I think you will see just how much you rely on the clarification skill. We'll go over your ratings in our next session.

Therapist: O.K.

Supervisor: Then, after rating the tape, choose three insight techniques that you are not now using. In particular, I think the analogy technique would work with this client because he's such a concrete thinker. O.K.? Then, find those points on your tape where these new skills could have been used. At each point, listen to the client, and then, in your imagination, practice one of the new skills. See yourself doing it, choose your words, and do it. Carry on a short interaction with the client. How does this sound?

Therapist: Interesting, and like a lot of work.

Supervisor: True, if we're going to turn this case around it will take work. And when we get together for our next supervision session, I'll role play the client's part and let you practice the skills you've rehearsed in imagery.

Therapist: Gee, I feel like this is exactly what I need, to force myself to practice new things.

Supervisor: Great! I'm optimistic that with a few different skills and less frustration you can make progress with this client. What we've done today is to dispute the ideas behind your frustration and anger, and a lowering of these emotions will enable you to loosen up and build more skills. Let's get together before you see the client again, and we'll practice some of the new techniques you've choosen.

These two supervision excerpts show how an RET supervisor can begin to help a therapist work-through a roadblock. Though much more supervision will be required before the supervisee has completely overcome his frustration and anger, and before his skill performance reaches a satisfactory level, this beginning is a step in the right direction. Other roadblocks can be approached in the same way because they, too, consist of emotional and/or skill problems.

RET Skill Rating Form. Experienced RET supervisors tend to collect and use a cadre' of aids and materials which are tangible accoutrements to their methods. Foremost among these are RET readings, modeling tapes, homework forms, skill practice exercise sheets, case studies, and self instructional packages. We consider skill rating devices to be particularly valuable aids in RET supervision, and although there are many such instruments for the rating of general therapy skills (Zytowski and Betz, 1972), these do not relate to the essential skills in RET. For this reason we developed the *RET Skill Rating Form* (SRF), an instrument which was mentioned in the preceding pitfall example and is presented in the Appendix.

The SRF is a versatile device having the main purpose of directing supervision toward RET skills. Among the many supervisory tasks that can be accomplished with the SRF are the following ones we have found to be profitable.

- *Supervisor critique*: By using the SRF the supervisor can do a thorough and objective job of critiquing a therapy tape; without the SRF, critiques are more unstructured and subjective.
- *Peer and self supervision*: Supervisees can accurately evaluate their therapy tapes with the SRF. It points them to essential RET skills, thereby improving the quality of self- or peer supervision.
- *Setting skill goals*: Together the supervisor and supervisee can critique a therapy session with the SRF and identify those skills to work on in supervision. See the previous roadblock example for an illustration.
- *Homework assignments*: After completing an SRF critique, a homework assignment can be written on the form and given to the supervisee. In one piece of material, the supervisee thus receives an objective evaluation of his/her therapy, skill goals to pursue, and a homework assignment by which the skill goals can be attained.
- *Refining skill performance*: The SRF is an excellent tool for supervising neophyte therapists, but it can also help experienced therapists to broaden their repertoire of skills, refine techniques, and overcome a stalemate in therapy by discovering and changing unproductive methods.

A critique example is offered here to show how the SRF can be used, and readers should read the SRF instructions in the Appendix for an understanding of our example. The ratings in Figure 7-2 are from the insight session by a therapist who was caught up in the roadblock of demanding cooperation from an uncooperative client (see previous topic—Supervisee Roadblocks).

Critique ratings such as these should be discussed with the supervisee because they are rather cryptic and can be misunderstood. But when SRF data is explained, the rating sheet becomes a training device around which the supervision session can revolve. Following supervision the therapist can use the ratings as he again reviews his tape and completes homework assignments.

RET Skill	Proficiency (+, −, 0)	Notes
INSIGHT		
Advancing Hypotheses	−	You used this skill category often but without much success.
Clarifying Ideas	−	When you tried to clarify, the client ignored your words, and then you seemed to get angry and give up.
Defining Terms	0	
Leading Techniques	0	Few leads used in session—do more of these.
ABC Formula	0	I have a hunch the client might understand the ABC paradigm if you go over it slowly.
Imagery	0	
Contrasting Technique	0	In supervision lets go to point 305 on the tape and see where this technique could be done.
Confronting Hidden Ideas	0	You missed the main ideas we diagnosed last week; check that diagnosis again before your next therapy session.
Rhetorical Question	0	
Incomplete Sentences	−	At point 235 on the tape, see where you started this technique but then quit in the middle.
Key Words	+	You interpreted several key "shoulds"—good job!!
In vivo Assignments	0	
Maultsby's Analogy	0	This technique is worth a try because it can cut through resistance and is less abstract than ordinary hypotheses and verbal interpretations.
		Don, you showed some anger and frustration during the session. Let's discuss this in supervision.

Figure 7-2. RET Skill Rating Form.

An examination of these ratings gives us some evidence of the supervisee's roadblock, though an observation of the session would be necessary to formulate a strong hypothesis. One can see that the supervisee's skill performance range is narrow; the 0 ratings indicate those skills that were not performed. The supervisor's notes indicate there were opportunities in the therapy session for other RET skills, and recommendations were offered as to which ones to attempt in the next session. Other helpful skill comments were things to listen for on the tape, and referral to the prior diagnosis.

The supervisor's comments also reveal an awareness of the supervisee's emotional problem (frustration and anger) and an intention to discuss it in supervision. From the data on the SRF, it would seem that the stage is set for RET supervision to deal with the supervisee's roadblock.

SUMMARY

Our skills-based approach to the training and supervision of RET therapists is an implementation of the ideas and principles stated in the preface. We have a high regard for the clinical artistry of great psychotherapists, but we do not believe this expertise is instinctual or inherited. Rather, we think it consists of actions—overt and covert skill-behaviors—which can be taught and learned through a deliberate program of training and supervision.

In Chapters 2 through 6 we discussed the essential skills of RET, and in this chapter we have explained a program for the training and practice of these skills. Through the training dimensions of experiential learning, didactic instruction, modeling, and skill shaping, we hope that instructors will impart RET skills and psychobehaviorally guide them into accountable RET practice.

8

RET With Women: Some Special Issues

Ingrid Zachary, Ed.D.

The purpose of this chapter is not to suggest that there are specific techniques or intervention strategies that are unique to doing RET with women. Rather, the purpose is to heighten the reader's awareness of some special issues that women bring into the therapeutic situation and to aid them in the facilitation of as humanistic and nonsexist a response as possible. This implies that the reader examine his/her own values vis-a-vis working with women in therapy, values that have been inculcated via acculturation and via therapeutic training, which is often fraught with Freudian baggage.

An exhaustive discussion of the psychoanalytic view of the etiology of neurosis in women is beyond the purview of this chapter. It will be noted, however, that the traditional psychoanalytic position has been that women are inherently passive, masochistic, narcissistic (Freud, 1974; Deutsch, 1973) and capable of reaching feminine maturity and a sense of identity only through marriage and child-bearing (Erikson, 1968; Freud, 1974). Deviations from this were regarded as "masculine protest" and were viewed as neurotic. Chesler (1972) has charged that the Freudian view of women as subordinate and men as dominant continues to influence the way in which psychotherapy is conducted and Broverman, Broverman, Clarkson, Rosenkrantz, and Vogel (1970) have found that a double standard of mental health for men and women continues to exist among clinicians.

Rational-emotive therapy has certainly discarded the Freudian view of women along with many other psychoanalytic constructs. It posits no separate etiology of neurosis unique to women nor does it support a standard of mental health for women which is different than that of men.   Nevertheless, there are some special women's issues which have not been discussed in the RET literature heretofore, and it is upon these issues that this chapter will focus. The discussion of these issues—rape, unwanted pregnancy/abortion, motherhood vs. career, and homosexuality—is by no means exhaustive, as each one merits volumes in and of itself.   Rather, this is an introductory discussion from within the RET framework of some of the significant concerns with which women currently contend.

RAPE

Rape is an assault on the body, mind and spirit of an individual. As women report this crime in increasing numbers and as law enforcement agencies become more sensitized to the emotional and psychological concomitants of rape, we will be seeing more and more rape victims in psychotherapy. When a woman comes into therapy immediately after a rape has occurred, the role of the therapist is largely crisis intervention and practical problem solving. This phase of therapy largely consists of giving support, helping the client to decide whether or not to report and prosecute, with a realistic, yet rational understanding of the possible consequences of doing so, and to help allay fears and become constructively mobilized again.   Often the women will request a female therapist and whenever possible it is best to accommodate this request.

At times, the effects of rape can be insidious and the woman may not be aware that she has an emotional disturbance about rape until months or even years after the actual event.   At this point the woman is often experiencing anger, often at receiving no satisfaction from our judicial system, and, more distinctively, feelings of guilt and shame. It is not unusual for a woman to note a personality change in herself in the direction of social withdrawal and timidity as well as sexual inhibition.   RET exploration of these concerns often reveals that the woman feels devalued, soiled, and ashamed of herself for having been raped. Often the response of law enforcement and judicial systems tend to reinforce her feelings. If she has not reported the crime, she often feels guilty and continues to question her own motives in refraining from doing so. The woman is often left with the nagging thought that she should have done something more, both at the time of the rape and in the aftermath.

The following excerpt from an initial RET session illustrates the issues delineated above.

Client: So I'm finding myself feeling really awkward at parties and in groups and people and I just don't like sex as much as I used to. I think it has to do with the rape a year and a half ago, but I'm not sure of the connection.

Therapist: You're feeling that your current problems are related to being raped.

Client: Uh huh. It was a guy I accepted a date with, but I barely knew him. He drives me out to a really disserted place, raped me, and left me out there. I hitched back into town, went to the police station, and had a medical exam. I even got myself a lawyer, but he told me that since I had accepted a date with the guy I wouldn't have a snowball's chance in hell of proving rape, so I dropped the whole thing.

Therapist: And what do you think about all of that now?

Client: Well, I go back and forth about it. Sometimes I think I should have prosecuted and other times I think it was better to drop it. I mean the police, the lawyer, they acted like I was asking for it by going out with the guy, and it would have been more humiliating to pursue it.

Therapist: So you're continuing to go over and over it in your mind and you're vascillating back and forth about what would have been the best thing to do.

Client: Yes, I think about it a lot. It's really pretty distracting.

Therapist: So you're thinking that there must have been a perfectly right thing to do and you continue to torture yourself with that thought.

Client: Uh, huh. I even think that maybe I could have avoided being raped.

Therapist: How could you have done that?

Client: I don't know exactly. He said he had a knife, but I never actually saw it. Maybe he didn't. Maybe I could have screamed or fought harder or tried to run away, but I was afraid he might stab me.

Therapist: So at the time, you believed that he had a knife and would really hurt you or even kill you if you didn't give in.

Client: Yes, but I don't know now if he would have. And it was just my word against his. He told the police that I had seduced him and they seemed to believe him. Even my lawyer seemed to question my story.

Therapist: And how you feel?

Client: This sounds crazy, but I feel guilty and ashamed of myself, like less of a person. He raped me and I feel guilty!

Therapist: So you're feeling guilty, ashamed and devalued as a person. And you're telling yourself that you should have fought him away at the time and you should have stuck by your story. Mostly you seem to be telling yourself that it's all your fault and that you're less of a person because you were raped and didn't do the right thing.

Client: Yes, that's all true, but what do we do with that?

Therapist: We begin by examining the beliefs you have, disputing them, and, hopefully eventually allowing you to put the incident to rest. Let's begin right now by looking at your belief that there is a perfectly right thing that you could have done at the time.

Comment

This excerpt is a good illustration of how RET's theory and skills are applied to the special issues that women often bring to therapy.

In the first few moments of this session, I diagnosed the client's problem via the ABC formula, as stemming primarily from her belief that she is less of a person because she should have done something other than what she did at the time of the rape. I then helped her gain insight into this, bringing the focus of the session out of the past and into the here and now, as it is the client's present rumination about the rape, rather than the event itself that occurred a year and a half previously, that is causing her difficulty right now. I also quickly started her disputations of her beliefs. And, in subsequent sessions we worked through the notions of perfect solutions, of whether or not we can even be devalued as human beings by what others do to us, and whether other people (in this case policemen and lawyers) have the right to define reality for us and to judge us. This client was able to let go of the rape incident and adjust to social and sexual situations to her satisfaction after four months in therapy. She was even able to constructively channel her anger about the judicial system by deciding to go to law school and by following through on this decision.

UNWANTED PREGNANCY/ABORTION

Despite the prolification of birth control information and the accessibility of birth control devices, unwanted pregnancy continues to be a physical and psychological problem for many women. If you are a counselor or a therapist at a junior or senior high school, a university, or a community mental health center, it is virtually certain that you will encounter women confronted by an unwanted pregnancy. Regardless of your psychotherapeutic persuasion, it is imperative that you be clear about your own values regarding this potentially sensitive issue, for the sake of your client and for your own peace of mind. In my experience, most young women confronted by an unwanted pregnancy choose to have an abortion and if you have moral, religious or ethical misgivings about this alternative, it would be advisable to refer this client to someone else. On the other hand, if you are particularly pro-abortion, it is equally important not to foist that choice on your client, but rather to let your client truly take control of her own body by allowing her to explore every alternative freely, helping her to understand the consequences of her choice, and making it clear that you will see her through any choice she makes.

It is also important to be aware of cultural differences vis-à-vis unwanted pregnancy. Again, in my experience, women of minority groups are more likely to have the child and keep it, and this choice is more likely to be accepted by her family. In the majority of cases, however, your client will opt for an abortion, as she will be extremely concerned about the negative reaction of her family to the pregnancy and will eventually not want to interrupt her life by caring for a child.

In most cases, emotional disturbances about abortion do not arise until it is a *fait accomplis*. The pregnant woman will usually be seeking advice about where to receive an abortion, the cost, and other pragmatic concerns. It is usually after the abortion that she will sometimes experience depression and/or guilt and will need the intervention of an RET therapist.

What are some of the more typical irrational beliefs that women hold that would cause them to feel depressed or guilty? The first and most obvious guilt producing thought is that the client is a terrible person for doing such a horrible thing as having an abortion. Even women who have sought the aid of a therapist in deciding to have an abortion have often not thought through their values about this choice. At that point they are too distracted by solving the immediate problem to examine their philosophic stance vis-à-vis this alternative, even if the therapist encourages them to do so. The goal of the RET therapist in working with a client experiencing feelings of guilt resultant of having an abortion is to help her separate her self, her person, from the particular action she has engaged in. Thus, even if she maintains the wrongness of her action, she can be helped in typical RET fashion to see that it does not make her a totally condemnable human being. At worst, she has made a mistake, one which is preventable in the future.

Beliefs about being a bad person for having had an abortion also tend to produce feelings of depression. Other depression producing beliefs surround magically thinking motherhood equals womanhood and magically thinking "if he (the potential father) really loved me he wouldn't have let me have an abortion" (despite the total disruption in their lives and their inability to support a child at this time). The work of the RET therapist, in these cases, is clearly to help the client dispute her magical ideas about the mystique of motherhood (which, by the way, is a subtle form of total self-rating), as well as to examine the shoulds she is placing on her boyfriend or husband as proof of his caring for her. Often an abortion does throw relationships into crisis, and RET then takes the direction of a reevaluation and examination of her primary relationship and/or couple counseling.

The following therapy excerpt is an illustration of how to work on guilt resultant of an abortion in the RET framework:

Client: So I had an abortion about three months ago and I'm feeling, I don't know, just sort of crummy.

Therapist: Can you tell me more about feeling crummy? How does that feel for you exactly?

Client: I don't know . . . sort of depressed, guilty maybe.

Therapist: So you had this abortion three months ago and now you're feeling depressed and guilty. What's going on in your mind to make you feel that way? What are you thinking?

Client: Well, I'm thinking that it's all wrong. At the time, I just didn't want to be pregnant anymore. My family would kill me. I'm in school. I didn't want to drop out, stuff like that. But now I feel so shitty about it.

Therapist: So at the time you thought you had some good reasons to have an abortion, but now you think you've made a mistake.

Client: To say the least!

Therapist: How's that?

Client: Well, it's a pretty big mistake. I mean I can't undo it now.

Therapist: Yes. That's true, it can't be undone. But you have some control over not making that mistake again in the future. I'm wondering if you have some feelings about yourself as a result of this.

Client: Well, I'm feeling kind of rotten. I mean, what kind of a person has an abortion first and then thinks about it later. And as I think about it now, I wonder if I haven't really destroyed a life. I mean the unborn child.

Therapist: So you're telling yourself that you're a rotten individual for destroying a life and especially without having thought about it.

Client: Yes, that's right.

Therapist: Well, let's say you did make a mistake, how does that make you a rotten person?

Client: Well, I did a rotten thing.

Therapist: O.K. Let's say that you as a person are a circle, O.K.? And inside this circle are many, many dots, each one representing one of your actions. Can you picture that?

Client: Yes.

Therapist: And one of your dots is having an abortion. Let's say that it was a mistake—a negative dot. Does it make sense to generalize from that one dot to your whole circle? Are you a totally rotten person because you made a mistake, even if it's a big one?

Client: I guess not.

Therapist: You sound unsure about that.

Client: Well, it's such a big dot! It's not like flunking a test or getting a parking ticket. I mean, it's a tremendous mistake.

Therapist: Yes, if your values now tell you that abortion is taking a life, then it is a very big mistake, but it's still *only* a mistake, and its only *one* dot, one action of the thousands you commit in your life.

Client: So even if I believe that I did something very, very rotten, I still don't have to put my whole self down. I can still feel O.K. about myself.

Therapist: That's right, you can. You can feel bad or regretful about the act, and, if you disvalue abortion, that would be logical. But, you need not condemn yourself, for that act is only a tiny part of you. See?

Comment

Clearly, this client was totally condemning herself because of her decision to have an abortion. By first knowing that guilt results from self-downing, or total self-condemning, by quickly facilitating her seeing this as the issue, and by using the circle and dot analogy (developed by Maxie Maultsby, Jr., M.D.), to get her to dispute her belief in her condemnability, I helped her to quickly delineate between one particular action she committed and her worth as a human being. This very simple and clear analogy is often quite powerful in helping clients make this sort of distinction. In the course of therapy with this particular client we did move on to examining other beliefs she held about abortion, motherhood, and her primary partner, and she was able to work on these concerns with much of her initial guilt alleviated.

MOTHERHOOD VS. CAREER

In our society, the right of a man to be both a father and a worker is never questioned; it is simply assumed that men will fulfill both of these roles. Yet, for women the choice of whether to be a mother and/or to have a career often poses a dilemma. Although more and more women are entering the labor force, the transition is rarely smooth, met with prejudices from society and from within themselves as well. Many working women continue to harbor questions as to the damage their working may be doing to their children. Often they find themselves trying to be superwomen—holding down a job, doing all the household chores, attending to the physical and emotional needs of their children, and attempting to do all of those things perfectly. It is an intricate juggling act, indeed, in which priorities are constantly reevaluated and energies scattered to the point of physical and psychological exhaustion.

Typically, the emotional disturbance which the client brings to RET is a profound and pervasive feeling of guilt. The client feels guilty that she is neglecting the children, that her house is less than spotless, that she is not working as efficiently as possible on the job; in short, that she has failed everyone in some way, including herself. In addition, the woman is often questioning her competence as a worker since, typically, many years have elapsed between her last job or her training and her current position. The role of the RET therapist with the client who is experiencing the mother/career role conflict and questioning her own abilities is to help her to establish the legitimacy of a woman's need or desire to work, to help her work through her perfectionistic notions by giving herself permission to make mistakes both at home and at work, and to help her get rid of the fantasy that everyone who is younger and just entering the labor force must surely be more competent than she is.

The following excerpt from an RET session illustrates major points in the foregoing discussion:

Client: Well, this week has been really bad—I remembered not to say "awful"—for me. A few nights ago I gave one of the terminal patients a larger dose of morphine than I should have. I realized my mistake immediately and told the doctor about it and he was really understanding. He reassured me that it wasn't a crucial mistake, but I've been kicking myself for it ever since. And I've been so tired that I've been feeding the kids T.V. dinners and asking them to do the laundry. And you should see the house; it's a holy mess! I just can't seem to get my act together anywhere.

Therapist: O.K., so you made a mistake at work and the house is a mess and the kids aren't getting gourmet meals; what's so terrible about that?

Client: Well, I keep telling myself that I shouldn't make mistakes and that I should be there for the kids. I'm really up-tight at work and I feel really guilty at home.

Therapist: So you're feeling guilty and anxious because you're laying all of these shoulds on yourself.

Client: Yep. I'm really laying this trip on my head and I can't stop it.

Therapist: Yes, you can stop it. Nancy, you're putting a lot of energy into telling yourself what you should and shouldn't be doing. You could be putting that energy into giving yourself a break and getting off your own back.

Client: How can I do that?

Therapist: First, by thinking through some of those shoulds with me right now, and then doing even more of it on your own before our next session.

Client:	O.K.
Therapist:	Let's take your "should" about never making mistakes at work.
Client:	O.K., but these kids just out of school aren't screwing up the way I am.
Therapist:	Nancy, do you really believe that kids just out of school never make mistakes?
Client:	Well, maybe they do, but I'm not current in my profession anymore.
Therapist:	Not being current in the profession is something you can remedy if you choose to. There are professional journals, seminars and workshops you can attend. But in the meantime let's you and I work on this notion you have about it being a sin to make a mistake. Do you know anyone who never makes a mistake?
Client:	No.
Therapist:	So how come Nancy isn't allowed to make a mistake?
Client:	Well, I'm a nurse. If I make a mistake, it could be a matter of life and death.
Therapist:	That's why it would be a pretty good idea not to screw up colossally. But, why should you never make any mistakes at all? It's generally not the end of the world when people make mistakes, even nurses.
Client:	OK, I get it, I don't have to be perfect. I'm only human.
Therapist:	That's right, Nancy. You're a human being and you're going to screw up sometimes just like I am and just like everyone else. We're all of us fallible human beings.
Client:	So I start telling myself, "Hey, Nancy, you're human. Everyone makes mistakes. It's not the end of the world."
Therapist:	That's right and the same kind of thinking applies at home. But, look, Nancy, why does everyone make mistakes? And why does that apply to you too? Put on your thinking cap and give me a few reasons why it's both OK and inevitable for everyone of us to make mistakes, regularly.

Comment

In this excerpt, I directly and quickly attacked the client's perfectionistic notion of "I should never make a mistake," as well as her awfulizing notion that it would be the end of the world if she did. I avoided getting embroiled in the "red herrings" she placed before me (kids just out of college, not being current in the profession) and focused on her primary mustabatory belief. With this particular client, this ground was covered again and again over several sessions, as perfectionistic beliefs are often clung to tenaciously. However, this client is now better able to relax and enjoy her work and her children without the constant, unrealistic demands she had been placing on herself.

HOMOSEXUALITY

Clearly, homosexuality can be a problem for both women and men in terms of discrimination by the public at large and privately by family and friends. Both female and male homosexuals often harbor feelings that they are "sick" and "perverted" and are extremely fearful of "coming out" with their gayness. Yet, women have the additional burden of the mystique of motherhood, a role that the female homosexual usually opts out of.

Here again, the therapist, regardless of psychotherapeutic persuasion, must be clear about his/her own values regarding the issue of homosexuality. If you do not believe that this is a legitimate, viable, and healthy sexual choice, it is best to refer the homosexual client to someone else. It is also important to be clear about what you are able and willing to do as a therapist vis-à-vis homosexuality. For example, a homosexual client will often ask you to make him/her "straight." If this is beyond your perview as a therapist, or contrary to your own values, it is best to make this clear to your client at the outset. My own stance is to share with my clients that I cannot make them "straight," but I can help them become more accepting of themselves as human beings who have gayness as one aspect of their being.

The gay female clients that I have worked with have serious questions about their femininity, as they often buy into the negative stereotypes of gay women. It should be noted that they seldom fit this stereotype themselves; however, they question profoundly why it is that they don't want to be wives and mothers and wonder what's wrong with them. They often hold ideal fantasies about heterosexual relationships, believing them to be simple and easy. They are extremely fearful of total rejection by friends and family if they were to "come out." They are often extremely depressed as they foresee an endless struggle to be accepted socially and professionally, and they predict a life of tremendous unhappiness for themselves.

In working with a gay female (or, for that matter, male) client, the initial goal of the RET therapist is usually to help her become more accepting of herself and to see her gayness in the context of her total life and being; that is, sexual choice is one aspect of a person's life rather than its totality. Other goals of the RET therapist in working with the gay client are to help her rid herself of high approval needs from friends and relatives, many of whom, realistically, will not approve of her gayness. The gay client can learn that if she can accept herself as a human being then the censure of others will become less painful. Additionally, the gay client can learn that most relationships are difficult to maintain over the long haul and require a great deal of work and energy, regardless of the gender of the individuals involved. Finally, the gay female client can be helped to accept herself as a woman without fitting traditional sex roles. It can be pointed out that many heterosexual women are choosing not to become wives and mothers and, that, in no way injures their femininity or womanhood.

Admittedly, the homosexual individual does have a more difficult time in our society. It is often very hard for a gay person to make appropriate social contacts. Even if s/he does find a primary partner, there are no formal celebrations and public acknowledgments of this event as there are with heterosexual partners. There is certainly discrimination on the job to contend with and the fear of being "discovered." Yet, despite these and other difficulties, there is no reason for the gay client to predict disaster. These are difficulties, inconveniences, and hassles, and they should be seen as such and kept in perspective.

The following excerpt from a therapy session is an example of helping a gay client work through her approval needs.

Client: I've been coming to see you a few weeks now and it really has helped me.

Therapist: That's nice to hear. How has it helped you?

Client: Well, I think that I really am beginning to accept myself. I'm not telling myself that I'm sick anymore and I see myself as a student, friend, softball player, lots of things besides a gay person. But, what I can't get past is what other people will think.

Therapist: Tell me about that.

Client: Well, yesterday in the dorm, a group of us were talking about homosexuality and one woman actually said that they should ship all queers to some island somewhere like lepers. Can you believe that?

Therapist: Well, that's certainly not one of the more enlightened views I've ever heard.

Client: The point is that she was talking about me! If I told her I was gay she'd want to ship me off to an island somewhere.

Therapist: She probably would. What would be so awful about that?

Client: She lives in my dorm! She's my friend! She would totally reject me if she knew I was gay.

Therapist: What would be awful about that?

Client: Well, I need her to be my friend. I couldn't stand it if everyone deserted me and stopped liking me because I'm gay.

Therapist: Well, if this particular friend rejects you, does that mean that everyone will do the same thing?

Client: No, not everyone, but I can't stand to have anyone not approve of me.

Therapist: Do you know anyone who is universally approved of?

Client: No.

Therapist: So, what makes you so special that everyone must approve of you?

Client: Nothing, but I want to be approved of!

Therapist: Now, that's a very rational statement. We all want approval, but you seem to be saying more than that! You're saying that you need approval, you absolutely must have it or it would be awful.

Client: Yes, I guess I am saying that. I need approval or I'll be miserable.

Therapist: Do you actually need approval? You need air, water, shelter, and so forth, but do you need approval?

Client: No, not in that sense. But it's nice to be approved of.

Therapist: Yes, it's very nice, but that doesn't mean we have to be miserable without it.

Client: It doesn't?

Therapist: Look, Terrie, I'd like you to try something this week. I'd like you to chose one person you trust and think is pretty reasonable and tell that person about you're being gay.

Client: Oh, shit! What if it blows their mind? What if they really put me down?

Therapist: What if they do? Let's assume the worst. Let's assume they say, "That's the most disgusting thing I've ever heard. Don't ever speak to me again, you pervert." What would happen?

Client: I would die.

Therapist: Would you?

Client: Not literally, but I'd be embarrassed.

Therapist: Would that be so awful to be embarrassed?

Client: I don't know.

Therapist: Would you be willing to take a risk and find out?

Client: O.K., I guess it's time.

Comment

In this session, I asked my client to do a risk exercise to experience for herself that the reaction of a friend would probably not be as negative as she anticipates and, even if it were, to see that she would survive it. The distinction between wanting and needing approval is often difficult to grasp cognitively and even more difficult to experience emotionally. It may require several therapeutic sessions and several risk exercises before the client can actually grasp and experience a desire, rather than a need, for approval. In the case of the gay client, who may realistically experience disapproval to an intense degree, it is crucial to get rid of high approval needs and become self-accepting.

CONCLUSION

This chapter has demonstrated some of the techniques of RET as applied to women's issues. You have probably noted that the basic mustubatory, awfulizing and self-downing themes were present here as they are in virtually all human concerns. Thus, although the A's can be very different for women, as delineated in this chapter, the B's and resultant C's are the same for all persons. Many women are still struggling for autonomy, for the right to control their own bodies, to make choices, and to define their roles in society. RET offers a humanistic, non-sexist vehicle for helping women to work through these issues via an objective, logical examination of their beliefs and philosophies. By ridding themselves of *shoulds, oughts,* and *musts,* women can make great strides in achieving personal freedom and control over their own destinies.

Bibliography

Adler, A. *Understanding human nature.* New York: Greenberg, 1927.

Adler, A. *The science of living.* New York: Greenberg, 1929.

Alberti, R.E., and Emmons, M.L. *Your perfect right: A guide to assertive behavior.* San Luis Obispo: Impact Press, 1974.

Bandura, A. *Aggression: A social learning theory.* Englewood Cliffs: Prentice-Hall, 1973.

Bandura, A. *Principles of behavior modification.* New York: Holt, Rinehart and Winston, 1969.

Bandura, A. *Social learning theory.* New York: Prentice-Hall, 1976.

Bard, J. Rational proselytizing. *Rational Living,* 1973, 8, 13–15.

Beck, A.T. A systematic investigation of depression. *Comparative Psychiatry,* 1961, 2, 162–170.

Beck, A.T. Thinking and depression: 1. Idiosyncratic and cognitive distortions. *Archives of General Psychiatry,* 1963, 9, 324–335.

Beck, A.T. Thinking and depression: 2. Theory and therapy. *Archives of General Psychiatry,* 1964, 10, 561–571.

Beck, A.T. *Depression: Causes and treatment.* Philadelphia: University of Pennsylvania Press, 1972.

Beck, A.T. *Cognitive therapy and the emotional disorders.* New York: International Universities Press, 1976.

Beck, A.T., and Shaw, B.F. Cognitive approaches to depression. In A. Ellis and R. Grieger (eds.). *Handbook of rational-emotive therapy.* New York: Springer Publishing Co., 1977.

Becker, I.M., and Rosenfeld, J.G. Rational-emotive therapy: A study of initial therapy sessions of Albert Ellis. *Journal of Clinical Psychology,* 1976, 32, 872–876.

Berkowitz, L. Experimental investigations of hostility catharsis. *Journal of Consulting and Clinical Psychology,* 1970, 35, 1–7.

Berne, E. *Games people play.* New York: Grove Press, 1964.

Bersoff, D.N. The "current functioning" myth: An overlooked fallacy in psychological assessment. *Journal of Consulting and Clinical Psychology,* 1971, **37**, 391–393.

Bersoff, D.N. Silk purses into sow's ears: The decline of psychological testing and a suggestion for its redemption. *American Psychologist,* 1973, **39**, 892–899.

Boker, S. *A study to determine the effects of a self-concept enhancement program in increasing self-concept in black, disadvantaged sixth grade boys.* Master's thesis, Queens College, 1971.

Boyd, J.D. *Counselor supervision.* Muncie: Accelerated Development, 1978.

Braaten, L.J. The main theories of "existentialism" from the viewpoint of a psychotherapist. *Mental Hygiene,* 1961, **45**, 10–17.

Broverman, I.K., Broverman, D.M., Clarkson, F.E., Rosenkrantz, P.S., and Vogel, S.R. Sex-role stereotypes and clinical judgements of mental health. *Journal of Consulting and Clinical Psychology,* 1970, **34**, 1–7.

Buber, M. *I and thou.* New York: Shocken, 1962.

Carkhuff, R.R. *Helping and human relations: Selection and training* (vol. 1). New York: Holt, Rinehart, and Winston, 1969.

Chesler, P. *Women and madness.* Garden City: Doubleday, 1972.

Delaney, D.J. A behavioral model for the practicum supervision of counselor candidates. *Counselor Education and Supervision,* 1972, **12**, 46–50.

Deutsch, H. *The psychology of women* (1944). New York: Bantam, 1973.

diGiuseppe, R., Miller, N., and Trexler, L. A review of rational-emotive psychotherapy outcome studies. *Counseling Psychologist,* 1977, **7**, 64–72.

D'Zurilla, T.J., and Goldfried, M.R. Problem solving and behavior modification. *Journal of Abnormal Psychology,* 1971, **78**, 107–126.

Ellis, A. *How to live with a "neurotic".* New York: Crown Publishers, 1957.

Ellis, A. *Reason and emotion in psychotherapy.* New York: Lyle Stuart, 1962.

Ellis, A. *The intelligent woman's guide to man-hunting.* New York: Lyle Stuart, and Dell Books, 1963.

Ellis, A. Rational therapy: A rational approach to interpretation. In *Use of interpretation in treatment,* edited by E. Hammer. New York: Greene & Stratton, 1966.

Ellis, A. Goals of psychotherapy. In *The goals of psychotherapy,* edited by A.R. Maurer. New York: Appleton-Century-Crofts, 1967.

Ellis, A. What *really* causes therapeutic change? *Voices: The Art and Science of Psychotherapy,* 1968, **4**, 90–97.

Ellis, A. A weekend of rational encounter. In *Encounter,* edited by A. Burton. New York: Jossey-Bass, 1969. (a)

Ellis, A. A cognitive approach to behavior therapy. *International Journal of Psychiatry,* 1969, **8**, 896–900. (b)

Ellis, A. *Growth through reason.* Palo Alto: Science and Behavior Books, and Hollywood: Wilshire Books, 1971.

Ellis, A. Psychotherapy and the value of a human being. In *Value and valuation,* edited by J.W. Davis. Knoxville: University of Tennessee Press, 1972. Reprinted: New York: Institute for Rational Living, 1972.

Ellis, A. *Humanistic psychotherapy: The rational-emotive approach.* New York: Julian Press, and McGraw-Hill Paperbacks, 1973. (a)

Ellis, A. Rational-emotive therapy. In *Current psychotherapies.* 2nd ed., edited by R.J. Corsini. Itasca, Ill.: Peacock Publishers, Inc., 1973. (b)

Ellis, A. The treatment of sex and love problems in women. In *Women in Therapy,* edited by V. Franks and V. Burtle. New York: Bruner/Mazel, 1974.

Ellis, A. The rational-emotive approach to sex counseling. *The Counseling Psychologist,* 1975, 5, 14–21.

Ellis, A. The biological basis of human irrationality. *Journal of Individual Psychology,* 1976, 32, 145–168. (a)

Ellis, A. *Sex and the liberated man.* New York: Lyle Stuart, 1976. (b)

Ellis, A. *How to live with—and without—anger.* New York: Reader's Digest Press, 1977. (a)

Ellis, A. Rational-emotive therapy: Research data that supports the clinical and personality hypotheses of RET and other modes of cognitive behavior therapy. *The Counseling Psychologist,* 1977, 7, 2–42. (b)

Ellis, A. *A garland of rational songs.* Songbook and cassette recording. New York: Institute for Rational Living, 1977. (c)

Ellis, A. Fun as psychotherapy. *Rational Living,* 1977, 12, 2–6. (d)

Ellis, A. Intimacy in psychotherapy. *Rational Living,* 1977, 12, 13–20. (e)

Ellis, A. A rejoinder: elegant and inelegant RET. *The Counseling Psychologist,* 1977, 7, 73–82. (f)

Ellis, A. Toward a theory of personality. In *Readings in current personality theories,* edited by R.J. Corsini. Itasca, Ill.: Peacock Publishers, Inc., 1978. (a)

Ellis, A. Cognitive techniques of psychotherapy. Talk presented at Rutgers University and the Annual Meeting of the American Association of Sex Educators, Counselors and Therapists, April, 1978. (b)

Ellis, A. Discomfort anxiety: A new cognitive-behavioral construct. Invited address to the Association for the Advancement of Behavior Therapy. Chicago, November 17, 1978. (c)

Ellis, A. *New developments in rational-emotive therapy.* Monterey: Brooks/Cole, 1979.

Ellis, A., and Abraham, E. *Brief psychotherapy in medical and health practice.* New York: Springer Publishing Co., 1978.

Ellis, A., and Grieger, R. *Handbook of rational-emotive therapy.* New York: Springer Publishing Co., 1977.

Ellis, A., and Harper, R.A. *A guide to rational living.* Englewood Cliffs: Prentice-Hall, Inc., 1961.

Ellis, A., and Harper, R.A. *A new guide to rational living.* Englewood Cliffs: Prentice-Hall, Inc., and Hollywood: Wilshire Book Co., 1975.

Ellis, A., and Knaus, W. *Overcoming procrastination.* New York: Institute for Rational Living, 1977.

Emmelkamp, P.M.G., Kuipers, A.L.M., and Eggeraat, J.B. Cognitive modification vs. prolonged exposure in vivo: A comparison with agoraphobics as subjects. *Behavior Research and Therapy,* 1978, **16,** 33–41.

Epictetus. *The works of Epictetus.* Boston: Little, Brown, 1899.

Erikson, E. Womanhood and the inner space. *Identity, youth and crisis.* W.W. Norton and Co., Inc., 1968.

Farrelly, F., and Brandsma, J. *Provocative therapy.* Fort Collins: Shields, 1974.

Frankl, V. *Man's search for meaning.* New York: Washington Square Press, 1966.

Frankl, V. *Psychotherapy and existentialism.* New York: Simon and Schuster, 1968.

Freud, S. *Standard edition of the complete psychological works of Sigmund Freud.* London: Hogarth, 1965.

Freud, S. Female sexuality (1931). In *Women and analysis,* edited by J. Strousse. New York: Crossman Publishers, 1974.

Freud, S. Femininity (1933). In *Women and analysis,* edited by J. Strousse. New York: Crossman Publishers, 1974.

Freud, A. *The ego and the mechanisms of defense.* New York: International Universities Press, 1975.

Garcia, E.J. Working in the E in RET. In *Twenty years of rational therapy: Proceedings of the first national conference on rational psychotherapy,* edited by J.L. Wolfe and E. Brand. New York: Institute for Rational Living, Inc., 1977.

Geen, R.G. *Human aggression.* Philadelphia: Bureau of Research and Training—Mental Health, 1976.

Girodo, M., and Roehl, J. Cognitive preparation and coping self-talk: Anxiety management during the stress of flying. *Journal of Consulting and Clinical Psychology,* 1978, **46,** 978–989.

Goldfried, M.R., and Davison, G.C. *Clinical behavior therapy.* New York: Holt, Rinehart and Winston, 1976.

Goldfried, M.R., and Goldfried, A. Cognitive change methods. In *Helping people change,* edited by F.H. Kanfer and A.P. Goldstein. New York: Holt, Rinehart and Winston, 1975.

Goldfried, M.R., and Merbaum, M. *Behavior change through self-control.* New York: Holt, Rinehart and Winston, 1973.

Goldstein, A.P. Relationship-enhancement methods. In *Helping people change,* edited by F.H. Kanfer and A.P. Goldstein. New York: Pergamon Press, Inc., 1975.

Greenwald, H. Humor in psychotherapy. *Journal of Contemporary Psychotherapy,* 1975, **7,** 113–116.

Greenwald, H. *Direct decision therapy.* San Diego: Edits, 1976.

Grieger, R., and Boyd, J. Psychotherapeutic responses to some critical incidents in RET. In *Handbook of rational-emotive therapy,* edited by A. Ellis and R. Grieger. New York: Springer Publishing Co., 1977.

Grieger, R.M., and Zachary, I. *Cognition and emotional disturbance.* New York: Human Sciences Press, in press.

Haley, J. *Strategies of psychotherapy.* New York: Grune and Stratton, 1963.

Haley, J. *Problem solving therapy.* San Francisco: Jossey-Bass, 1976.

Harris, R. Rational-emotive therapy: Simple but not easy. *Rational Living,* 1977, **12**, 9–12.

Hartman, R. *The measurement of value.* Carbondale: Southern Illinois University Press, 1967.

Hauck, P.A. *Overcoming depression.* Philadelphia: Westminister Press, 1973.

Hauck, P. *Overcoming frustration and anger.* Philadelphia: Westminister Press, 1974.

Heidigger, M. *Being and time.* London: SCM Press, 1962.

Hogan, R.A. Issues and approaches in supervision. *Psychotherapy: Theory, Research and Practice,* 1964, **1**, 139–141.

Horney, K. *Collected works.* New York: Norton, 1965.

Horowitz, R. The concept of responsibility. *Etc.,* 1971, **28**, 399–407.

Ivey, A.E. *Microcounseling.* Springfield: C.C. Thomas, 1976.

Jacobson, E. *Progressive relaxation.* Chicago: University of Chicago Press, 1929.

Jakubowski-Spector, P. Facilitating the growth of women through assertive training. *The Counseling Psychologist,* 1973, **4**, 75–86.

Kanfer, J.F.H., and Goldstein, A.P., eds. *Helping people change.* New York: Holt, Rinehart and Winston, 1975.

Kaslow, F.W., ed. *Supervision, consultation, and staff training in the helping professions.* San Francisco: Jossey-Bass, 1977.

Kassinove, H. The effect of learning rational-emotive therapy on graduate student adjustment. *Rational Living,* 1974, **9**, 12–13.

Kassinove, H. and DiGiuseppe, R. Rational role reversal. *Rational Living,* 1975, **10**, 44–45.

Kell, B.L. and Burow, J.M. *Developmental counseling and therapy.* Boston: Houghton Mifflin Co., 1970.

Kell, B.L., and Mueller, W.J. *Impact and change: A study of counseling relationships.* New York: Appleton-Century-Crofts, 1966.

Kelly, G.B. *A theory of personality: The psychology of personal constructs.* New York: W.W. Norton and Co., Inc., 1955.

Kempel, L.T. Identifying and confronting ways of prematurely terminating therapy. *Rational Living,* 1973, **8**, 6–9.

Klein, J.P. On the use of humor in counseling. *Canadian Counsellor,* 1974, **8**, 233–237.

Knaus, W. Personal communication: RET Supervision Practicum, Institute for Rational-Emotive Therapy, New York, 1976.

Knight, R.P., and Friedman, C.R. *Psychoanalytic psychiatry and psychology: Clinical and theoretical papers* vol. 1. New York: International Universities Press, 1962.

Krumboltz, J.D. Changing the behavior of behavior changers. *Counselor Education and Supervision,* 1967, **6**, 222–229.

Kutash, S. Modified psychoanalytic therapies. In *The therapist's handbook,* edited by B. Wolman. New York: Van Nostrand Reinhold, 1976.

Lang, P.J., Melamed, B.G., and Hart, J. A psychophysical analysis of fear modification using an automated desensitization procedure. *Journal of Abnormal Psychology,* 1970, **76**, 220–234.

Lange, A. Cognitive-behavioral assertion training. In *Handbook of rational-emotive therapy,* edited by A. Ellis and R. Grieger. New York: Springer Publishing Co., 1977.

Lange, A., and Jakubowski, P. *Responsible assertive behavior: Cognitive-behavioral procedures for trainers.* Champaign: Research Press, 1976.

Laughlin, H.P. *The neurosis.* Washington: Butterworth Press, 1967.

Lazarus, A.A. *Behavior therapy and beyond.* New York: McGraw-Hill, 1971.

Levine, F.M., and Tilker, H.A. A behavior modification approach to supervision of psychotherapy. *Psychotherapy: Theory, Research and Practice,* 1974, **11**(2), 182–188.

Liberman, R.P., King, L.W., DeRist, W.J., and McCann, M. *Personal effectiveness.* Champaign: Research Press, 1975.

Liberman, R.P., Kuehnel, J., Kuehnel, T., Wheeler, E., and DeVisser, L. *Marital therapy: A positive approach to helping troubled relationships.* Kalamazoo: Behaviordelia, 1978.

Mahoney, M.J. Reflections on the cognitive-learning trend in psychotherapy. *American Psychologist,* 1977, **32**, 5–13.

Maslow, A.H. *Towards a psychology of being.* 2nd ed. New York: Van Nostrand Reinhold, 1974.

Maultsby, M.C., Jr. *More personal happiness through rational self-counseling.* Author copyright, 1974.

Maultsby, M.C., Jr. *Help yourself to happiness.* New York: Institute for Rational Living, 1975.

Maultsby, M.C., Jr. Emotional re-education. In *Handbook of rational-emotive therapy,* edited by A. Ellis and R. Grieger. New York: Springer Publishing Co., 1977. (a)

Maultsby, M.C., Jr. Rational-emotive imagery. In *Handbook of rational-emotive therapy,* edited by A. Ellis and R. Grieger. New York: Springer Publishing Co., 1977. (b)

Maultsby, M.C., Jr., and Ellis, A. *Techniques for using rational-emotive imagery (RET).* New York: Institute for Rational Living, 1974.

May, R. *Existential psychology.* New York: Random House, 1961.

May, R. *Love and will.* New York: Norton, 1969.

Meehl, P. Schizotaxia, schizotype, and schizophrenia. *American Psychologist,* 1962, **17**, 827–838.

Meichenbaum, D. Cognitive modification of test anxious college students. *Journal of Consulting and Clinical Psychology,* 1972, **39**, 370–380.

Meichenbaum, D. *Therapist manual for cognitive behavior modification.* Unpublished manuscript, Univeristy Waterloo, 1973.

Meichenbaum, D. A self-instructional approach to stress management: A proposal for stress innoculation. In *Stress and anxiety in modern life,* edited by C. Spielberger and I. Sarason. New York: Winston and Sons, 1976. a

Meichenbaum, D. Towards a cognitive theory of self-control. In *Consciousness and self-regulation: Advances in research.* vol. 1, edited by G. Schwartz and D. Shapiro. New York: Plenum Press, 1976. b

Meichenbaum, D. *Cognitive behavior modification.* New York: Plenum Press, 1977.

Meichenbaum, D., and Cameron, R. *Stress innoculation: A skills training approach to anxiety management.* Unpublished manuscript, University of Waterloo, 1972.

Mischel, W. On the empirical dilemmas of psychodynamic approaches: Issues and alternatives. *Journal of Abnormal Psychology,* 1973, **82**, 335–344.

Mischel, W. *Introduction to personality.* New York: Holt, Rinehart and Winston, 1976.

Morris, K.T., and Kanitz, J.M. *Rational-emotive therapy.* Boston: Houghton-Mifflin, 1975.

Murphy, R., and Ellis, A. *A bibliography of articles and books on rational-emotive therapy and cognitive-behavior therapy.* New York: Institute for Rational Living, 1979.

Novaco, R.W. Treatment of chronic anger through cognitive and relaxation controls. *Journal of Consulting and Clinical Psychology,* 1976, **44**, 681.

Paul, G.L. Outcome of systematic desensitization. II. Controlled investigations of individual treatment, technique variations, and current status. In *Behavior therapy: Appraisal and status,* edited by C.M. Franks. New York: McGraw-Hill, 1969.

Peterson, D.R. *The clinical study of social behavior.* New York: Appleton-Century-Crofts, 1968.

Phillips, E.L. *Psychotherapy.* Englewood Cliffs: Prentice-Hall, 1956.

Raimy, U. *Misunderstanding of self.* San Francisco: Jossey-Bass Publishers, 1975.

Rogers, C.R. *On becoming a person.* Boston: Houghton-Mifflin, 1961.

Rotter, J.B. *Social learning and clinical psychology.* New York: Prentice-Hall, 1954.

Rotter, J.B. Generalized expectancies for internal vs. external control of reinforcement. *Psychological Monographs: General and Applied,* 1966, **80**(1) (whole No. 609).

Rychlak, J.P. Can psychology be objective about free will? *Philosophical Psychologist,* 1976, **10,** 2–9.

Salter, A. *Conditioned reflex therapy.* New York: Farrar, Straus, and Giroux, 1949.

Seligman, M. *Helplessness: On depression, development and death.* San Francisco: W.H. Freeman and Co., 1975.

Smith, M.L., and Glass, G.V. Meta-analysis of psychotherapy outcome studies. *American Psychologist,* 1977, **32,** 752–760.

Spice, C.G., Jr., and Spice, W.H. A triadic method of supervision in the training of counselors and counseling supervisors. *Counselor Education and Supervision,* 1976, **15**(4), 251–258.

Spivack, G., Platt, J.J., and Shure, M.B. *The problem solving approach to adjustment.* San Francisco: Jossey-Bass, 1976.

Stevens, J.O. *Awareness: Exploring, experimenting, experiencing.* Maob: Real People Press, 1971.

Sydel, A. *A study to determine the effects of emotional education on fifth grade children.* Master's thesis, Queens College, New York, 1972.

Taylor, M.H. A rational-emotive workshop on overcoming study blocks. *Personnel and Guidance Journal,* 1975, **53,** 458–462.

Turk, D. *Cognitive control of pain: A skills training approach.* Unpublished manuscript, University of Waterloo, Waterloo, Ontario, Canada, 1974.

Watzlawick, P., Weakland, J.H., and Fisch, R. *Change: Principles of problem formation and problem resolution.* New York: W.W. Norton and Co., Inc., 1974.

Whitaker, C. Psychotherapy of the absurd: With special emphasis on the psychotherapy of aggression. *Family Process,* 1975, **14,** 1–16.

Wolpe, J., and Lazarus, A.A. *Behavior therapy techniques.* New York: Pergamon Press, 1966.

Zingle, H.W. *Therapy approach to counseling underachievers.* Doctoral dissertation, University of Alberta, 1965.

Zingle, H.W., and Mallett, M. *A bibliography of RET materials, articles, and theses.* Edmonton: University of Alberta, 1976.

Zytowski, D.G., and Betz, E.Z. Measurement in counseling: A review. *The Counseling Psychologist,* 1972, **3,** 72–86.

Appendix

INSTRUCTIONS
RET SKILL RATING FORM

The RET Skill Rating Form (SRF) is a device for rating and commenting upon the performance of rational-emotive therapists. Though not a sophisticated psychometric device, the SRF does require an understanding of the skills-based RET model as described in this text. Also, reference to particular skill descriptions and illustrations in the text may be helpful during SRF critiques.

Ratings on the SRF are an evaluation of skill proficiency, or, "how well a skill was performed." A competent or satisfactory skill performance is rated with a (+), skill performances needing improvement are given a (-), and when a skill is not performed the rating is (0). Ratings can be given to individual skills and the skill categories to which they belong. An illustration of SRF ratings is offered in Chapter 7 (see Figure 7-2).

Notes from the rater should accompany and explain ratings. Included in this feedback are things such as references to certain portions of a video or audiotape, praise, suggested techniques, hypotheses, clarification of a rating, etc.

The last page of the SRF is devoted to a summary of SRF ratings and homework assignments. Here the therapist's entire RET performance can be overviewed, and self instructional activities are directed at needed skill improvements.

RET SKILL RATING FORM

RET Skill	Proficiency (+, −, 0)	Notes
PSYCHODIAGNOSIS		
Relationship	____	
Problem Exploration	____	
Categorization	____	
ABC Focus	____	
Pointed Leads	____	
Reflective Responses	____	
Psychodiagnosis Proper	____	
Goal Setting	____	
ADDITIONAL SKILLS		
	____	
	____	
INSIGHT		
Advancing Hypotheses	____	
Clarifying Ideas	____	
Defining Terms	____	

RET SKILL RATING FORM
(Continued)

RET Skill	Proficiency (+, -, 0)	Notes
INSIGHT (Continued)		
Leading Techniques	_____	
ABC Formula	_____	
Imagery	_____	
Contrasting Technique	_____	
Confronting Hidden Ideas	_____	
Rhetorical Question	_____	
Incomplete Sentences	_____	
Key Words	_____	
In-vivo Assignments	_____	
Maultsby's Analogy	_____	
_____	_____	
_____	_____	
WORKING-THROUGH		
Cognitive Methods	_____	
Disputation	_____	
Written Homework	_____	
Role Reversal	_____	
Information Giving	_____	
RE Imagery	_____	
_____	_____	

RET SKILL RATING FORM
(Continued)

RET Skill	Proficiency (+, −, 0)	Notes
WORKING-THROUGH (Continued)		
Emotive Methods		
Empathy & Acceptance	——	
Shame Exercises	——	
Humor	——	
Bibliotherapy	——	
Behavioral-Activities		
Stay-In-There	——	
Doing It/Risk Exercises	——	
Self Management	——	
Desensitization	——	
RE-EDUCATION		
R-E Imagery	——	
Role Reversal	——	
Proselytizing	——	
Reinforcing Rational Thinking	——	

RET SKILL RATING FORM
(Continued)

RET Skill	Proficiency (+, −, 0)	Notes
RE-EDUCATION (Continued)		
Rational Indoctrination	____	
Stress Inoculation	____	
Skill Training	____	
	____	
	____	

Summary:

Homework:

Author Index

279

Subject Index

Imagery, 98. *See also* Rational-Emotive Imagery (REI)
Imagery, use in supervision, 221
Information giving, 25, 146–147
Insight, 81–83, 91, 123, 220, 221–222. *See also* Rational-emotive insight
Inventories, rational belief scales, 220
Irrational beliefs, 5–8, 12, 19, 39, 63, 254
Irrational beliefs, debating, *See* Disputation
Irrational ideas, 36–37, 45, 46–47, 49, 63–64, 71, 163–165. *See also* Irrational beliefs
Irrational ideas, giving them up, 82, 122, 161, 162, 163–165
Irrational ideas, themes, 8, 37, 63

Leads, pointed, 65–67
examples, 66
Learning, modeling/observational
focal skills, 224
guidelines, 225
gross effects, 223–224
preparation for modeling, 224–225
specific effects, 224
Learning theory, 20. *See also* Social learning theory
Lecturing, 115–116, 172
Limitations of RET, 28–29
Listening skills, 59, 226–227
for activating events, 59–60
for consequences, 60–62
for irrational ideas, 62–65
Low frustration tolerance (LFT), 7–8, 11, 15, 19, 40, 49–50, 63, 99–101

Multimodal approach, 18, 20–21, 24, 125, 129–130, 155–156
Musturbation, 5, 6–7, 8, 114–115

Operant conditioning, 145, 150, 159

Past history, 9, 76–77, 84, 118–119, 124
Peer supervision, 237, 246
Perfectionism, 39, 167, 169–170, 235, 260
transcript, 167–169
Personal power, 84, 86, 119–120
Personality change, theory of, 12–13
Phobia, 20, 40
Primary symptoms, 19, 40, 42, 50–51. *See also* Problems, levels of

Problems, categories, 34–36, 53, 56. *See also* Psychodiagnosis
career, 35–36, 56
emotional-behavioral, 35–36, 50, 56, 56–57, 117, 120, 196
environmental, 35–36, 56, 116–117
Problems, levels of. *See also* Problems, categories
primary symptoms, 50–52
secondary symptoms, 47–48, 49–50, 51–52, 120
tertiary symptoms, 51, 52
Procrastination, 18–19, 158–159
Proselytizing, 180
Psychoanalysis, 11, 12, 59, 81, 124, 249
Psychodiagnosis, 199–200, 201–202
facilitation of, 33–34
skills
A-B-C paradigm, 59–67
categorizing client problems, 56–59
transcript, 57–59
client-therapist relationship, 53–56
Psychodiagnosis proper, 80
defined, 70
illustrated, 71–72
Psychodiagnosis, roadblocks
client, 78–80
therapist, 76–78
Psychodynamic theory, 11
Psychopathology, understanding, 34–37, 62, 84. *See also* Anger and aggression, dynamics of; Anxiety, dynamics of; Depression, dynamics of; Guilt and self-downing, dynamics of

Questions, 114, 172, 174. *See also* Rhetorical questions

RET Skill Rating Form. *See* Skill Rating Form (SRF)
Rapport. *See* Relationship, client-therapist
Rational-Emotive Imagery (REI), 147–148, 149–150, 178–179
transcript, 148–149
Rational-emotive insight, 121, 199–200, 201–202
benefits, 86–88
defined, 83